The Sequence of Late Formative Ceremonial Structures at Salango, Coastal Ecuador

A Reconstruction and Interpretation

RICHARD LUNNISS

BAR INTERNATIONAL SERIES 3117 | 2023

BAR
PUBLISHING

Published in 2023 by
BAR Publishing, Oxford, UK

BAR International Series 3117

The Sequence of Late Formative Ceremonial Structures at Salango, Coastal Ecuador

ISBN 978 1 4073 5995 3   paperback
ISBN 978 1 4073 5996 0   e-format

DOI https://doi.org/10.30861/9781407359953

A catalogue record for this book is available from the British Library

COVER IMAGE *Pendant figurines of shell, marble, and tusk from Late Formative Salango. Photograph by Richard Lunniss.*

BAR
PUBLISHING

BAR titles are available from:

BAR Publishing
122 Banbury Rd, Oxford, OX2 7BP, UK
info@barpublishing.com
www.barpublishing.com

By the Same Author

Cultural Identity, Transition, and Interaction at Salango, Coastal Ecuador
A Study of Pottery from the Early Regional Development Funerary Precinct
BAR International Series **3109** | 2022

Of Related Interest

Vessels Explored: Applying Archaeometry to South American Ceramics and their Production
Edited by Emily M. Stovel and Guillermo De La Fuente
BAR International Series **2808** | 2016

Sex, Metaphor, and Ideology in Moche Pottery of Ancient Peru
Andrew Turner
BAR International Series **2739** | 2015

Chaupisawakasi y la formación del estado Pukara (400 a.C. - 350 d.C.) en la Cuenca norte del Titicaca, Perú
Henry Tantaleán and Carlos Zapata Benites
BAR International / British Series **2687** | 2014

The Pottery Figurines of Pre-Columbian Peru
Volume II : The Figurines of the Central Coast
Alexandra Morgan
BAR International Series **2845** | 2017

The Pottery Figurines of Pre-Columbian Peru
Volume III: The Figurines of the South Coast the Highlands and the Selva
Alexandra Morgan
BAR International / British Series **2441** | 2012

Frayer la route d'un monde inversé
Sacrifice et offrandes animales dans la culture Mochica (100–800 apr. J.-C.), côte nord du Pérou
Nicolas Goepfert
BAR International Series **2278** | 2011

The Pottery Figurines of Pre-Columbian Peru
Volume I: The figurines of the North Coast
Alexandra Morgan
BAR International Series **1941** | 2009

Mortuary Practices and Ritual Associations
Shamanic Elements in Prehistoric Funerary Contexts in South America
Edited by John E. Staller and Elizabeth J. Currie
BAR International Series **982** | 2001

Prehistory of the Southern Manabí Coast, Ecuador. López Viejo
Elizabeth J. Currie
BAR International Series **618** | 1995

For more information, or to purchase these titles, please visit **www.barpublishing.com**

Contents

List of Figures

2022 Preface and Acknowledgements

Revisiting this study, I remembered the excitement of identifying the central axis of the house of Episode 2 and seeing that that this line was the main organising principle of the Late Formative structures at Salango. Even so, it was a while before I could begin to appreciate its fuller implications. At the time, the task was to make a first, general account of the complex mass of evidence and of the process by which I achieved the reconstruction of the designs presented, and to make some preliminary interpretations. Subsequently, it has been possible to focus on aspects that were then already suggesting themselves but still far from clear. Other themes of importance in turn became apparent and have been discussed. Much else awaits treatment and likely even recognition.

The monograph was originally submitted in draft form to the Banco Central del Ecuador in 2006 and now follows as a companion volume to an earlier study of material from Salango originally finished in 2004 and recently also published by BAR Publishing. My thanks again then to Jacqueline Senior and the other editors for agreeing to carry out the publication, and to them, three reviewers, and Tansy Branscombe for their advice on making improvements to the text and presentation. Once more also, my thanks to the Universidad Técnica de Manabí for supporting this work, and to my neighbours for their friendship.

UNIVERSIDAD TÉCNICA DE MANABÍ

Instituto Nacional de
Patrimonio Cultural

INSTITUTO NACIONAL DE
PATRIMONIO CULTURAL

2006 Preface and Acknowledgements

In May 1989, excavation of site OMJPLP–141B Salango, in the province of Manabí, Ecuador, was halted. Now, at last, it has been possible to draw on the records made and artefacts recovered during seven years of field work, and so reconstruct the unique sequence of ceremonial buildings that arose there during the Middle and Late Engoroy phases of occupation. Although the interpretation made here is mine, it is based on the careful and detailed observations made by the many archaeologists and field assistants who worked with the Programa de Antropología para el Ecuador under the general direction of Presley Norton over that time. Those involved in the excavation of T3 I have previously acknowledged. Now I should thank those who carried out the work on the Late Formative components at T4, including Freddy Acuña, José Chancay, Florencio Delgado, Hugo Gómez, Diego Jara, Telmo López, Mark Pierce, Marco Vargas, Adam Weissman, and in particular John Johnson, who directed the excavations, thus providing the essential data on the front halves and entranceways to the buildings discussed in this monograph. Conditions in Salango were never exactly easy or ideal, but John carried out his work with great dedication, obviously fuelled by his own recognition of the worth of this site. Later, he was only too happy to advise me on his experience of the excavations, and to encourage me in carrying out the analysis.

Both the field work and this study were carried out with financing from the Banco Central del Ecuador. I thank Mariella García Caputi, Regional Director of Cultural Programs for the Banco Central in Guayaquil, for having encouraged and supported me in carrying out the post-excavation analysis. I also thank Diego Zapater and others of the staff at the Museo Antropológico y de Arte Contemporáneo, Guayaquil, for their friendship and help. In Salango and Puerto López, I was supported by many acts of generosity, particularly when money was short. Edison Muenala digitised the line drawings. The Comuna Salango kindly gave me full and free access to all the materials and space I needed at the Centro de Investigaciones y Museo Salango. Patrick Gay, as he has done for many years, steered me through frequent moments of stress and lent me his precious Black Beauty whenever I needed her. Throughout my work, Karen Stothert has been both a friend and mentor. She has provided the example of commitment necessary to stay the course, as well as books and articles necessary for me to develop my thoughts. Most of all, I owe thanks to Deirdre and to all our children for their love and smiling welcome at the end of each day.

1

Introduction

Abstract: A sequence of Middle and Late Engoroy ceremonial structures dating to 600–100 BC that were excavated at OMJPLP–141B Salango, on the central coast of Ecuador, presents the most detailed and complete examples of architectural settings for ritual practice so far known for the Late Formative. Ecuadorian coastal Late Formative cultures such as Chorrera and Engoroy are best known for their often brilliant ceramics, and the socio-cultural traditions behind this pottery are relatively understudied. Likewise, architecture is principally understood based on looted pottery models of houses. Salango thus offers a major addition to knowledge of Late Formative ceremonial architecture and the sequence of change in ritual practices. Salango sits midway between the Santa Elena Peninsula and Cabo San Lorenzo, in a zone of deciduous tropical dry forest, and its Pre-Columbian settlement lay at the south end of a sandy bay opposite Salango Island. Evidence for Engoroy occupation shows, especially at sector OMJPLP–141B, that Middle Engoroy saw reconfiguration of the site for ceremonial purposes. Excavation of OMJPLP–141B from 1983 to 1986 focused at Trench 3 (T3) on a series of Regional Development and, under these, Late Formative ceremonial structures. Seven main structures were identified for the Late Formative Middle and Late Engoroy phases at T3. From October 1988 to May 1989, the Late Formative components at Trench 4 (T4) were excavated. Details of the rear left quarters of the structures identified at T3 have previously been published. This monograph now presents the evidence for the front, northeast-facing halves recovered at T4, reconstructs the overall design of each of the structures at OMJPLP–141B, and assesses their meaning and function.

Resumen: Una secuencia de estructuras ceremoniales Engoroy Medio y Tardío fechadas en 600–100 a.C. que se excavaron en OMJPLP–141B Salango, en la costa central del Ecuador, presenta los ejemplos más detallados y completos de escenarios arquitectónicos para prácticas rituales conocidos hasta ahora para el Formativo Tardío. Las culturas Formativo Tardío de la costa ecuatoriana, como Chorrera y Engoroy, son mejor conocidas por sus cerámicas a menudo brillantes, y las tradiciones socioculturales detrás de estas cerámicas son relativamente poco estudiadas. Asimismo, la arquitectura Formativo Tardío se entiende principalmente a partir de huaqueados modelos cerámicos de casas. Salango ofrece así una importante contribución al conocimiento de la arquitectura ceremonial del Formativo Tardío y la secuencia de cambios en prácticas rituales. Salango se encuentra a mitad de camino entre la Península de Santa Elena y Cabo San Lorenzo, en una zona de bosque seco tropical caducifolio, y su asentamiento precolombino se encuentra en el extremo sur de una bahía arenosa frente a la Isla Salango. La evidencia de la ocupación Engoroy muestra, en particular en el sector OMJPLP–141B, que Engoroy Medio vio la reconfiguración del sitio con fines ceremoniales. La excavación de OMJPLP–141B desde 1983 a 1986 se centró en la Trinchera 3 (T3) en una serie de estructuras ceremoniales Desarrollo Regional y, debajo de estas, Formativo Tardío. Se identificaron siete estructuras principales para las fases Engoroy Medio y Tardío del Formativo Tardío en T3. Desde octubre de 1988 hasta mayo de 1989, se excavaron los componentes Formativo Tardío de la Trinchera 4 (T4). Los detalles de los cuartos traseros izquierdos de las estructuras identificadas en T3 se han publicado anteriormente. Esta monografía ahora presenta la evidencia de las mitades delanteras orientadas al noreste recuperadas en T4, reconstruye el diseño general de cada una de las estructuras de OMJPLP–141B, y evalúa su significado y función.

1.1. Aims and Scope of the Study

The multi-component archaeological site at Salango, on the south coast of the province of Manabí, Ecuador, has previously been reported for a sequence of ceremonial structures belonging to the Late Formative and Early and Middle Regional Development periods excavated in sector OMJPLP–141B (Lunniss 2001, 2022; Norton et al. 1983).

These structures comprise the most detailed and completely excavated examples of architectural settings for ritual practice on the central coast so far available for this time span. Specifically, they are associated with Middle and Late Engoroy ceramics (Beckwith 1996; Bischof 1982; Bushnell 1951; Paulsen 1982; Paulsen & McDougle 1974, 1981; Simmons 1970; Zeller & Bischof 1960), dating to 600–300 BC and 300–100 BC respectively, for the Late

Formative, and with Bahia II (Huerta 1940; Estrada 1957, 1962) and Early Guangala (Bischof 1982; Bushnell 1951; Estrada 1957, 1962; Masucci 1992; Paulsen 1970; Simmons 1970; Stothert 1993), and then Middle Guangala (Zeller & Bischof 1960; Paulsen 1970) ceramics, at 100 BC–AD 300 and AD 300–600 respectively, for the Regional Development.

Remains of the rear southwest quarters of the structures were excavated as Trench 3 (T3) of OMJPLP–141B, and these have already been described (Lunniss 2001). This monograph now presents evidence of the northeast-facing front halves of the buildings of the Late Formative stage of the sequence, excavated as Trench 4 (T4) of OMJPLP–141B, reconstructs the overall design of each of the structures, and assesses their meaning and function.

The rest of the chapter reviews previous research into the Ecuadorian coastal Late Formative and its ceremonial architecture and practice, describes the general setting of Salango, considers local topography and Engoroy settlement pattern, summarizes the results of excavation at OMJPLP–141B–T3, and introduces OMJPLP–141B–T4. Chapter 2 then describes the methodology applied to the analysis and interpretation of the data from T4. In Chapter 3, the stratigraphic sequence for T4 is described, treating first of the building sequence and then of features and artefacts associated with the structures. In Chapter 4, the data from T4 are combined with those from T3 in a reconstruction of the overall design and dimensions of each of the structures, with summary accounts of the human burials of the later episodes and of the anthropomorphic figurine depositions. In Chapter 5, these results are then assessed in terms of the likely use of the site, the principles of spatial organisation that underlay the structures, and the meaning of the site for those who created and used it. Finally, in Chapter 6 I consider the significance of Salango for understanding of Late Formative ceremonial architecture, ideology, and ritual practice.

1.2. Previous Research into the Late Formative of Coastal Ecuador

The Late Formative period of coastal Ecuador is represented by a mosaic of diverse cultures themselves largely defined based on often brilliantly decorated and technically superb pottery vessels and pottery figurines (Beckwith 1996; Cummins 2003; Lunniss 2001; Meggers 1966:55–66; Marcos 2003; Zeidler 2003; Zeidler & Isaacson 2003; Zeidler & Sutliff 1994). General dating remains problematic on account of the variability (and availability) of the start and end points of the different cultural manifestations, including Chévele, Tachina, Mafa, Early Selva Alegre, Early Tolita, Tabuchila, Bahía I, Chorrera, Engoroy, San Pedro de Guayaquil, and Bella Vista, that are gathered under this umbrella term, but Chorrera and related cultures of central and northern Manabí can be placed at ca. 1300/1200–300 BC, while in south Manabí and down to the Santa Elena Peninsula, Engoroy can be dated overall, though with caveats, to 900–100 BC (Zeidler 2003). Likewise, after decades of mostly sporadic

field work, beginning with Bushnell's isolation of Engoroy ceramics on the Santa Elena Peninsula in the 1930's (Bushnell 1951), and Evans and Meggers' identification of Chorrera ceramics at Hacienda La Chorrera, upriver from Guayaquil, in the 1950's (Evans & Meggers 1957), we are still far from an understanding of the inter-relationships that held between the different socio-cultural traditions implied by the ceramics, and even, for the most part, of the nature of those traditions themselves (Figure 1.1). The most systematic analysis of the coastal Late Formative so far has been undertaken by Zeidler and colleagues (Zeidler & Pearsall 1994) in research into the Tabuchila complex of the Jama Valley of north Manabí, up and down river from San Isidro, where extensive surveys and sampling have allowed identification of settlement patterns through time and of a major ash fall, produced by the eruption of the highland Pululahua volcano around 467 cal BC, that brought about the end of Late Formative occupation of that region (Zeidler & Isaacson 2003; Zeidler & Sutliff 1994).

One of the striking, indeed definitive, aspects of the coastal Ecuadorian Late Formative was the intensification of ceremonial activity and the foregrounding of sacred power and authority, supporting the idea that this period saw the emergence of incipient chiefdoms (Stothert 2003a; Zeidler & Isaacson 2003:92). Much of the evidence comes in the form of looted artefacts probably taken in most cases from unregistered burial grounds in Manabí. Some reconstruction of coastal Late Formative ideology has been carried out with reference to such objects, using ethnographic analogy as well as stylistic and iconographic analysis to provide clues as to their cultural significance (Lathrap et al. 1975; Cummins 1992, 2003; Weinstein 1999; Stothert 2003a). More specifically, certain of these vessels perhaps represent ceremonial houses (Holm 1985:12–15; Cummins 2003:451, 452, Fig. 32). Meanwhile, the Chorrera type site (Evans and Meggers 1954, 1957) appears on the basis of artefacts recovered there to have been the village of a local chief (Stothert 2003b:44), and San Isidro, in northern Manabí, was evidently a major political and ceremonial centre for Tabuchila occupation of the Jama valley with a large central ceremonial platform (Estrada 1957; Zeidler 1994).

Nevertheless, the absence of information on Chorrera or Chorreroid ceremonial structures has been a leitmotif of recent Ecuadorian Formative studies (Stothert 2003a:347, footnote 5; Cummins 2003:424, 451 footnote 29; Burger 2003:479). And although the already large Piquigua (Valdivia) phase platform mound at the centre of the San Isidro site was enlarged (Zeidler & Isaacson 2003:93), the nature of the new, Tabuchila phase mound at San Isidro and of any accompanying structures on top of it remain to be determined. Thus, Late Formative ceremonial houses and platforms, with clear evidence for them, are so far best represented at Salango.

Meanwhile, several Engoroy cemeteries have been documented along the coast at La Libertad (Bushnell

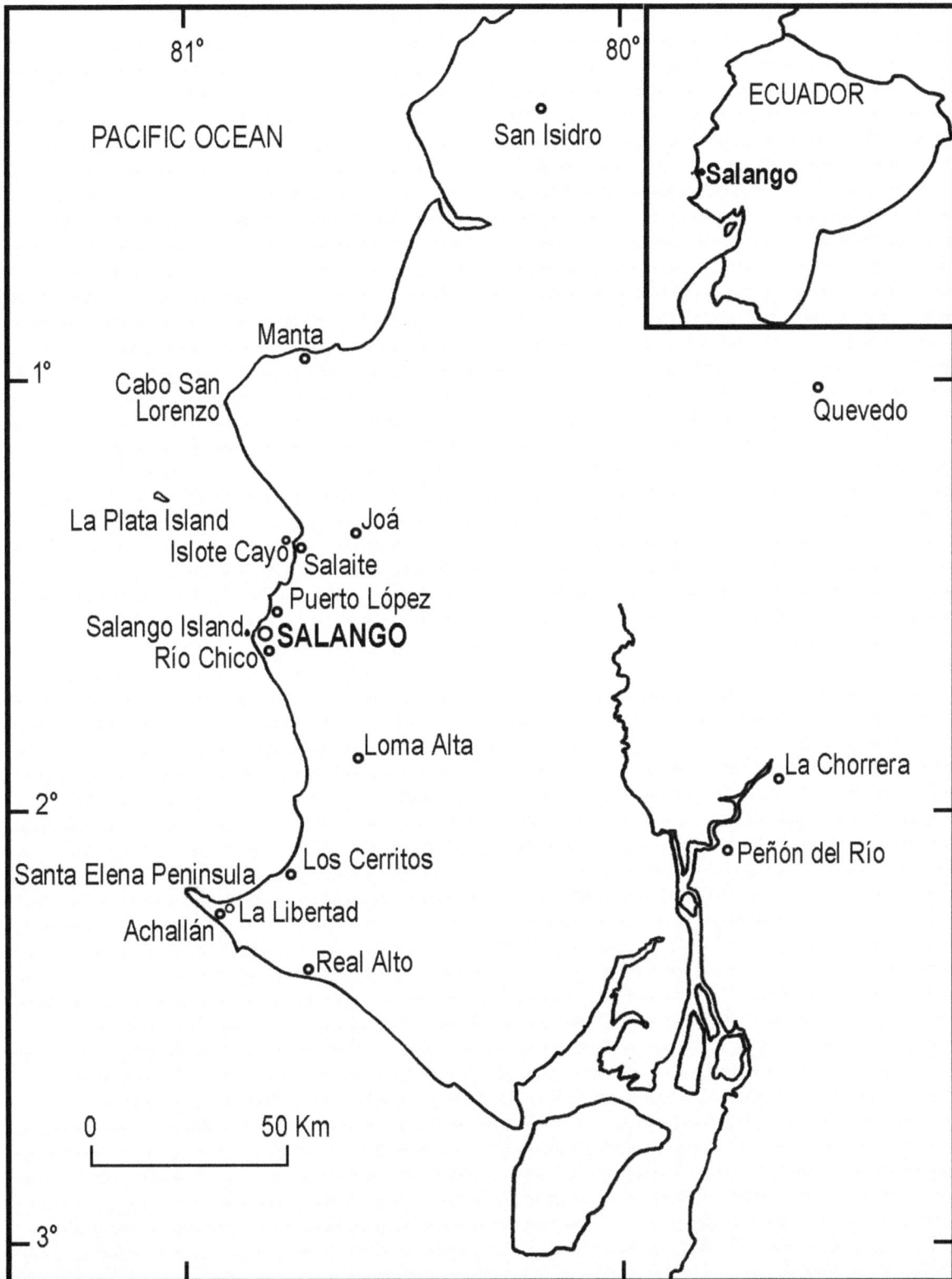

Figure 1.1. The Ecuadorian coast with sites mentioned in the text. Reprinted by permission from Springer Nature Customer Service Centre GmbH: Springer, Pre-Columbian Landscapes of Creation and Origin, by J. Staller, ed. © (2008).

1951; Ubleaker 1988), Los Cerritos (Zevallos 1965/66; 1995) and Loma Alta (Beckwith 1996:47, 48, 83, 84), and the Guayaquil Phase settlement and cemetery at San Pedro, Guayaquil (Parducci & Parducci 1970, 1972, 1975), appear to correlate with very late Engoroy as well as Early Regional Development at Salango, as does a

cemetery at Joá (Holm 1969). A cemetery at Bahía de Caráquez was partially excavated (Huerta 1940; Estrada 1962:19, 20), though it is unclear whether it was of Bahía I or Bahía II affiliation, or both. Evidence for other forms of Late Formative ceremonial activity has been reported elsewhere. At the Achallán *albarrada* (Stothert 1995),

3

Engoroy offerings of pottery and shell were deposited in the body of the massive reservoir wall to ensure successful capture and retention of water (Stothert 2003a:364). And on La Plata Island, Bahía cliff-top rituals culminated in the breaking of hundreds of anthropomorphic whistling figurines and their deposition in caches along with decorated and undecorated stone plaques and beads as well as blocks and beads of exotic coloured stone (Dorsey 1901), while at the back of the single beach where a landing could be made, there were further offerings of stone and pottery figurines, stone plaques, coloured stone beads, and fishhooks (Carluci 1966; Marcos & Norton 1981, 1984).

Many of these and other Late Formative artefact types, often identified elsewhere in isolated fashion or recovered with no record of archaeological context, appear at Salango as integrated elements of a complex yet ordered and fully documented architectural setting. The register of the sequence of ceremonial structures at Salango is itself a major addition to knowledge of ceremonial architecture of the period. But as the site was occupied over the entire Middle and Late Engoroy span, a time of great ideological experiment among coastal society, it is also possible to use Salango as a point of reference for a more precise definition of the sequence of change in ritual practices, thus providing a more solid base for subsequent interpretation of their significance.

1.3. Salango: The Setting and Engoroy Settlement Patterns

The fishing village of Salango sits at 1° 35' 30" S, 80° 50' 30" W (IGM Map CT MIV–3), roughly halfway between the Santa Elena Peninsula and Cabo San Lorenzo, each approximately 70 km away. It lies on the north side of Punta Piedra Verde, the headland, which, with Salango Island, constitutes the most westward point of the shoreline between those two larger promontories. The coastal strip itself is mostly vegetated with deciduous tropical dry forest and scrub, with wetter regimes further inland and at the higher altitudes of hills which reach 800 m asl. But a few miles south of Salango, the Cinco Cerros, a westward extension of the Cordillera Chongón-Colonche, attracts enough rainfall to support permanent tropical cloud forest right to the cliffs above the ocean. The effects of this relatively high precipitation reach as far as Salango, whose year-round greenery is in refreshing and colourful contrast

Figure 1.2. Salango: view of the bay, the island, and the headland, Punta Piedra Verde. The site lies under the factory installations visible at the base of the headland to the left. Reprinted by permission from Springer Nature Customer Service Centre GmbH: Springer, Pre-Columbian Landscapes of Creation and Origin, by J. Staller, ed. © (2008).

to the more arid conditions that prevail from Puerto López northwards.

The Pre-Columbian settlement, throughout its history, was focused on the south end of Salango's sandy beach (Figure 1.2). From this site, now largely occupied by a fish meal factory, the view is dominated by the ocean and points of land that mark its limits. While Salango Island, a few hundred metres offshore, marks the horizon to the west, La Plata Island, 44 km to the northwest, and Cabo San Lorenzo, just west of north, are also visible on clear days. Otherwise, cliff promontories block off the view of the northern shoreline immediately beyond, just as Punta Piedra Verde shuts the bay off from the coastline to the south.

Salango is pressed close by low hills reaching down from the east, and the flat land of the Río Salango flood plain is not extensive. In earlier times, much of this land was rather lower than it is now, and the details of the beachline have altered also, partly though natural processes, partly as the result of human action. It is clear, though, that there was never any large area of land suitable for settlement within these confined spaces.

The evidence for Engoroy occupation of Salango derives from various sources. In the first place, there are the results of excavation at sectors OMJPLP–140, OMJPLP–141A, 141B, including both T3 and T4, and 141C (Allan 1988; Beckwith 1996; Kurc 1984; Lunniss 2001; Norton et al. 1983). Second, there are two sets of data gathered during field surveys of the Salango valley (Allan & Allan 1989; Graber 2004). Third are observations made by the author during two community construction projects undertaken in the village of Salango in 2004–5.[1] There are no data available for the area between 141B and the beach since this is occupied by the main fish factory buildings, which were constructed in 1975.

The focus of Engoroy occupation lay at the foot of Punta Piedra Verde, an area excavated as sectors OMJPLP–140 and OMJPLP–141A, 141B, and 141C (Figures 1.3, 1.4). Its full extent was about 3 ha and corresponds to the land from the base of the headland to the top of the slope leading down to the old estuary of the Río Salango 300 m to the northeast, reaching at its widest point 200 m in from the beach.[2] Additionally, four small Engoroy habitation sites have been identified on low spurs along the north side of the valley of the Río Salango (Allan & Allan 1988).[3]

There were three distinct phases of Engoroy occupation for the main site, each characterised by different ceramics, and with different patterns of use. For Early Engoroy, the main evidence is habitation refuse and one or more human graves located at OMJPLP–141C. Almost no Early Engoroy ceramics have been identified amongst the material examined from 141B–T3.[4] Early Engoroy ceramics did not appear either in the material recovered from non-archaeological pits and trenches dug to the north and east of 141C, 141A, and 141B. It appears that in its early phase, Engoroy Salango was a relatively small settlement dedicated to the same fishing activities as characterised the preceding Machalilla period.

With Middle Engoroy, there was a major change in settlement organisation and use. Most important of all, at 141B, to the southwest of the earlier habitation site identified at 141C, there was constructed first a ceremonial floor, and then over that a northeast-facing ceremonial house.[5] This house was to be the first of the series of ceremonial structures that dominated Salango from 600 BC to AD 600.

While refuse layers surrounded the house and subsequent Engoroy platforms at 141B, no Middle or Late Engoroy refuse was identified at site 141C. However, Engoroy period floors of yellow clay with posthole alignments, apparently oriented northeast-southwest and northwest-southeast, and hearths, were found at 141A.[6] Their similarity with contexts excavated at 141B suggests that they may have formed part of a sequence of structures of middle or late phase Engoroy closely associated with those at 141B. Late Engoroy pottery was recovered both northeast from 141C, at 141A, and a little to the east beyond 141A. Additionally, ritually deposited stone figurines, such as those found in the floor surrounding the final Late Engoroy platform at 141B, were recovered at 141C and 141A, and also from private land 80 m to the south.[7]

The overall pattern of artefact distribution and of excavated structures suggests that by Late Engoroy the ceremonial precinct or centre consisted of the main platform at 141B and a surrounding plaza, also dedicated to ceremonial performance, that extended at least 50 m to the northeast as far as 141C, at least 20 m east, reaching or perhaps passing beyond a secondary structure at 141A, and at least 80 m to the south. Beyond that, a further zone as far as the edge of the settlement was possibly occupied by habitation structures.

---

[1] In one case, 200 holes, 2 m deep and 1.20 m across, were dug at various spots throughout the village as latrine pits. Artefacts from nine of these pits were brought to the museum for me to see. In the second case, every street in the village was trenched along one side to accommodate new water pipes, and I was able to inspect over 2 km of trenches so created.

[2] This spot lies close to the Bongo restaurant, owned by Rita Guillén, where the largest sample of Late Engoroy and Early Regional Development pottery was found during the latrine project.

[3] Graber (2004:151–152) casts doubt on the existence of these sites, indicating that he was unable to confirm the cultural affiliation of any of them as Engoroy. He was also unable to identify any other Engoroy sites in the Salango valley (Graber 2004:163).

[4] No ceramic analysis has been carried out yet on the Engoroy material from OMJPLP–141A.

[5] It is possible that the space occupied by the Middle Engoroy structures had in Early Engoroy times been some sort of plaza, itself given over to public events. Equally, although there is no sign of Early Engoroy structures under the Middle Engoroy house, there may have been some ceremonial building elsewhere in this area during that phase.

[6] This material has not yet been systematically analysed.

[7] These figurines were found in the yard of Sr. Colón Figueroa during a latrine project conducted in 2000 by the Programa de Manejo de Recursos Costeros.

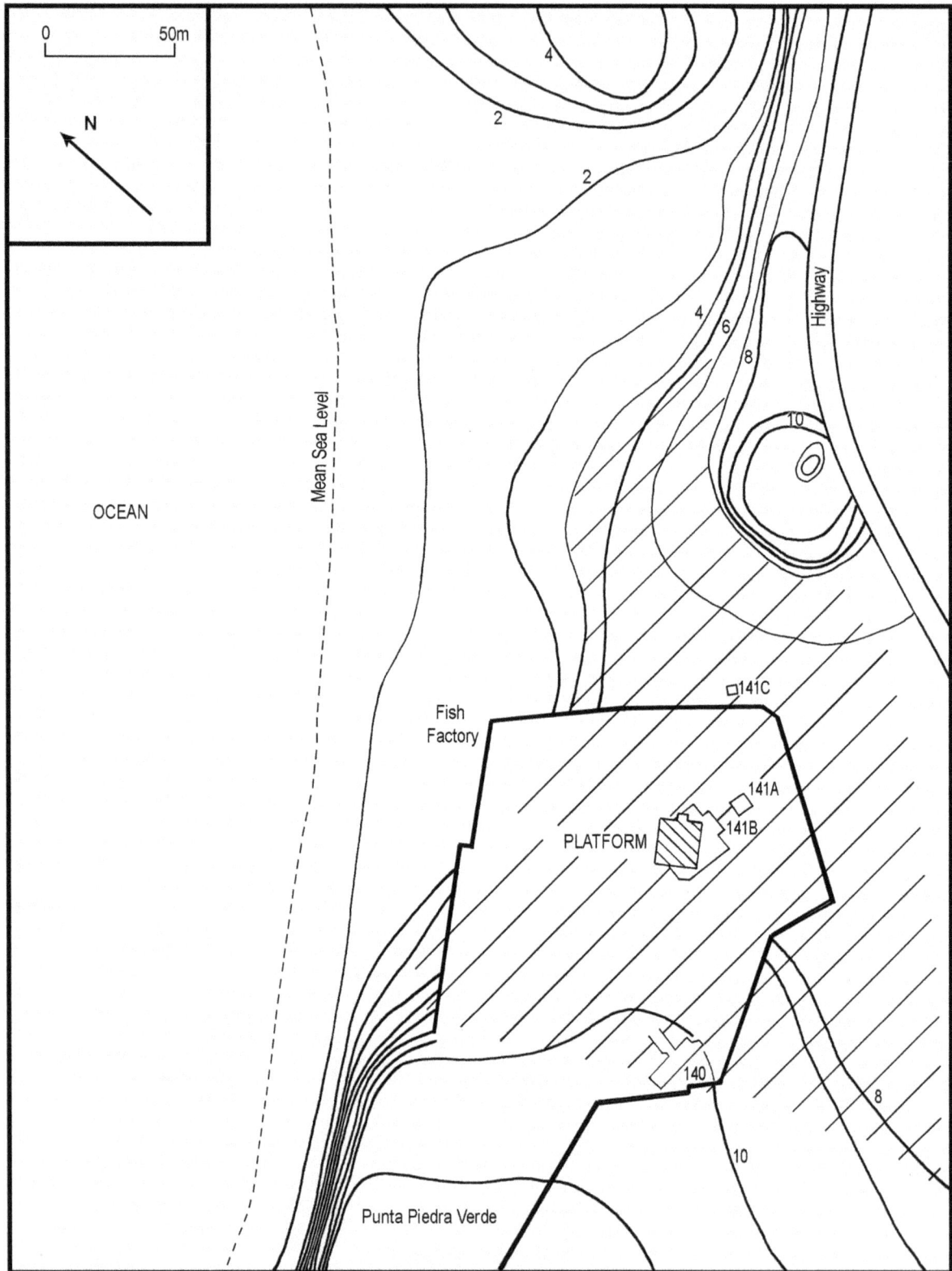

Figure 1.3. Salango: approximate area of Engoroy occupation (shaded) in relation to sectors OMJPLP–140, 141A, 141B, and 141C, and to the local topography (contours at metre intervals). Reprinted by permission from Springer Nature Customer Service Centre GmbH: Springer, Pre-Columbian Landscapes of Creation and Origin, by J. Staller, ed. © (2008).

1.4. OMJPLP–141B–T3 Salango

Sector OMJPLP–141B was opened for excavation in June 1982 as part of the field research currently being undertaken by the Programa de Antropología para el Ecuador (PAE). Initially, it took the form of a series of small and independent units, which were subsequently amalgamated within a broader area excavation ultimately covering 550 m². Beneath Manteño period surface remains was a culturally sterile layer that in turn capped

Figure 1.4. OMJPLP–141B in May 1983. View to the southwest showing the headland rising behind the site, the beach, and the fish factory installations.

the Regional Development contexts. Principal amongst the latter were elaborate primary burials set within a low platform comprised by a complex arrangement of rectangular clay structures oriented to the northeast. However, certain units reached Late Formative levels, and while the evidence is partly compromised by the presence of intrusive Regional Development tombs, in unit L–82, which area was subsequently included as part of Trench 4, there was clear indication of the yellow clay layers typical of the Late Formative structures to be described below.

From 11th November 1983, investigation focused on the westward rear corner of the platform with the aim of defining the nature of the structures, their relation to the burials, and their cultural affiliations. This area of the site, encompassing 88 m², was designated Trench 3 (T3). The results of the field work, which continued more or less without interruption through to 7th October 1986, are reported in detail elsewhere (Lunniss 2001; Lunniss & Mudd 1987). Here, a summary of the evidence at T3 for the Late Formative period occupation will help explain the specific goals of this paper.

A sequence of seven Late Formative period structures was identified, Structures 1 to 5 corresponding to Middle Engoroy, and Structures 6 and 7 corresponding to Late Engoroy. Each structure was oriented on a northeast-southwest axis, with the entrance assumed to be to the northeast. In the case of Structures 1, 2, 3, and 6, it was possible to recover direct evidence for both their southwest and their northwest sides. For Structures 4, 5, and 7, only the southwest side lay within the confines of the excavation area. Between Structure 7 and the first of the Regional Development structures was a brief transitional phase with no building carried out.

The structures showed considerable changes in overall configuration as the sequence evolved. Structure 1 consisted of a yellow clay floor with a rectangular wooden superstructure. For Structure 2, the floor was replaced with a low platform of the same material. With Structure 3 the platform was extended, and its perimeter was defined by a sunken wall of a different coloured clay, this in turn connecting to an area of clay floor around the outside of the wall. With Structures 4 and 5, further clay walls were built, and the platform edge was recapped. With Structure 6, a much more substantial clay wall extended away from the platform as a deep, tapering layer, so creating a broader expanse of exterior clay floor than had previously existed, and the platform centre was recapped. Structure 7 consisted of another large wall, set flush with the Structure 6 wall and exterior floor surface, with further recapping of the platform. No large rectangular wooden superstructures were found for Structures 4 to 7.

In addition to the elements of the structures themselves, there were many associated features of different types, including, principally, human burials, stone figurine depositions, animal and bird burials, and structured depositions or offerings of a variety of other artefacts and materials. There were two groups of human burials. One was associated with Structure 1. The other corresponded on purely stratigraphic grounds to Structures 3 to 7 and the transition phase, though it is likely that all the graves post-dated Structure 6. This second group was also associated with funerary fire pits and rubbish pits. The stone figurine depositions were all associated with Structure 7. The other depositions fell at different points through the sequence.

In short, there was evidence not only for a unique sequence of ceremonial structures, but also for a wide variety of features and artefacts in direct and intentional association with them. However, the view gained of the site was obviously far from complete. It was just a rear quarter that was in each case recovered of the structures, and the building elements were in some cases either only partially preserved or not present within the excavation area. To achieve a more complete view of the configuration and design of each of the structures of the entire sequence, along with their entrance ways, it was necessary to excavate their front halves to the northeast. Accordingly, Trench 4 (T4) was opened for excavation on 23rd March 1987 (Figure 1.5).

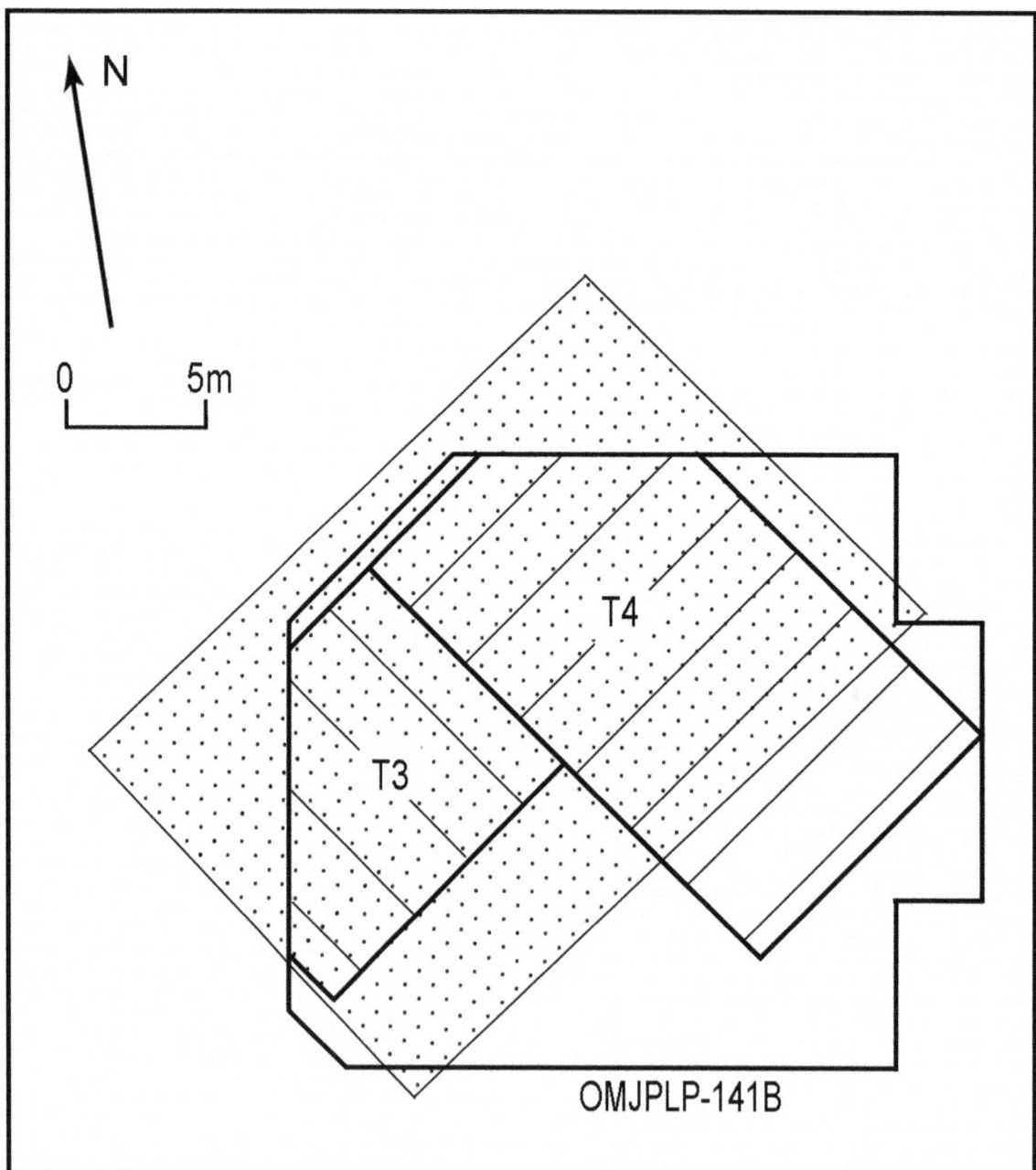

Figure 1.5. Site OMJPLP–141B, with Trenches 3 y 4, and the area (stippled) represented by the reconstructed building plans. Reprinted by permission from Springer Nature Customer Service Centre GmbH: Springer, Pre-Columbian Landscapes of Creation and Origin, by J. Staller, ed. © (2008).

1.5. Excavation of OMJPLP–141B–T4 Salango

The excavation of T4, like that of T3, began with the structures of the Regional Development Period, and by June 1988 these had been mostly removed, under the direction of Andy Mudd and Ian Mays. Later that year, John Johnson was appointed field director, with the brief to follow the sequence down through the Late Formative levels as far as that of the first building identified in T3, i.e., Structure 1. Beginning field work on 19th October 1988 and assisted by local workers as well as professional archaeologists and archaeology students, Johnson completed his task on 27th May 1989. The site was then handed back to the Empresa Pesquera Polar, which owns the land, and subsequently buried under the foundations of a fish meal warehouse. Any visitor to the site today would not be able even to guess from the appearance of things that the modern factory hides from sight and enquiry one of the most interesting and informative archaeological sites to have been identified on the Ecuadorian coast.

For T3, the very complex stratigraphic sequence had been excavated and recorded using single context planning (Harris 1979; Lunniss 2001:55–61). The same methodology was applied to the excavation of T4. Contexts 10001 to 11986 having been excavated by Mudd and Mays, Johnson proceeded to excavate contexts 11987 to 13397.

2

Methodology

Abstract: The principal aims of the study of the data from OMJPLP–141B–T4 were to: 1) identify the sequence of Late Formative ceremonial structural elements recorded in that area; 2) correlate those elements with the sequence obtained for OMJPLP–141B–T3; and 3) reconstruct the full design and dimensions of each of the structures. All available documentary material relating to the excavation of Late Formative period contexts at T4 was gathered and reviewed. Analysis and reconstruction of the stratigraphic sequence at T4 followed the order of procedures applied to T3: preliminary interpretations were made of the nature and function of the contexts; full context plans were drawn up for each of the structural elements identified; the elements were sorted into a sequence of eight structural episodes; major features and potential posthole patterns associated with the structures were identified; and composite plans were then drawn up for the eight structural episodes at T4. The seven structures and elements thereof at T3 were now correlated with those episodes. With the integrated stratigraphic sequence determined, the respective plans of the elements from T3 and T4 were combined on plan drawings for each of the episodes. And from these, complete schematized plan outlines and profiles were produced for the reconstructions of the ceremonial structures.

Resumen: Los objetivos principales del estudio de los datos de OMJPLP–141B–T4 fueron 1) identificar la secuencia de elementos estructurales ceremoniales del Formativo Tardío registrados en esa área; 2) correlacionar esos elementos con la secuencia obtenida para OMJPLP–141B–T3; y, 3) reconstruir el diseño completo y las dimensiones de cada una de las estructuras. Se reunió y revisó todo el material documental disponible relacionado con la excavación de contextos del período Formativo Tardío en T4. El análisis y reconstrucción de la secuencia estratigráfica en T4 siguió el orden de los procedimientos aplicados a T3: se hicieron interpretaciones preliminares de la naturaleza y función de los contextos; se elaboraron planos de contexto completos para cada uno de los elementos estructurales identificados; los elementos se ordenaron en una secuencia de ocho episodios estructurales; se identificaron los rasgos principales y los posibles patrones de hoyos de poste asociados con las estructuras; y luego se elaboraron planos compuestos para los ocho episodios estructurales en T4. Las siete estructuras y elementos de estas en T3 ahora se correlacionaron con esos episodios. Con la secuencia estratigráfica integrada así determinada, los planos respectivos de los elementos de T3 y T4 se combinaron en dibujos de plano para cada uno de los episodios. Y de estos se produjeron planos y perfiles esquematizados completos de las reconstrucciones de las estructuras ceremoniales.

The principal aims of the study of the data from OMJPLP–141B–T4 were to:

1. identify the sequence of Late Formative ceremonial structural elements recorded in that area;
2. correlate those elements with the sequence obtained for OMJPLP–141B–T3; and
3. reconstruct the full design and dimensions of each of the structures.

That done, additional analysis would incorporate evidence for important features associated with the structures.

The first step was to locate and gather all the available documentary material relating to the excavation of Late Formative period contexts at T4. These, for the most part, belonged to that part of the sequence excavated by Johnson. Initial efforts, then, were directed to contexts 11987 to 13397. Although sixteen years had passed since the end of the field work, the original field record was almost entirely intact, and consisted of: context sheets, context plans, the Harris Matrixes, the context register, the levels register, profile drawings of the trench walls recorded at the end of the excavation, the photographic register, the finds inventory, the special finds register, the worked shell register, and the accession cards with descriptions of the special finds. Unfortunately, however, although colour slides and black and white photographs were taken throughout the excavation, only one set of black and white negatives could be traced amongst the PAE archives at Salango.

Analysis and reconstruction of the stratigraphic sequence at T4 then followed the order of procedures applied to T3 (Lunniss 2001:62–69). Throughout, much reliance was placed on the observations and interpretations made in the field and recorded by Johnson and his excavators on the context sheets, or by Johnson on the various Harris Matrixes which he drew up during and after excavation. First, all context sheets were reviewed, and a preliminary interpretation was made wherever possible of the nature and function of each context. A skeleton matrix was then drawn up of all deposits that appeared to represent elements of structures, principally clay layers, clay walls, components of the entranceways, i.e., clay steps and clay ramps, and clay floors surrounding the main structures. This was achieved using the stratigraphic data compiled by Johnson, consisting of one complete Matrix for all contexts from 11197 to 12495, an outline Matrix for the remaining sequence, and rough but detailed Matrixes for the various subsequences of his outline Matrix. Third, full context plans were drawn up for each of the structural elements identified and then their stratigraphic relations were re-examined. At this stage it became possible to sort the elements into a more ordered sequence of eight structural episodes, each consisting of one or more structural elements.

Next, a review was made of other contexts that appeared to represent major features associated with the structures. Attention was focused principally on human burials, stone figurine depositions, and depositions involving other materials and artefact types. The stratigraphic and spatial relations of these contexts to the structures were then defined. As it turned out, the human burials excavated by Johnson did not, in fact, belong to the Late Formative stage of the sequence, but were intrusive features from Early Regional Development levels. At this point, a review was then made of contexts excavated by Mudd and Mays for any graves of Late Formative type that they might have excavated, and four were identified. And negative features other than those just mentioned were reviewed to identify possible posthole patterns associated with the floors, platform layers and clay walls. Out of this material, composite plans were drawn up for the eight structural episodes identified for T4, each including the main elements of the structure, the main associated features such as human burials, figurine depositions, etc., and associated postholes. Postholes not directly or clearly related to a major structural component were excluded from these plans.

Finally, a review was made of the inventory of special finds recovered from T4. At T3, certain artefact types were commonly associated with ritual offerings (Lunniss 2001:158). It was expected that the overall pattern of special artefact distribution at T4 would not only provide useful comparative background for analysis of structured depositions already identified but might also lead to the identification of others that had escaped notice. Both expectations were met.

With the data from T4 in place, the next step was to correlate the sequence with that obtained for T3. As a start, contexts that extended across the line dividing T3 from T4 were used to link the sequences of those two sectors.

That done, the relative positions of the other contexts were compared, and descriptive data and context levels were then used to assess the possible correlations between the remaining walls and layers of the two trenches. Here it was seen not only that the T4 sequence began before that for T3, but also that the interpretation given to the T3 sequence needed to be in some places modified.

Based on the evidence from T3, the stratigraphic sequence for Middle and Late Engoroy was seen to consist of seven successive Structures. T4, however, presents evidence for the creation of at least one ritual space prior to the construction of the first structure excavated in T3. Furthermore, the data from T4 demonstrated that the internal correlation of several important contexts within T3 itself were not entirely correct. Rather than attempt to recast the Structures identified for T3 in accordance with the requirements of the new data, it seemed easier to create a new term for the stages of construction identified for T4, and to reallocate the contexts from T3 accordingly. The term used is Episode.

Broadly speaking, Episode 1 consists of the evidence from T4 for a clay floor that predates Structure 1 as identified in T3, and Structure 1 is relabelled Episode 2. Episode 3 correlates directly and simply with Structure 2, while all the elements of Structure 3 fall in Episode 4. The elements of Structures 4 and 5 are less certainly correlated, respectively, with Episodes 5 and 6. Episode 6 also includes a platform cap (5409) that had earlier been linked to Structure 6. Episode 7 includes the walls of Structure 6 (4642 and 4632) and the platform cap (4344) of Structure 7. Finally, Episode 8 includes the wall (4622) of Structure 7. The outline sequence is shown in more detail in Figure 2.1 where, in the left-hand columns, Episode numbers (e.g., E2) for T4 are given alongside the corresponding Structure numbers (e.g., ST1) for T3. In parentheses to the right are the specific contexts of T3 that correlate unambiguously with main contexts of T4, along with the numbers of the structures with which they were originally identified (Lunniss 2001: Sequence Diagram 2).

With the stratigraphic sequence determined, the respective plans of the elements from T3 and T4 were combined on single plan drawings for each of the structural episodes, each one showing the total set of relevant information obtained through excavation. These plans, which are not included in this report, then formed the basis for reconstruction of the complete design and dimensions for each building. Thus, the recovered data were used both to project the likely positions of building outlines or elements that lay outside T3 and T4, and to reconstruct elements that had been destroyed by later features. Using the excavated data and the projections based on them, complete schematized plan outlines were produced for the structures of each episode, save Episode 5, where the data were insufficiently complete and secure. In addition, complete schematized profiles were reconstructed, again excepting Episode 5. For each episode, save Episode 1, there are two such drawings, one showing the central

T4 Episode	T3 Structure	T4 Contexts	T3 Corresponding Context: Structure
E8	ST7	12321 Ramp	
		12344 Ramp	
		12380 Ramp	
		12388 Ramp	
- - - - - - -		12385 Outer Floor ═══12348 Ramp	4622:ST7
		12407 Steps	
		12546 Ramp	
E7	ST6	12567 Ramp	
		12482 Platform Cap	4344:ST7
- - - - - - -		12501 Wall	4632/4642:ST6
		12584 Steps	
E6	ST5	12677 Outer Floor 12598 Entrance Wall 12693 Wall	
		12570 Platform Cap	5409:ST6
- - - - - - -		12855 Entrance Wall 12632 Entrance Wall	
E5	ST4	12791 Platform Cap	
		12876 Platform Cap	
		12899 Wall	
- - - - - - -		12849 Outer Floor	5705:ST3
E4	ST3	12936 Platform Cap	5776:ST3
		12878 Wall	5805:ST3
		12983 Wall	
E3	ST2	12953 Platform	6500:ST2
E2	ST1	13316 House Floor	7300:ST1
E1		13360 Central Floor	

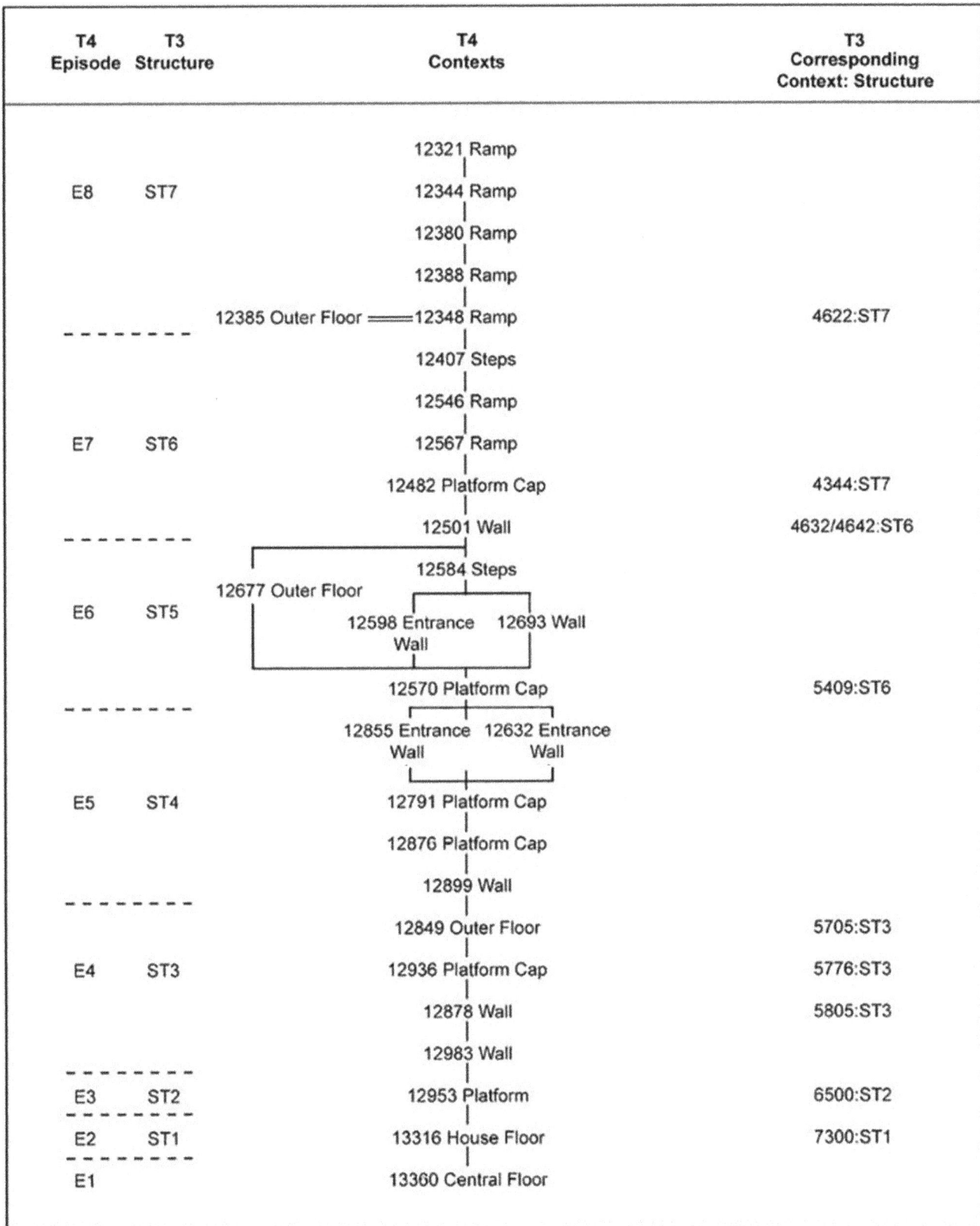

Figure 2.1. Harris Matrix showing key depositional events associated with the Late Formative ceremonial structures at OMJPLP–141B–T4.

axis and entranceway, the other showing a parallel cross-section that passes to the northwest of the entrance. For Episode 1, there is just the cross-section of its suggested central axis. The end points of each profile are indicated on the respective reconstructed plan outlines.

In Chapter 3, the written text describes the basic form and elements of each of the structures as encountered in T4. It also includes not only the burials and ritual offerings, but also describes the slightly more complicated sequences of deposition associated with the entrance ways. Footnotes are used for alternative readings of the stratigraphy or to present qualifying statements. But for this presentation, there has had to be a great deal of compromise. The sheer quantity of data recorded was enormous, and some drastic process of selection had to be followed to make a readable text with clear focus on the ceremonial structures and the principal associated features. Excluded, then, is discussion of the many layers and features that could not, within the time allowed, be properly interpreted. The drawn plans are also simplified, in that they show just the main solid elements of each structure (i.e., clay layers and clay walls), the most important identified posthole patterns, and main associated features. Postholes not obviously in any pattern, and uninterpreted negative features are all excluded, save for Episode 2, where it is necessary to show all the features of T4 as background to the selection made in the reconstruction of the building.

In Chapter 4, combining the evidence from T3 and T4 and following the sequence presented in Figure 2.1, the overall structural design for each episode is described. Focus is once more put on the structures, their integral components, and the relation with them had by secondary features such as graves and artefact offerings. Many features such as rubbish pits and firepits associated with the later human burials, rectangular pits possibly used for mixing clay, evidence for the use of fire and ash over the platforms and for the process of accumulation of discarded material around the platforms, and the secondary or ephemeral structures represented by postholes either on or outside the platforms, especially as represented in T3, have been left out of the discussion. The reconstructed schematic profile and plan drawings present simplified images that, distilling the available contextual evidence, aim to convey the overall design of each structure, the major associated features, including human burials, of Episode 2, and the main offerings of the remaining episodes. They also include the location of major features associated with the central axes of the structures.

A major initial working hypothesis adopted when reconstructing the building outlines was that they would each follow a pattern of bilateral symmetry either side of a main northeast-southwest axis. This assumption seemed to be justified by the ceramic models of temples, whether they represent actual or ideal structures (Cummins 2003:451–456), which all present this symmetric form. It also allowed for a simpler process of reconstruction. Thus, given that there was usually adequate data for one side of the structure, after first identifying the position of the central axis it would be in theory relatively easy in any instance to account for the undocumented side. However, as the reconstruction advanced, it became apparent that although the principle of symmetry either side of a central axis was maintained as a general guide, absolute symmetry was not always sought. For example, the front wall might be wider or further forward on one side of the entrance than on the other, or the entrance might not be at the true centre of the front wall.

The Datum point for T3 was at approximate contemporary ground level (Lunniss 2001:58), and all levels were referenced directly to this. For T4, a temporary benchmark was established, 1.13 m below the T3 Datum point, and levels were added to the plans without correction for this difference. It was reassuring to find, when I came to compare the levels of contexts that crossed from T3 to T4, that the data from each sector correlated perfectly once the difference had been corrected for. Importantly, this allowed me to be confident in combining the levels from each sector when reconstructing the structure profiles.

Finally, a word about the different series of numbers used in the text. Numbers without a prefix, e.g., 13316, are used to designate specific excavated contexts. Numbers prefixed with a B, e.g., B1192, refer to individual artefacts, save in the case of shell artefacts, which are prefixed with CT, e.g., CT831.

3

The Stratigraphic Sequence at OMJPLP–141B–T4

Abstract: The stratigraphic sequence at OMJPLP–141B–T4 presents evidence for eight episodes of construction and use of a series of yellow clay floors and platforms mostly and variously associated with upstanding wooden structures, low clay perimetral walls, and exterior clay floors, all designed for ceremonial purposes. Episode 1 involved a yellow clay floor with an open hearth. In Episode 2, a yellow clay floor was associated with elements of a rectangular wooden structure that went through two main phases of use. Over the floor were layers of ash derived from open hearths, including a central oval hearth, as well as patches of yellow clay covering the hearths. While the surface of the floor was generally clean of artefacts, outside it were extensive deposits of discarded material. After dismantling of the Episode 2 house, Episode 3 saw construction of a yellow clay platform up to 35 cm thick with a ramp on the northeast side, and a surface marked by burning and ash scatters, with extensive build-up of discard around the outside. In Episode 4, the existing platform was surrounded by a low clay wall supporting a row of posts set in holes at intervals of 40 to 70 cm, more yellow clay was added to the platform, and a layer of clay was laid outside the wall. In Episode 5, the old wall was replaced by a new clay deposit, and more yellow clay was added to the platform on two separate occasions, ultimately being covered by ash derived from open hearths situated directly on the surface of the clay. For Episode 6, a thick new cap of yellow clay was added to the northeast front and the top of the platform, the outer floor was resurfaced, and a complex new entrance was built into the front slope, involving a low front wall and, up from that, a flight of clay steps bracketed by and flush with a clay wall to either side and at the top. Offerings were incorporated in the steps. With Episode 7, a clay wall up to 80 cm tall and 120 cm thick was built around the existing platform, leaving a 2.80 m wide entrance, and a new platform cap of yellow clay was laid. The entrance was the setting for a complex series of ramps and steps, along with offerings and offering pits. For Episode 8, the old clay wall was augmented by a new wall outside it and clay infill between, resulting in an overall width of 3 m at the front and 2.50 m along the sides. A series of ramps were added to the entranceway steps, again with offerings and offering pits, along with a gateway and large central post. The final ramp and area outside it were covered directly by a 1–3 cm layer of ash most likely of volcanic origin.

From Episode 2 onwards, 19 shell, stone, and pottery anthropomorphic figurines and pendants were found, several of them incorporated in platform entranceways. Three human burials and a grave-like pit set into the final platform may have been of Episode 7, 8, or later. Stone discs, and beads of greenstone, shell, and ceramic were found, notably in human burials, offering pits, and scattered in soil layers at the entrance. There were two small pottery lime containers, and a zoomorphic whistling bottle.

Resumen: La secuencia estratigráfica de OMJPLP–141B–T4 presenta evidencia de ocho episodios de construcción y uso de una serie de pisos y plataformas de arcilla amarilla mayoritaria y diversamente asociados con estructuras verticales de madera, muros perimetrales bajos de arcilla, y pisos exteriores de arcilla, todos diseñados para propósitos ceremoniales. El Episodio 1 involucró un piso de arcilla amarilla con un hogar abierto. En el Episodio 2, se asoció un piso de arcilla amarilla con elementos de una estructura rectangular de madera que pasó por dos fases principales de uso. Sobre el piso había capas de ceniza derivadas de hogares abiertos, incluido un hogar ovalado central, así como parches de arcilla amarilla que cubrían los hogares. Si bien la superficie del piso estaba generalmente limpia de artefactos, afuera había extensos depósitos de desechos. Después del desmantelamiento de la casa del Episodio 2, el Episodio 3 vio la construcción de una plataforma de arcilla amarilla de hasta 35 cm de espesor con una rampa en el lado noreste y una superficie marcada por quema y cenizas dispersas, con una gran acumulación de desechos alrededor del exterior. En el Episodio 4, la plataforma existente estuvo rodeada por un muro bajo de arcilla que sostenía una fila de postes colocados en hoyos a intervalos de 40 a 70 cm, se agregó más arcilla amarilla a la plataforma, y se colocó una capa de arcilla fuera del muro. En el Episodio 5, el antiguo muro fue reemplazado por un nuevo depósito de arcilla, y se agregó a la plataforma en dos ocasiones distintas más arcilla amarilla que finalmente quedó cubierta por cenizas derivadas de hogares abiertos situados directamente en la superficie de la arcilla. Para el Episodio 6, se agregó una capa nueva y gruesa de arcilla amarilla al frente noreste y a la parte superior de la plataforma, se repavimentó el piso exterior, y se construyó una entrada nueva y compleja en la pendiente frontal, que involucró una pared frontal baja y, hacia arriba desde esta, un tramo de gradas de arcilla rodeadas por y al ras con una pared de arcilla a cada lado y en la parte superior. Se incorporaron ofrendas en las gradas. Con el Episodio 7, se construyó un muro de arcilla de hasta 80 cm de altura y 120 cm de espesor alrededor de la plataforma existente, dejando una entrada de 2,80 m de ancho, y se colocó una nueva capa de arcilla amarilla sobre la plataforma. La entrada fue el escenario de una serie compleja de rampas y gradas, junto con ofrendas y pozos de ofrenda. Para el Episodio 8, el antiguo muro de arcilla se amplió con un nuevo muro en el exterior y un relleno de arcilla en el medio, lo que resultó en un ancho total de 3 m en el frente y 2,50 m en los lados. Se agregaron una serie de rampas a las gradas de la entrada, nuevamente con ofrendas y pozos de ofrenda, junto con un portón y un gran poste central. La rampa final y el área exterior estuvieron cubiertas directamente por una capa de ceniza de 1 a 3 cm, muy probablemente de origen volcánico.

Desde el Episodio 2 en adelante, se encontraron 19 figurines y colgantes antropomorfos de concha, piedra, y cerámica, varios de ellos incorporados en las entradas de las plataformas. Tres entierros humanos y un pozo con forma de tumba ubicados en la plataforma final pueden haber sido del Episodio 7, 8, o después. Se encontraron discos de piedra y cuentas de piedra verde, concha, y cerámica, especialmente en entierros humanos, pozos de ofrenda, y esparcidos en capas de tierra en la entrada. Había dos pequeños recipientes de cal cerámicos y una botella silbato zoomorfa.

3.1. The Ceremonial Structures

3.1.1. Episode 1: Floor 13360

The earliest clear evidence for the deliberate creation of a physical setting for the enactment of ritual is context 13360, a 3 cm thick layer of hard yellow (10YR 5/6) clay (Figures 3.1, 3.2). This floor was of irregular outline and had been truncated to the south and east. Its surviving dimensions were 5.10 m (east-west) by 3.40 m (north-south). Towards the south was an open hearth (13361), represented by a roughly 1-m-wide oval area of burnt clay overlain by grey-white ash. No other features were associated with the clay.[8]

3.1.2. Episode 2: Floor 13316

Overlying and extending beyond the edges of that first floor, 13316 was also a surface of hard yellow (10YR 6/6) clay (Figure 3.3). Up to 15 cm thick, it measured 10.50 m (northwest-southeast) by 5.60 m (northeast-southwest). With an overall rectangular form, it had a rounded corner to the north, while the east corner, along with the southeast side, had been lost to intrusion by later features. Associated with the floor were 43 layers and approximately 140

AP	Ash pit		
BB	Bird burial		
CF	Clay floor		
CP	Circular pit		
CW	Clay wall		
DB	Dog burial	○	Registered posthole
F	Figurine deposition	——	Edge of context
GR	Grave	—··—··—	Truncated context edge
GU	Gully	- - - - -	Edge of buried context
H	Hearth	——→	Burial orientation
HB	Human burial	▶——	Slope
OF	Outer clay floor	——	Change of slope
P	Platform	⊙	Postulated posthole
PC	Platform Cap		
PH	Posthole		
R	Ramp		
RD	Ritual deposition		
S	Steps		

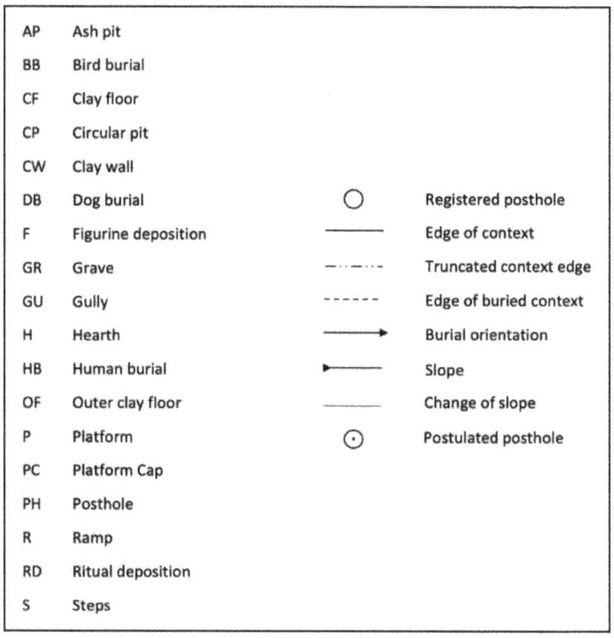

Figure 3.1. Key to plans and profiles.

postholes and other features. The layers directly over the floor area were either of ash or yellow clay. The ash was derived from open hearths situated on the floor, where burning has turned the originally yellow clay a deep red. Over these areas of burning, the ash tended to be crusted, thick, and white, while away from the burning, it was rather finer, lighter, more powdery, and grey. The yellow clay layers seem mostly to have been designed to cap the areas of burning and layers of ash.

Embedded in the clay floor was a pendant (CT831) made of white spondylus shell, and a small greenstone

---

[8] There is mention in the register for an earlier yellow clay floor, context 13043. In Johnson's outline Matrix, 13043 lies at the very bottom of the stratigraphic sequence and is marked as a "Chorrera Floor". There are then six negative features, all probably postholes, five of which are recorded as having cut 13043 while underlying 13316. Additionally, 13043 is recorded as underlying two other layers: one was of ashy midden material (13365), while the other (13362) was itself cut by a further two small negative features, which in turn underlay 13316. There is, however, no plan or context sheet available to provide specific details of these contexts. A further nine postholes in the area of the eight just mentioned are also recorded on context sheets, and these may also be related to 13043, but there are no plans available for them either.

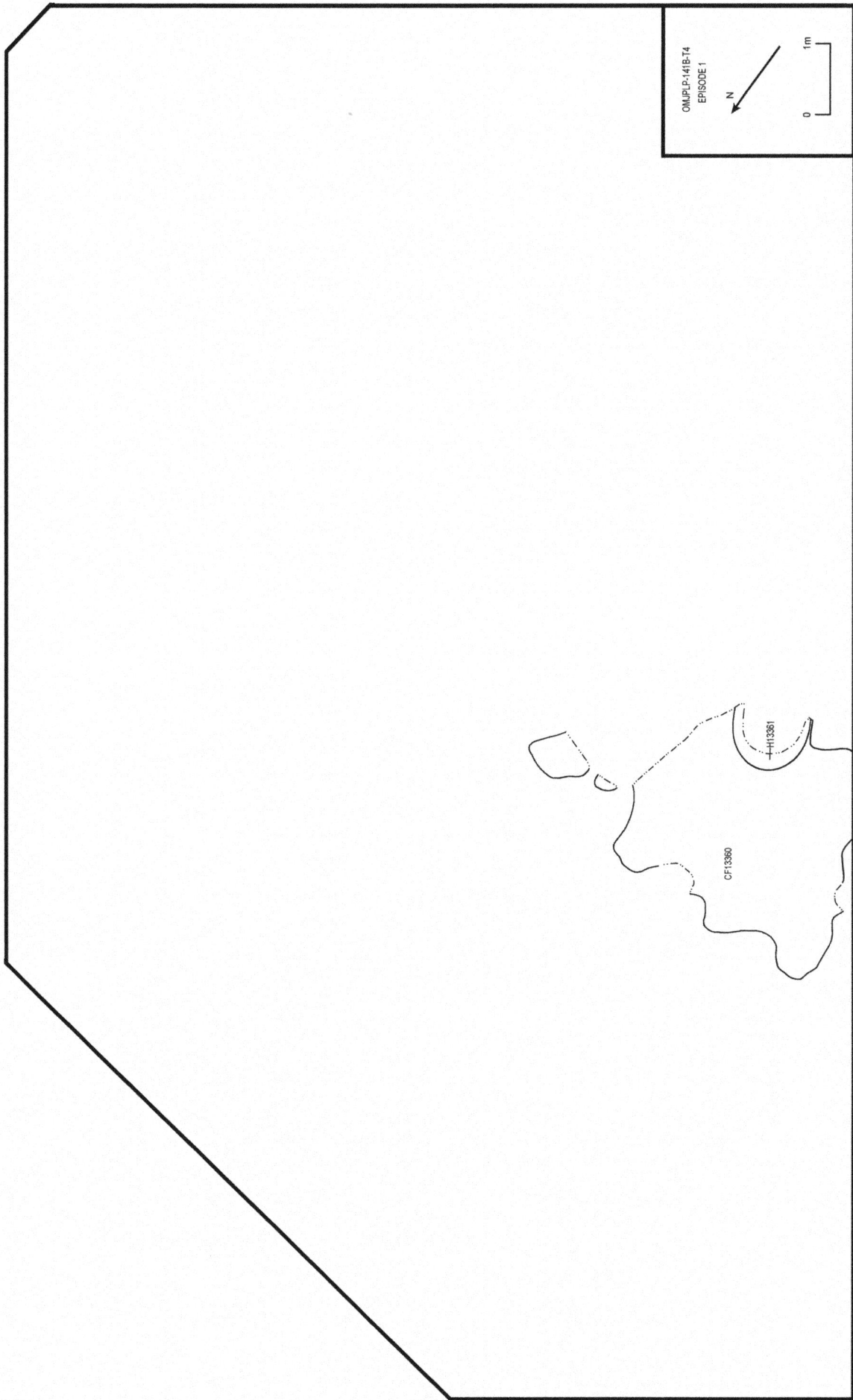

OMJPLP-141B-T4
EPISODE 1

N

0   1m

Figure 3.2. OMJPLP–141B–T4 Episode 1: Plan of the main excavated contexts.

CF13361

CF13360

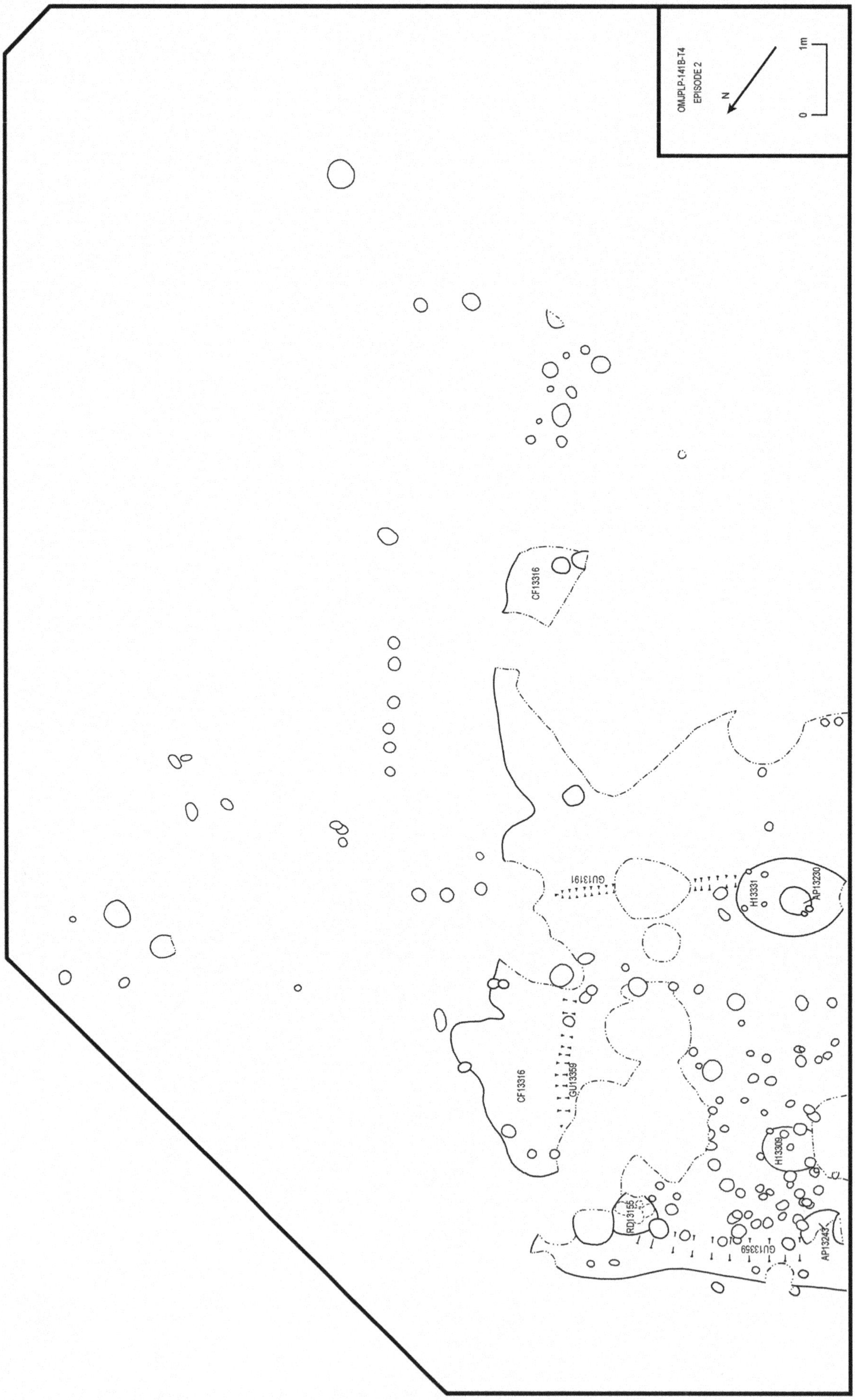

Figure 3.3. OMJPLP–141B–T4 Episode 2: Plan of the main excavated contexts.

disc (B1258). In one of the layers of ash was a small greenstone disc (B1259, very similar to B1258), while another contained a small fragment of copper (B1276). In general, very few artefacts were found directly over the floor. By contrast, around the outside of the floor, and extending onto it over its edges, were extensive deposits of discarded material containing large quantities of pottery sherds, bone, shell, and other artefacts. Amongst these were a solid pottery figurine (B1226) and a tiny tear-drop pendant made of purple spondylus (CT822).

Along the northwest and northeast sides of 13316, though interrupted at the north corner by a later feature, there was a shallow gully, 13359. Up to 35 cm wide and 3 cm deep along the northwest side, along the northeast side the gully was narrower, at 20 cm, but of the same depth. To the southeast, its end was also truncated. A further 1.30 m on, a second gully, 13191, up to 6 cm deep and also 20 cm wide, headed 2.70 m to the southwest, i.e., at a right angle to 13359. Between the northeast end of 13191 and the feature that truncated 13359, there was a gap of 70 cm, while further to the southeast, there was another space of 1.80 m without sign of a gully, beyond which point the floor had been lost.

Gully 13191 lay 5.50 m from the northwest side of the floor, and 5.00 m from the surviving southeast edge. The evidence suggests that the original southeast side of the floor probably lay not much beyond its surviving point, and that 13191 more or less bisected the northeast half of the floor. The spaces either side of the northeast end of gully 13191 can be interpreted as twin openings from the outside into discrete interior spaces, separated from each other by whatever fixture is represented now by that gully.

The southwest end of gully 13191 ended at an open hearth, 13331, whose oval outline measured 1.10 m by 1.60 m. This hearth sat at the centre of the building, and probably represents one of the first events conducted in the interior of the building. Like the other hearths, it was marked by the heavy red colour of the fired clay at the base and was overlain by a series of alternating layers of ash residue and clay resurfacing, the latter fired to red also.

Many of the postholes were cut directly into the material of the floor itself, others were cut into one or other of the ash and clay layers overlying the floor, while a third set lay beyond the edges of the floor. They represent elements both of a wooden structure built over the floor and of secondary structures outside it. The overall form of the building was rectangular. There appear to have been two principal phases of use, though the overall sequence is rather more complicated. Since interpretation of the posthole patterns depends largely on combination of the data with those from T3, fuller discussion of details of the design suggested by them will be left till Chapter 4.

At the end of the first phase of construction and use of the building, a group of postholes along the northwest side were emptied of their posts, and a shallow scoop (13155) was dug across the tops of the holes. Into this feature were deposited 31 small stones, along with 19 pottery sherds, 11 complete shells and some shell fragments. Further to the southwest along the line of the perimeter gully, a pit (13243) measuring 60 cm across by 4 cm deep, was dug and then filled with ash.

3.1.3. Episode 3: Platform 12953

The final version of the wooden superstructure rising from 13316 was dismantled, and over the floor was laid a 30 to 35 cm thick layer of yellow (10YR 6/4) gravelly clay, so creating a low platform as the foundation for another building (Figure 3.4). The clay layer, 12953, was irregular in its surviving outline, again heavily truncated to the south and east, and its main body measured 7.80 m northwest-southeast by 4.20 m northeast-southwest. On the long northeast side, access to the platform was granted via a ramp about 3.10 m wide, which reached to 2.40 m away. Assuming that the ramp lay at the centre of the front, the overall length of the platform on the northeast side would have been about 11.00 m.

Amongst the artefacts directly associated with 12953 were a small pottery lime container jar (B1232) in the form of a tree snail (*Strophocheilus popelairianus*), a stone figurine (B1231), and two stone discs (B1229, B1230).[9]

There were just eleven features registered that may have been postholes cut into the surface of the cap and ramp, but there was no obvious pattern to suggest any precise form of superstructure. The surface of 12953 was marked by patches of burning and ash scatters. And again, there was extensive build-up of occupation debris around the outside.

3.1.4. Episode 4: Walls 12983 and 12878

The yellow clay platform 12953 was eventually surrounded by a low clay wall (Figure 3.5). On the northeast side, a truncated 2.20 m long section of clay-filled U-shaped trench, 12983, was found to the northwest of the ramp. What survived of the trench was up to 42 cm wide and 25 to 30 cm deep. Its fill was hard yellowish clay. This section of wall may represent a first, independent episode of construction, for which further evidence has been lost. But it is also possible that it was the first part of a two-part episode, in which the greater effort is represented by the more extensive wall 12878.

Wall 12878 was of hard yellowish (10YR 5/4) clay, very similar to that of 12983, and was built immediately after it. Surviving dimensions were 11.80 m along the northeast side and 2.80 m along the southeast.[10] On the northeast side, 12878 appears to have respected the earlier ramp,

---

[9] See Cummins (2003:Fig. 14) for a Chorrera vessel representing a snail shell on top of a stepped platform.
[10] Much of the wall on the southeast side had been removed by earlier excavation.

OMJPLP-141B-T4
EPISODE 3

N

0   1m

PI2963

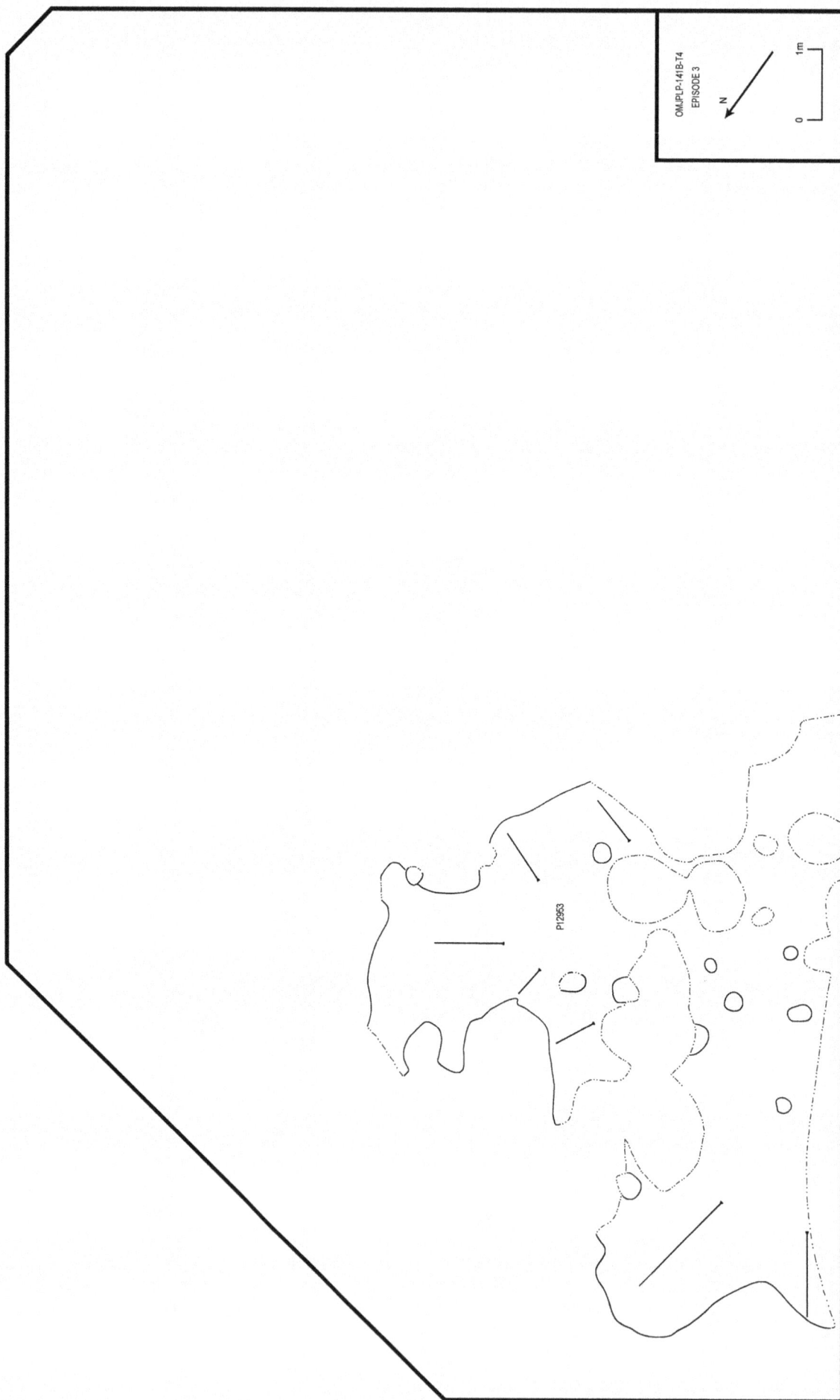

Figure 3.4. OMJPLP–141B–T4 Episode 3: Plan of the main excavated contexts.

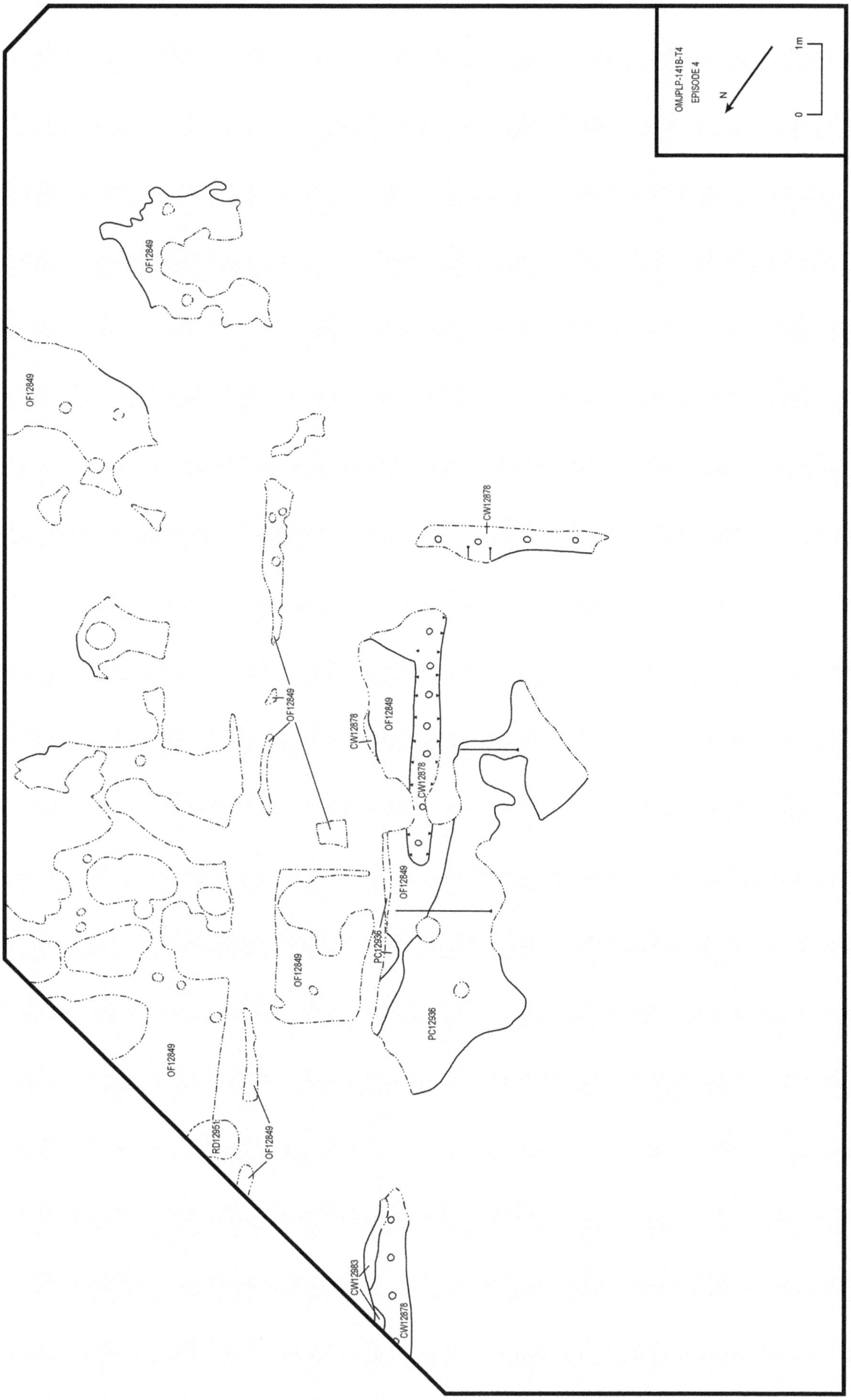

OMJPLP-141B-T4
EPISODE 4

N

0 1m

OF12849

OF12849

OF12849

CW12878

CW12878

OF12849

OF12849

OF12849

CW12878

OF12849

PC12936

PC12936

OF12849

OF12849

OF12849

RD12951

CW12983

CW12878

Figure 3.5. OMJPLP–141B–T4 Episode 4: Plan of the main excavated contexts.

running up to it at its foot, but not cutting into it. Thus, the entrance remained in the same location as before, with a probable width of around 3.00 m. Northwest from the entrance, wall 12878 cut into the top of the earlier 12983, lying slightly inside it. Its trench had a simple U-shape. The clay rose about 15 cm above the top of the trench, extending back slightly over its inside edge, and running forward over its outer lip and edge to cap the top of wall 12983.[11] To the southeast of the entrance, the trench of wall 12878 had a composite profile, with a deeper section about 20 cm wide on the outside and a shallower shelf, again about 20 cm wide, on the inside. The wall rose about 10 cm above the trench top to gain a maximum depth of about 30 cm, and on the outside its clay extended as a thin layer that reached up to at least 70 cm away to the northeast. Along the southeast side of the platform, the trench was a simple U-shape (though the outside edge was truncated), 30 to 40 cm wide, with the wall rising perhaps only a few centimetres above the top of the trench. The top of wall 12878 was flat, and up to 30 cm wide. Cut into the top of the wall, at intervals of 40 to 70 cm, was a row of postholes, each around 12 cm diameter and up to 35 cm deep.

3.1.5. Episode 4: Platform Cap 12936

The creation of wall 12878 was followed by the laying of more yellow (10YR 5/6) gravelly clay over the interior area. This layer, 12936, was found to extend from just outside the entrance on the northeast side, up the old ramp, and along the inside of the wall. Although the layer was truncated or worn, it appears to have served to extend the main body of the platform further to the northeast, so linking it to the wall. It was also overlain by extensive ash deposits most likely deriving from fires burnt directly on the platform surface.

3.1.6. Episode 4: Outer Floor 12849

Next, a layer of silt clay, 12849, was laid over the area outside wall 12878, reaching up the ramp and just inside the line of the wall over the recently laid clay of 12936. This layer created an outer floor that reached up to at least 5.80 m away on the northeast side, and probably extended along the southeast side as well.[12]

3.1.7. Episode 5: Wall 12899

12899 was a truncated deposit of hard, dark yellow brown (10YR 3/6) clay, 1.60 m wide, that lay directly over wall 12878 but probably left the ramp untouched (Figure 3.6). This clay ran northwest to southeast, capping the postholes of 12878 and thus indicating that the fence along that wall had by then been dismantled. While the clay is like that

found in walls, it did not fill a trench. Rather, it probably just sat over 12878, reaching 50 cm back and 50 cm forwards from the edges of the earlier wall, and raising the level along that line by about 15 cm. While it seems then to have been designed to present a more consolidated front, there is no evidence of any sort of fence along it. Nor is it clear whether it was limited to the front of the platform or extended along its sides as well.[13]

3.1.8. Episode 5: Platform Cap 12876

Next, 12876 was a layer of yellow brown gravelly clay that ran from the bottom of the ramp back to the forward edge of the high central area of the platform. The layer was truncated to the south and east, and it did not survive northwest from the top of the ramp, but it seems clear that the purpose of the layer was to bridge the gap between the high ground at the centre of the platform and the newly defined perimeter established by 12899, capping the earlier yellow clay of 12936 with a slightly raised slope.

3.1.9. Episode 5: Platform Cap 12791

A further capping event is represented by 12791, a more extensive layer of yellow gravelly clay, measuring 11.90 m by 3.10 m, that survived across much of the width of the platform, though it was truncated to either side by the perimeter wall of Episode 7. 12791 reached out from the forward edge of the high central area of the platform, buried the old ramp, buried and reached forward from the perimeter established by 12899 to the northeast, and buried also the southeast perimeter. This layer was also covered by an extensive layer of ash that most likely derived from open hearths situated directly over the clay surface.

3.1.10. Episode 5: Entrance Walls 12855 and 12632

Cut into 12791 on the southeast side of the ramp were two short, badly truncated sections of hard clay walls, each filling a U-shaped trench and running northeast-southwest, i.e., parallel to the side of the ramp. One wall, 12855, of brown (10YR 4/3) clay, survived as two short sections, 1.05 m long overall, 0.50 m wide, and up to 30 cm deep. Its rounded southwest end was partially preserved. The other, 12632, was of a similar brown (10YR 3/4) clay and lay slightly to the northwest. Neither end survived. It rose slightly over the top of its trench, which measured 1.05 m long by 32 cm wide, with a depth of 12 cm. The base of 12632 was level along its length.

There is no stratigraphic relation between the trenches, nor is there any surviving evidence for possible correlates on the other side of the ramp. However, it seems likely that these features represented successive events in which the ramped approach to the platform was consolidated and further defined by the addition of a clay wall on each side.[14]

---

[11] 12983, in this section, might correspond to the deeper outer section of the trench for 12878 on the other side of the ramp.

[12] It is not clear whether the elements 12878, 12936, and 12849 were added as parts of a single, if composite, modification to the original design of 12953, or whether they were added as separate modifications, each of which would have been considered complete in itself.

[13] Plans survive only for the northwest section of this context, and it is not known how far 12899 reached to the southeast of the entranceway.

[14] Entrance wall 12598 in Episode 6 is a clearer example of such treatment of the approach.

OMJPLP-141B-T4
EPISODE 5

N

0 — 1m

PC12791

PC12791

CW12855

CW12632

PC12791

PC12876

PC12791

CW12899

PC12791

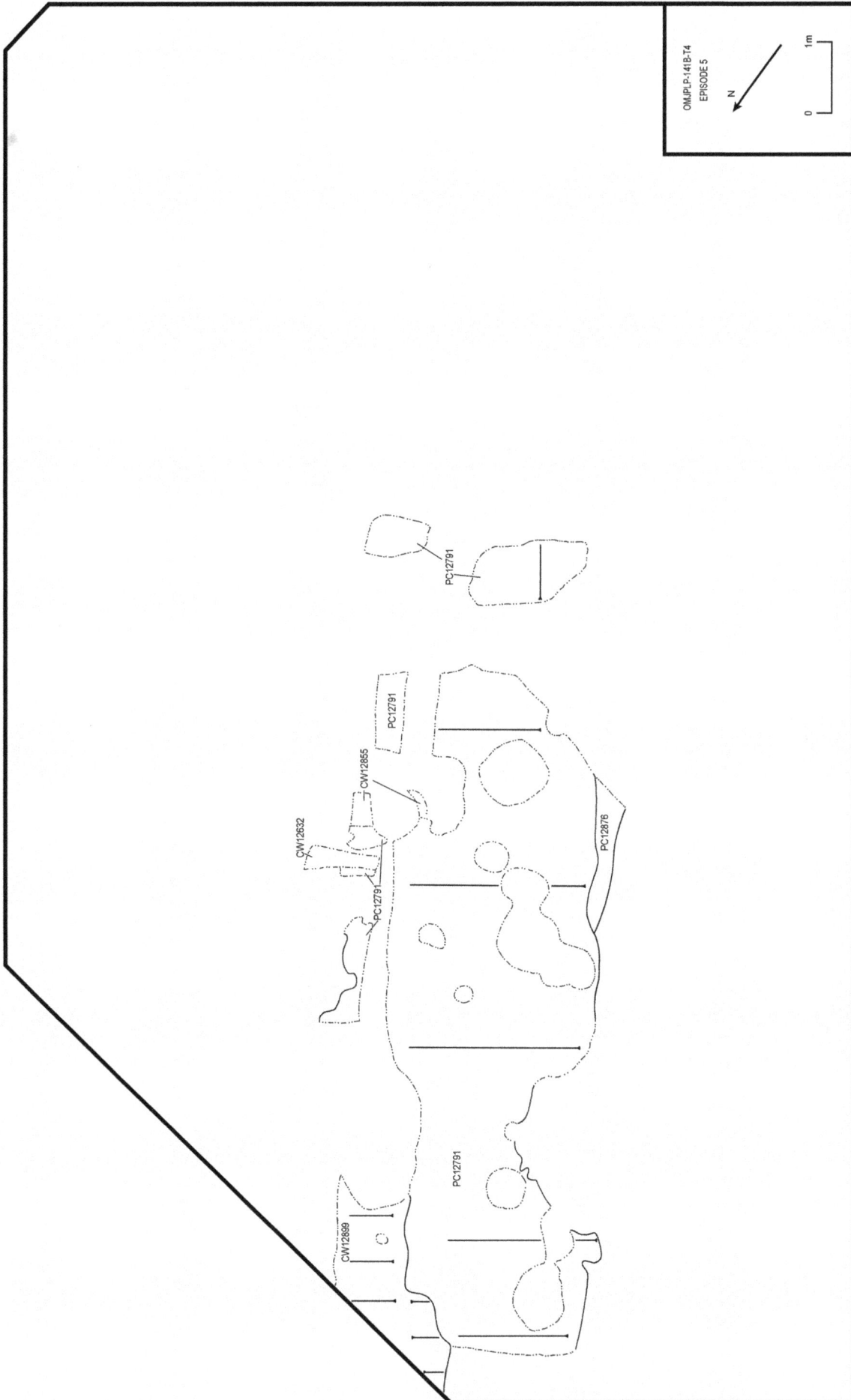

Figure 3.6. OMJPLP–141B–T4 Episode 5: Plan of the main excavated contexts.

3.1.11. Episode 6: Platform Cap 12570

The next major alteration to the platform came with the deposition of 12570, a yellow (10YR 6/4) gravelly clay cap up to 60 cm thick (Figure 3.7). This extended from the southwest edge of T4 to a line approximately 7 m to the northeast, from which point it sloped down to the surrounding floor before running level again for another 2.00 m over the outer area. The height of the platform top relative to the floor to the northeast rose, with this event, to over 80 cm. As the northeast front of the platform was heavily truncated by later wall trenches, we do not have a completely clear picture of how it was structured and cannot say what means were used to give access to the platform top during its initial period of use, but the area inside the entrance was likely higher than what lay to either side and further to the rear. The northwest and southeast sides were also severely truncated, and we have no picture of their precise structure either. However, the width of the platform, i.e., from northwest to southeast, must have been at least 11.40 m. The new platform thus completely covered all earlier platform material but respected both the general orientation of the previous structures and the position of their entrances. In a layer (12579) overlying this platform there was a rather worn stone figurine (B1192).

3.1.12. Episode 6: Outer Floor 12677

To the southeast of the entrance, a fragmented layer of yellow brown clay, 12677, may represent the remains of a resurfacing of the outer floor, and indeed was of the same material as the outer layer of 12570, which it overlay.

3.1.13. Episode 6: Wall 12693, Entrance Wall 12598, and Steps 12584

Sometime after, a clay wall was built at the base of the slope along the front of the platform. This wall, 12693, was of dark brown (10YR 3/3) hard clay. It filled and rose about 12 cm above the top of a simple U-shaped trench subsequently truncated along its northeast side by one later wall trench, and at the southeast end by another. What survived of the trench was 5.30 m long, with a width of 25 cm and a depth of about 20 cm. It is likely that while the wall fronted the platform, it did not reach or turn its corners and would have had an overall length of about 7 m. This wall effectively presented a slightly raised curb along the front of the platform and was the first element of a relatively elaborate restructuring of the approach to the platform top.

The second element was another wall, 12598, built along the top of the ramp and down either side of the entrance way, not quite reaching the first wall at its base. The clay of this second wall was also hard and of a similar dark brown (10YR 3/3) colour. The overall configuration seems to have involved a simple U-shaped trench, about 40 cm wide, with steep to vertical sides and a rounded bottom.[15] The base of the trench was roughly horizontal from end to end. The top length of trench would have measured 3.50 m long by about 60 cm deep, while the arms were about 1.25 m long but only 20 cm deep at the ends. Along the top, the wall rose over 20 cm above the trench, spreading back from the trench as a layer up to 30 cm thick, so creating a consolidated surface level with the top of the platform.

This second wall bracketing the ramp, and the first wall running across its base, were the foundations of a series of steps, 12584, built from the bottom of the ramp to the top. The first wall (12693) itself acted as the bottom step. From its back edge, four step-like cuts, were made up the ramp and into the forward edge of the wall at the top. Five separate blocks of clay were then set into these cuts: first one block (12599) into the lowermost cut and one (12596) in the uppermost, then one (12593) into the second cut from the top and a fourth (12595) into the second cut from the bottom, and then the fifth and last (12592) onto the block already set on the second cut down. The blocks were of similar clay to that of the walls, matching them in texture and colour. The steps as found were from 25 to 40 cm from front to back, and from 13 to 18 cm tall. They abutted the clay of the arms of the wall bracketing the stairway, and the clay of those arms was shaped to match the contours of the steps, so that, embracing them, they also acted as extensions of the steps. Overall, the steps were 3.50 m wide.

Associated with the entrance were two buried offerings. In the bottom step (i.e., wall 12693), there were 5 greenstone beads (B1194–B1198). In the top of the stairway (i.e., in wall 12598), there was an anthropomorphic figurine pendant (CT786), carved out of white shell.

Of various features cut or worn into the steps and subsequently backfilled, one (12625) was another figurine deposition. In this case, a small hole was cut into the outer edge of the bottom step, and in the hole was placed upright, facing northeast, a simple tusk-shaped tuff figurine (B1199).[16] Around the figurine, at roughly waist height, were 34 greenstone beads (B1200). Second, there was a circular hole (12587) of 8 cm diameter and 13 cm depth, filled with a dark brown (10YR 3/4) silt loam, cut into the middle of the bottom step. It may have been designed either to support a single, independent post that defined the centre line of the entrance, or perhaps to receive some sort of offering, long since perished.

3.1.14. Episode 7: Wall 12501

The next major addition to the ever-growing body of the platform was a massive wall, 12501, of very hard grey

---

[15] The northwest arm of the wall was completely truncated, and there were other parts destroyed, but the southeast arm of the trench survived intact, as did the rear section.

[16] The exact position is not recorded.

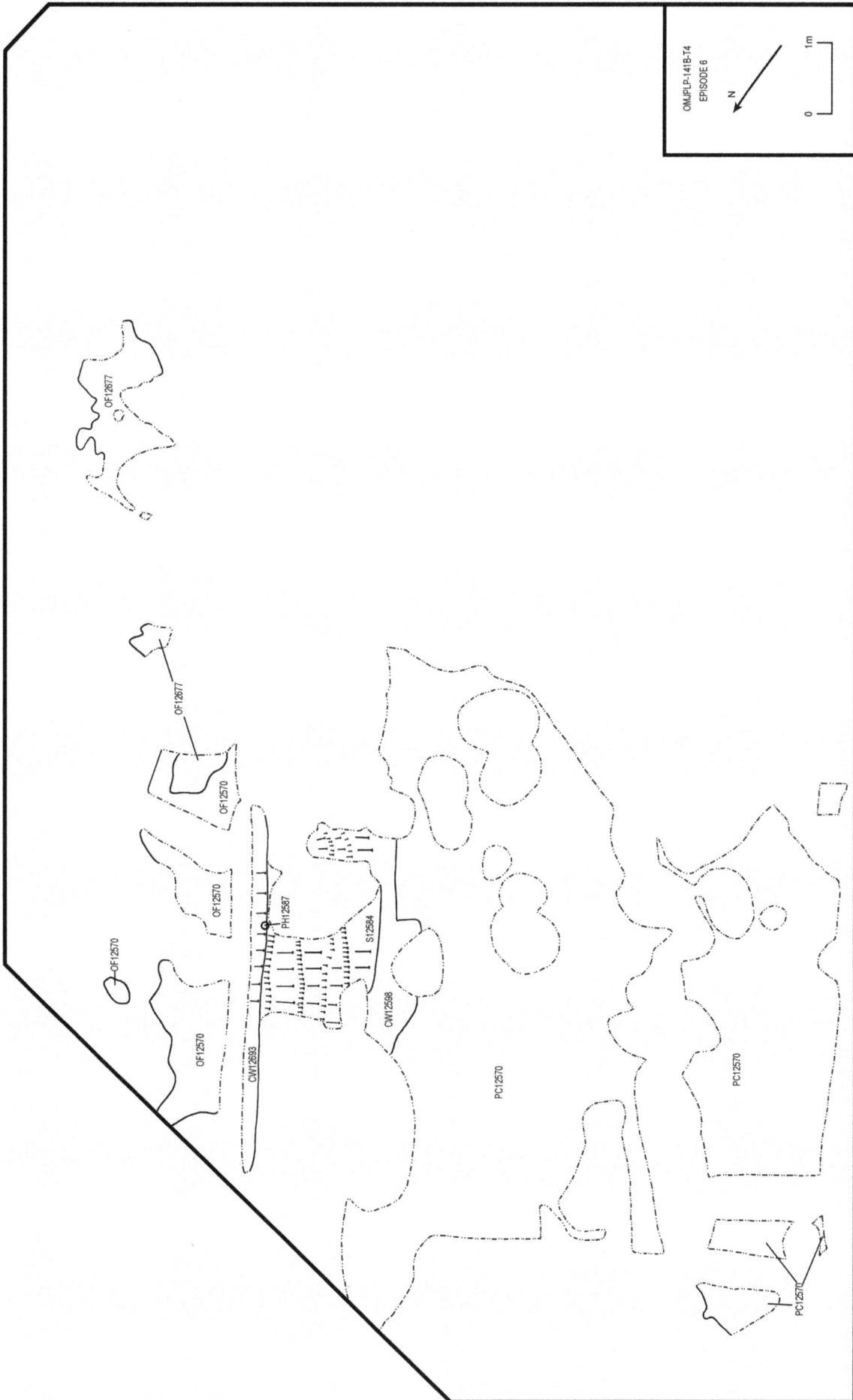

Figure 3.7. OMJPLP–141B–T4 Episode 6: Plan of the main excavated contexts.

brown (10YR 4/2) clay, that completely enclosed the earlier structures (Figure 3.8). Most of the northeast front, with the entrance, was recovered, as well as the inside edge of the northwest side and part of the southeast side. The foundation trench was U-shaped. On the inside, it cut through the outer edges of the earlier platform cap 12570 and had a face up to 65 cm deep, while the outer face cut from about 20 cm lower down. The main body of the trench was 1 m to 1.20 m wide. Along the northeast front, the top inside edge of the trench ended in a shallow lip about 30 cm wide. The clay of the wall filled the trench and rose above it vertically.[17] The clay also extended out as a shallow layer from the base of the wall.[18]

Seen from the outside, the wall stood about 80 cm above ground level, and its top lay at about the same level as the top of the platform at its highest point.[19] It appears that the northwest and southeast sides were about 30 cm lower than the front. The transition from the front to the lower sides may either have been a gradual slope at the corners, or some sort of stepped arrangement.

The entrance through the wall to the top of the platform was 2.80 m across on the outside, widening on the inside to 3.10 m. It was made with straight edges and sharply cut corners. It appears to have respected the earlier stairway and perhaps incorporated it as an initial approach to the newly defined interior.

Just in front of the wall, and slightly to the southeast of the entranceway, was an oval pit (12681) that contained a carefully deposited marble pendant, directly associated with three greenstone beads (B1212). Also in the pit were a small pottery lime container (B1209) and a tuff disc (B1210).

3.1.15. Episode 7: Platform Cap 12482

The construction of wall 12501 was followed by the laying of 12482, a new layer of yellow clay over the interior area that completely covered the earlier cap (12570). In the centre of the platform, 12482 was about 5 cm thick, while behind the entrance up to 10 cm of clay were added. Overall, the clay seems likely to have entirely filled the area contained by wall 12501, lying level with it along the northwest and southeast sides and inside the north and east corners and, as with Episode 6, rising higher in the area immediately inside the entrance.

Three human graves (10392, 10877, and 10755), and a grave-like pit (10708) lacking bones but containing typical grave goods were cut into the top of the platform, the first two along the northwest side, the other two close to the centre, a few metres back from the entrance.

3.1.16. Episode 7: The Entrance to 12482, and Ramps 12567 and 12546

Outside and to the southeast of the entrance through wall 12501, 12673 was a mixed layer of brown sandy silt that sloped lightly down towards the northeast. Its main point of interest is its artefact content, in particular a set of 68 unusual shell beads (CT794), 13 beads of coloured stone (B1207, B1208), and a stone disc (B1218). This layer was not an obviously prepared surface but rather a foundation for subsequent deposits. The stratigraphy overlying 12673 is divided into two parts by trench 12409 (see below), with one part to the southwest, and the other to the northeast. These parts will be described separately, as it is not certain how they should be correlated.[20]

To the southwest of 12409, the bottom two steps of 12584 were covered with a sloping layer of dark brown loam (12572), and over this 12567, a layer of hard dark grey brown clay, was laid from near the top step to the bottom. Two or three features and two small patches of soil in the lower right corner, all buried by 12567, indicate some sort of activity there, but offer no real clue as to what that might have been. Subsequently, six small patches of different soil types were covered by another more extensive mixed layer (12559) which ran from close to the still-exposed top of the steps down to the bottom. A circular feature (12558) in the middle of the ramp, measuring 80 cm across and up to 30 cm deep, is also hard to explain, though again it is evidence of some activity.

Next, 12546 was another brown clay layer, reaching from the very top of the old steps down to the bottom and designed to present a hard, even surface to the ramp. After the formation of two more patches of soil over 12546, one of them (12534) being co-extensive with it, the lower part of the ramp was cut out and filled with hard light yellow brown clay (12531). In addition, a pit (12526), measuring 62 cm by 70 cm across, and with an overall depth of 70 cm deep, was cut into the southeast side of the entranceway, immediately adjacent to the end of the clay wall 12501. The pit fill, of mixed soil, contained the lower half of a tuff figurine (B1181). Four more deposits of soil followed, with three more pits cut into the entrance. The last of these pits (12503), measuring 30 cm by 22 cm by 19 cm deep, contained a broken tuff figurine (B1179). The pit also directly overlay the earlier and larger feature (12526) which had contained the figurine fragment, but

---

[17] This assertion is directly supported by observed evidence for the inner face only. However, although the outer face was truncated along the entire length of both northeast and southeast sides by later wall trenches, it seems likely that it too was vertical, rather than sloped or stepped.
[18] Evidence only survives for this on the southeast side, the northeast having been truncated by a later wall trench.
[19] The tops of this wall, of those following it, and of the platform cap shortly to be laid inside it, were all affected by the digging of trenches cut to accommodate later walls. The conclusions stated here, then, must be to some degree tentative.

---

[20] An alternative interpretation would place 12673 earlier, in association with use of the mound 12570, whose outer face it in part abutted.

OMJPLP-141B-T4
EPISODE 7

N

0   1m

CWI2501

PC12482

F12681

R12638

F12503

R12640

F12682

S12407

F12526

PC12482

GR10708

HB10756

CWI2501

PC12482

PC12482

HB10933

HB10877

PC12482

CWI2501

Figure 3.8. OMJPLP–141B–T4 Episode 7: Plan of the main excavated contexts.

was separated from it by an intervening soil layer.[21] The ramp was then covered with a layer of clay (12498), before being cut by a series of three or four steps (12497) that led steeply down from the top of the entranceway to the bottom.[22] The purpose of the steps may either have been to provide access up on to the platform, or alternatively to provide a secure footing for the clay to be set in trench 12409.

To the northeast of 12409, the stratigraphic sequence is shorter and simpler. Of the eight features and seven layers comprising the remaining evidence for the leading edge of the ramp, two patches of soil (12659 and 12656) contained two beads of different greenstone (B1203 and B1204, the former being of malachite) and half a tuff bead (B1202). More importantly, at about 1.40 m to the northeast of the entrance, and on a line running from its centre, a pit (12662) contained a tusk-shaped figurine of shell (CT789), capped by a broken tuff disc (B1210). This feature was in turn overlaid by two separate and more extensive layers of clay (12640 and 12638) that would have been originally part of the ramp surfaces found to the southwest. These last two layers show that the ramp reached a minimum of 2.30 m away from the front line of the wall 12501. It is possible that the ramp was not of a single gradient, but that it rose more gradually as far as the line of the wall, and then became steeper as it passed between the walls.

In sum, an extensive ramped surface was created on at least two occasions. Other layers or patches of soil were either material trampled over the ramp or material used preparatory to the laying of the prepared surfaces. Several of the features cannot be explained but add to the picture of activity in and over the entranceway. Two of them set in the entranceway, however, and a third just outside, served as repositories for complete or broken figurines which would themselves have acted as guardians protecting the approach to the platform.

3.1.17. Episode 7: Steps 12407

Along the bottom of the steps (12497) that had been cut into the ramp, and immediately outside the line of outer face of wall 12501, a U-shaped trench (12409) was then dug. This trench extended slightly in front of the ends of the wall and was 2.90 m long and up to 50 cm wide, over 50 cm deep on its inside face, and about 25 cm deep on the outer face. While the inner face was entirely vertical before curving to meet the rounded bottom, the outer had a shallow lip at the top.

The trench was filled with hard dark brown clay, 12407, that rose vertically above the trench top and then reached

back over the steps (12497) previously cut into the layers filling the entrance. The top of the clay rose marginally higher than the top of the platform and the walls to either side. The northeast-facing surface of the clay itself presented as a series of steps that dropped roughly 20 cm, 20 cm, and 30 cm (or more) respectively down from its top. On either side, the bottom step reached just in front of the wall.

3.1.18. Episode 8: Wall 12348

A second major wall, 12348, was built soon after 12407, completely enclosing the earlier structures (Figure 3.9).[23] The foundation trench was a relatively shallow, simple U-shape. Much truncated, its deepest point it was less than 40 cm deep.[24] On the northeast front, it was from 100 cm to 105 cm wide, and on the southeast side from 80 cm to 100 cm wide. To the northwest, the trench and wall lay completely outside the excavation area. The wall itself was of hard dark brown (10YR 3/3) clay like both that of the recently built stairway and that of the earlier wall that it enclosed. Along the front it rose vertically to a flat top 65 cm above the trench top and outer floor, while on the southeast side it may have been up to 15 cm lower.

The trench for 12348 was cut 50 to 60 cm outside wall 12501 along the northeast front. The gap or interface between the walls was destroyed by later trenching, but it seems likely that the new wall not only filled the new trench, but also filled the space of 60 cm between it and the old wall, such that the two walls combined to provide a single massive front almost 3 m thick, while along the sides they would have been together at least 2.50 m thick.

The wall left an entrance this time slightly wider, at 3.60 m, on the outside than on the inside, where it measured 3.40 m. Furthermore, not only was its entrance wider than that of 12501, but it was also shifted slightly to the southeast. Thus, to the northwest, 12347 encroached in front of the earlier stairway 12407, while to the southeast it left 90 cm of the front of 12501 exposed. The wall, therefore, incorporated the earlier structure, but did not wholly respect it, and required a new approach to the platform top (see below).

In front of the wall, and running away directly from its base, was a new clay floor (12385) that dropped around 10 cm along the 2.50 m slope to the northeast. And just outside the east corner, two small holes (12926, 12477) each contained an upright stone figurine (B1228 and B1176 respectively).

---

[21] Alternatively, 12526 may have cut from higher up the sequence, and may belong to Episode 8. In which case, feature 12503 would also be of Episode 8, or later.

[22] The number of steps is not certain as the possible fourth step may have been produced by the cutting of the later trench 12409.

---

[23] The trench for the wall cut the steps 12407 with no sign of any intervening depositional activity.

[24] Later wall trenches cut the interior of the northeast front and both the interior and exterior of the southeast side.

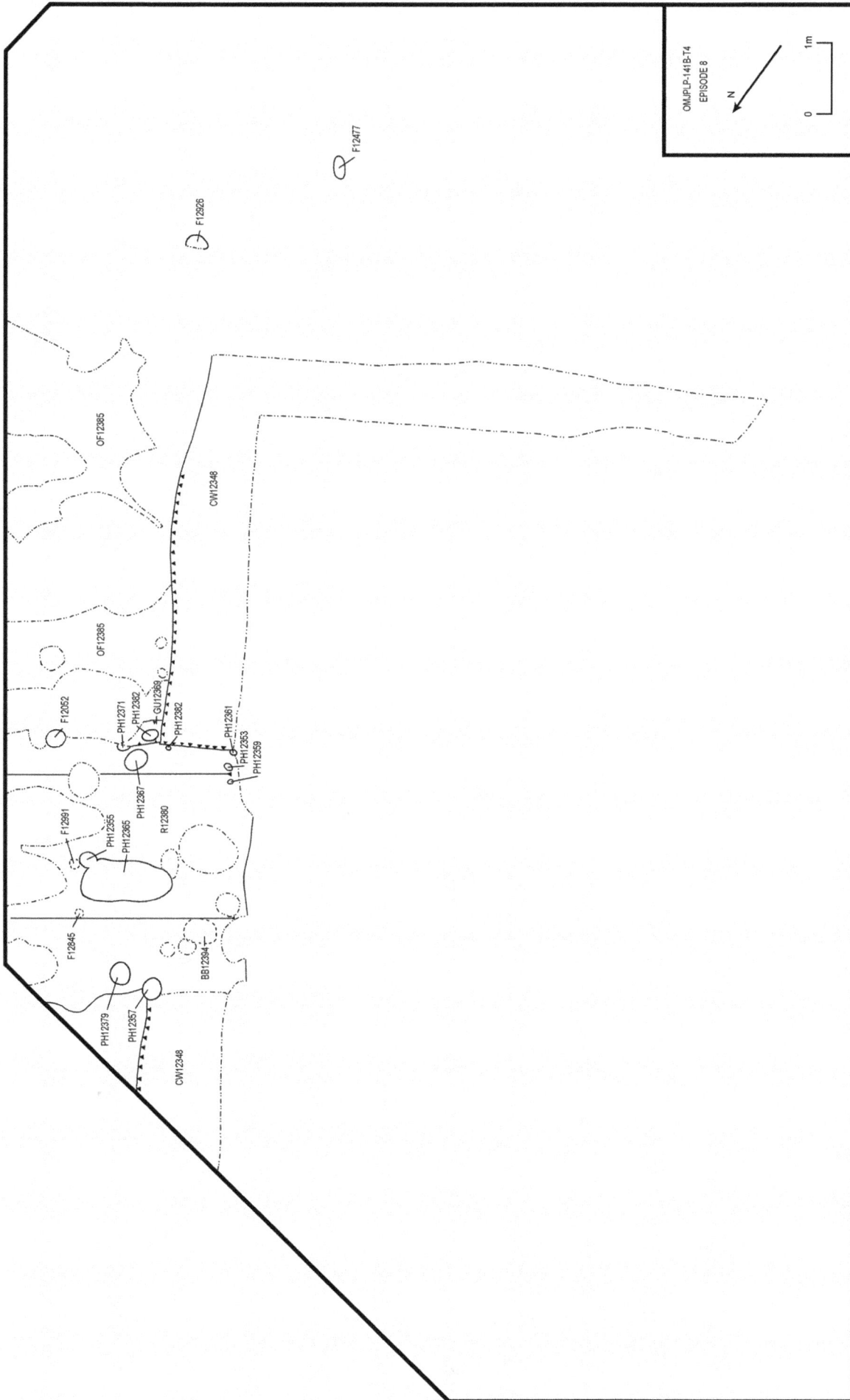

Figure 3.9. OMJPLP–141B–T4 Episode 8: Plan of the main excavated contexts.

3.1.19. Episode 8: Ramps 12388, 12380, 12344, and 12321

The construction of wall 12348 was followed by the creation of a ramped approach, in conjunction with the old stairway, through the new entrance to the platform. The ramp itself went through several stages of construction and modification. First, two stone figurines (B1223, B1247) were placed in holes (12845 and 12991 respectively), 70 cm apart, that had been cut into the ground about 2.20 m to the northeast of the entranceway. The holes were then covered with a deposit of dark yellow brown silt loam (12398) that was laid down from over the bottom step of 12407, dropping 20 cm through the entrance and out to the northeast over the first 2.50 m, before continuing further as a horizontal layer. With a depth of about 4 cm, it was scorched, in patches, to a dark red brown through the upper 2 cm. It also contained a shell bead (CT770) and two fragments of shell fishhooks (CT768, CT769).

Second, another sloping layer of similar soil (12395) was laid out from the bottom of the steps for 1.50 m to the northeast, so mainly occupying the space at the entrance and only just reaching beyond the face of the wall. Two complete shell beads (CT763, CT765), one half shell bead (CT766), and two fragments of shell rattles (CT762, CT764) were found in the layer.

Third, a new surface (12392) was laid coextensive with 12398, though reaching from slightly higher up the steps, so that over a distance of 3.10 m it dropped perhaps 35 cm. Composed of hard dark grey brown clay loam, this was the most durable of the surfaces so far laid down the approach to the entrance. It contained a single shell bead (CT761).

Following the repair (12389) to a patch of the ramp against the southeast end of the wall, 12392 was covered by yellow brown clay that this time reached down from the second step of 12407. This layer, 12388, contained a notable quantity of ash, whose source may have been the two small patches of burning found at the top end of the slope. It also contained a shell bead (CT760). One of the patches of burning covered a well-defined pit, 12394. The main section of the pit was of circular outline, 30 cm in diameter and just over 50 cm deep, while to the southwest there was a 20 cm wide lip, running up from about 10 cm below the top of the hole. The fill was yellow brown clay, and it contained the skeleton of a bird. There are no other recorded details of how the skeleton was positioned, but this was a deliberate burial offering in the manner of the stone figurines associated with the earlier ramps and clay steps. The original field notes have 12394 cutting from the earlier layer 12395. But the matching outlines of the pit and the burnt soil seem too close to be coincidental, and I suggest that the burial of the bird was followed directly by the burning of a small fire on top of the pit fill.

Completely covering 12388, 12380 was a sloping layer of similar clay, without signs of burning or ash, but cut by several pits.[25] At the centre of the ramp thus resurfaced, 12365 was the largest feature, and probably served as a posthole. 128 cm long (northeast-southwest) and 62 cm wide (northwest-southeast), it had an oval top, with a deeper section to the southwest that reached a depth of 109 cm. Its lower fill (12376) contained three pieces of worked shell, including a disc (CT757), a fishhook fragment (CT758), and a complete rattle (CT759). The upper fill (12364) was of yellow gravelly clay. At one side of the northeast end of the pit, 12355 was a smaller feature (24 cm by 20 cm by 22 cm), also filled with yellow gravelly clay.

Either side of the large central feature, were two sets of smaller holes. To the northwest, just outside the corner of the wall, there were two roughly circular postholes, 20 cm apart. 12357 measured 25 cm by 24 cm by 22 cm, and was filled by a yellow brown clay, while 12379 was 30 cm across and 50 cm deep, with a similarly coloured gravelly clay. On the other side of the ramp, two more features may have corresponded with these. 12367, at 32 cm by 24 cm by 26 cm, was of similar proportions to 12357. Next to it, 12371 was mostly truncated. Their yellow brown clay fills were like those of the others, though less clayey.

Immediately to the southeast, there was a linear feature (12369) which ran southwest-northeast from the outside face of the wall 12348. Truncated to the northeast by a later massive posthole, the feature survived to 60 cm long by 30 cm wide, with a depth of about 20 cm. Its flat bottom sloped down towards the northeast. At its upper end it was cut by a posthole, 12382, measuring 16 cm by 22 cm across, whose own base lay 10 cm below that of the trench.

Finally, there were four even narrower holes recorded just inside the southeast end of the wall. Three lie together near the top of the ramp. Next to the outer corner of the wall, 12361 was the deepest, measuring about 8 cm across by over 30 cm deep, while 12353 was 11 cm across and 7 cm deep, and 12359 measured 5 cm by 3 cm by 12 cm deep. Next to the lower corner of the wall, 12382 measured 7 cm by 6 cm by 8 cm deep.

These features collectively suggest that the ramp was furnished with a gateway at the point where it met the wall. The structure would have had a main central post, up to 30

[25] 12380 was also cut by the trench for a later wall, 12374, of yellow brown clay, that ran along the interface between walls 12348 and 12501 along the northeast front. This later wall, which evidently respected the entrance as defined by wall 12501 of Episode 7 and wall 12348, may have been of Late Engoroy origin. However, it has been excluded from this report as it postdates Episode 8 and makes no difference to the interpretation given to the sequence up to the creation of wall 12348 and its entrance. Similar comments would apply to a wall-like linear feature, 12341, that ran along the interface between 12501 and 12348 on the southeast side.

cm in diameter and possibly several meters tall, to judge by the depth of the setting for its base. Either side were two pairs of smaller posts, with a further element indicated on the southeast side by the linear feature and its posthole.

The gateway was eventually dismantled, and a new layer of yellow gravelly clay, 12344, was put down, again from the second step, and incidentally filling several of the just-emptied postholes. But this time, instead of presenting a steady slope directly from that step, this layer created a level shelf over the whole area between the ends of the walls, and only at the outer face of the walls did the slope begin. Thus, the ascent included first a yellow clay ramp that started about 1.50 m outside the wall and rose 50 to 55 cm, and then a broad step of the same yellow clay.[26] After this, there was the dark brown clay of the upper steps of 12407, the one rising 10 cm, and the last rising another 15 cm.

There was no sign of any wooden structure over the new ramp. But in the clay there were lenses of ash, from 10 to 30 cm across, with many small fish bone fragments, as well as the left humerus of a medium sized bird and the right tarsometatarsus of a small bird. In view of the burial of the bird with the overlying ash scatter in the earlier ramp, these ash lenses with their bones would appear to have been deliberately added inclusions, designed to give the ramp some spiritual protection. There was just one feature associated with the layer. 12338 (30 cm by 25 cm by 6 cm) was the base of a truncated hole cut into the centre of the ramp a meter out from the wall, its long axis oriented with that of the entranceway. There were no artefacts found in its fill of mixed soils, but its position is significant considering the treatment of earlier ramps.

Of the remaining episodes of soil deposition over the ramp, 12334/12333 was of dark brown clay, 5 to 8 cm thick, with frequent small bone fragments (</= 3 mm) and flecks of charcoal. Two separate patches, 12326 and 12330, were each about 4 cm thick, and were of lighter, more yellow soil, the latter containing ash and charcoal but no bone. 12327 and 12323 were two successive patches of yellow gravelly clay, and 12321 was the final ramp layer, again consisting of yellow gravelly clay with some flecks of charcoal.[27]

This last ramp surface, and the rest of the area outside the wall, was then covered in a 1 to 3 cm thick layer of white ash, 12255.[28] There was no charcoal visible in the ash, nor any sign of burning underneath, and comparison

with similar material on top of the final platform as recovered in T3 (Lunniss 2001:86, 292) suggests that these deposits collectively represent a single volcanic ash fall that effectively capped the sequence of Late Formative ceremonial structures at OMJPLP–141B.

3.2. Associated Features and Artefacts

3.2.1. Figurines and Pendants

Associated with the building sequence just outlined was a series of shell, stone, and pottery figurines and pendants. Nineteen such artefacts were recovered from Late Formative contexts in Trench 4.[29]

The earliest relevant objects belonged to Episode 2. From the clay floor 13316, CT831 is a slender and very elegant pendant of white spondylus shell, 67 mm tall, and weighing a little over 27 g (Figures 3.10a, 3.11). It is the first of a sequence of tusk-shaped pendants and figurines of shell and stone that evolved through the succeeding occupation of the site up to and including Episode 8.

From a layer (12948) outside the wooden structure that was set over 13316, there was a pottery figurine and small shell pendant. The figurine (B1226) is of solid modelled clay (Figures 3.12a, 3.13). It has two short arms and two short legs, but its head is missing. Somewhat crudely made, it is of a fine fabric, and its surface, variably brown and black, is polished. Its surviving height is 66 mm. The pendant (CT822), made of purple spondylus, has a tear-drop shape and measures 19 mm in length (Figures 3.12b, 3.14). The upper rear section is flat, with a circular hollow cut into the body. From the top of the pendant, a hole was drilled down to the hollow just mentioned, while a second hole leads from the hollow back down and out to the base of the flat rear section.

Next, associated with platform 12953 of Episode 3, was a pre-figurine or proto-figurine of white volcanic tuff (B1231). 59 mm tall and weighing 25 g, it is flat-backed and has sides that taper from top to bottom (Figures 3.12c, 3.15). The interpretation of this artefact as a representation of the human form is suggested by comparison with the general shapes of other, more obviously anthropomorphic objects, such as B1161 (Figures 3.12d, 3.33).

We now jump to Episode 6, when a pendant figurine (CT786) was set in the topmost of the steps (12584) built

---

[26] This interpretation is not completely certain as much of the pertinent material was lost to truncation from above by later wall trenches. An alternative scenario has the flat step extending some distance out from the entranceway.

[27] Much of each of these layers was lost through truncation, and only the section at the bottom of the ramp survived.

[28] The ash fell directly over the last ramp surface, with no sign of intervening features.

[29] Johnson found five more tuff figurines (B1171–B1175) in a massive posthole of the Early Regional Development, where they had probably been redeposited. A further 18 tuff figurines or figurine fragments had earlier been recovered by Mudd from later contexts of T4. From a review of the contextual data for these artefacts, it is likely that they had all been removed from their original settings and subsequently redeposited. Twelve of these contexts were without doubt of the Early Regional Development Period occupation, and the remaining six also probably post-dated the Late Engoroy occupation.

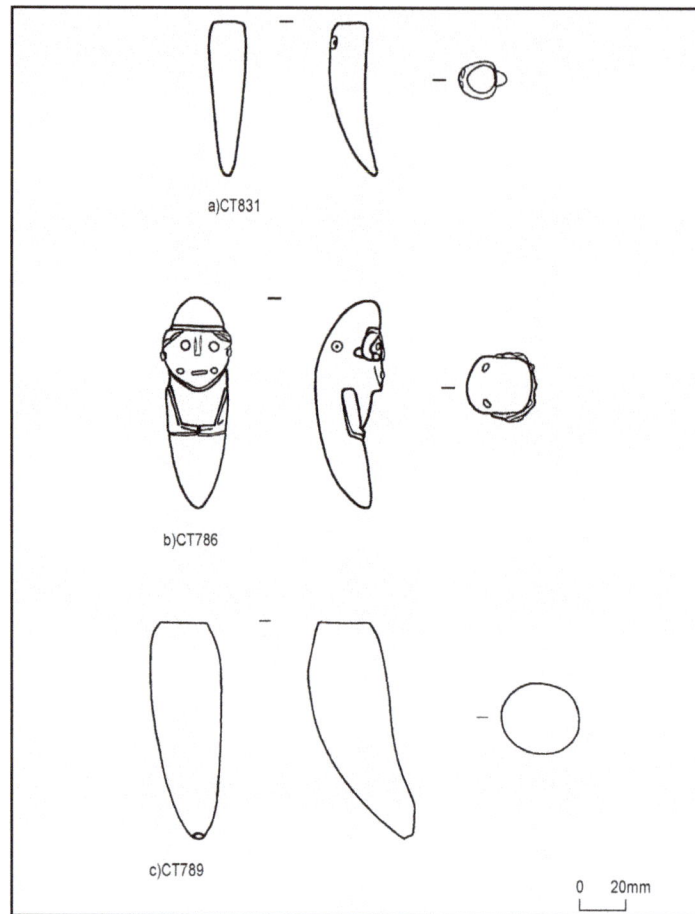

Figure 3.10. a) White spondylus pendant incorporated in the Episode 2 house floor; b) shell figurine pendant incorporated in the top of the Episode 6 stairway; c) white and orange *Spondylus calcifer* figurine buried in the centre of the Episode 7 ramp.

Figure 3.11. Pendant of *Spondylus calcifer* CT831, deposited within the floor of the Episode 2 ceremonial house. Reprinted by permission from Springer Nature Customer Service Centre GmbH: Springer, Pre-Columbian Landscapes of Creation and Origin, by J. Staller, ed. © (2008).

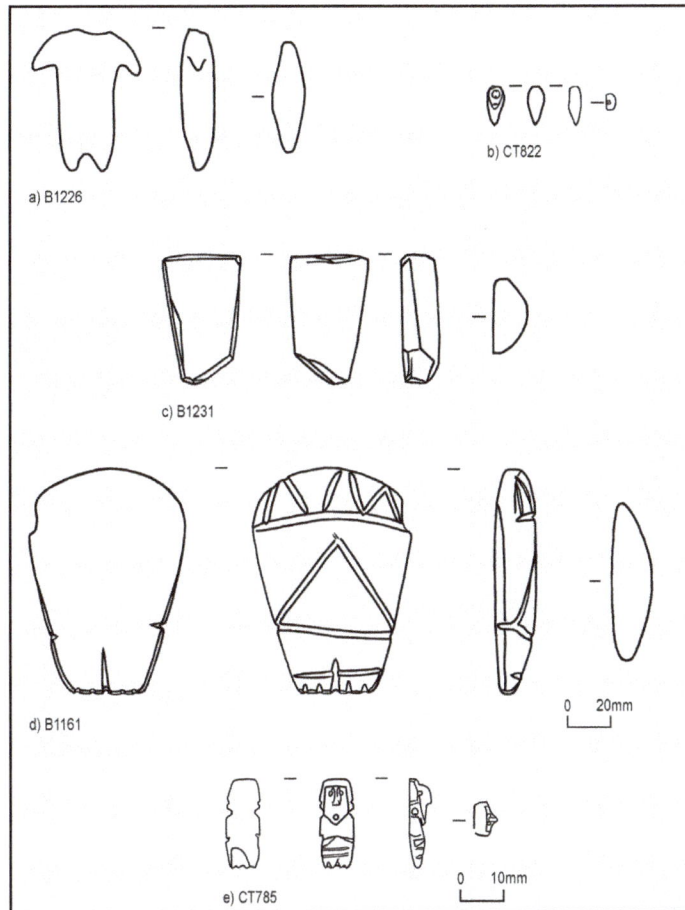

Figure 3.12. a) Pottery figurine and b) purple *Spondylus calcifer* pendant discarded outside the Episode 2 house; c) proto-figurine of tuff from the Episode 3 platform; d) tuff figurine and e) red *Spondylus princeps* figurines from T4 but lacking precise context.

Figure 3.13. Pottery figurine B1226, discarded outside the Episode 2 ceremonial house. Reprinted from Late Formative Shamans of the Ecuadorian Coast: Architectural, Mortuary, and Artifactual Evidence from Salango in the Middle and Late Engoroy Phases (600–100 BC), by R. Lunniss, Ñawpa Pacha 41(2), 2021, by permission of Taylor & Francis Ltd, http://www.tandfonline.com.

Figure 3.14. Tiny pendant of *Spondylus calcifer* CT822, discarded outside the Episode 2 ceremonial house.

33

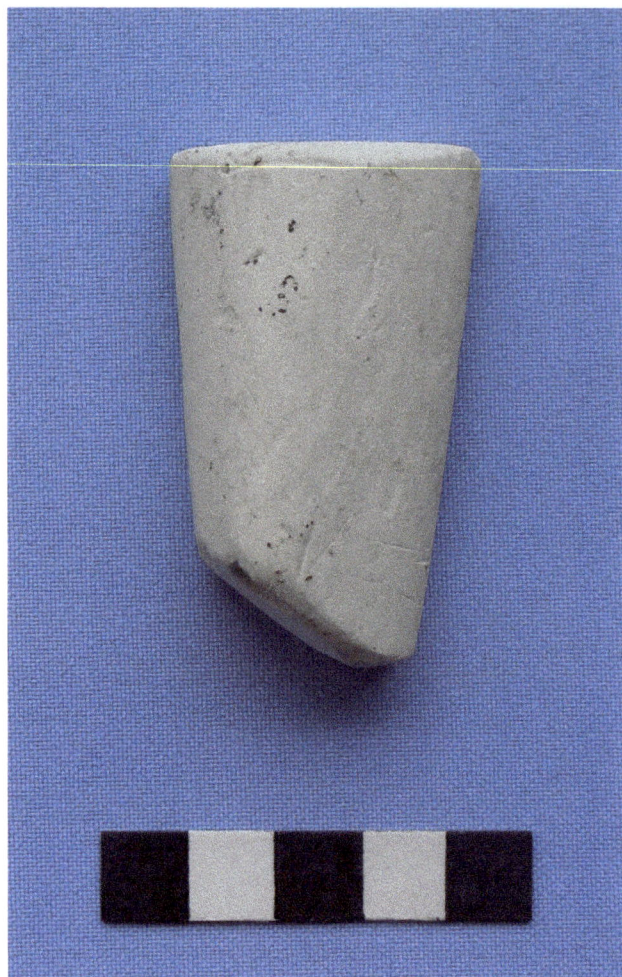

Figure 3.15. Tuff proto-figurine B1231 deposited within the clay of the Episode 3 platform.

Figure 3.16. Anthropomorphic shell pendant CT786 and five greenstone beads B1194–B1198, buried at the top and bottom respectively of the Episode 6 stairway. Reprinted from Late Formative Shamans of the Ecuadorian Coast: Architectural, Mortuary, and Artifactual Evidence from Salango in the Middle and Late Engoroy Phases (600–100 BC), by R. Lunniss, Ñawpa Pacha 41(2), 2021, by permission of Taylor & Francis Ltd, http://www.tandfonline.com.

to give access to platform 12570 (Figures 3.10b, 3.16 left). The figurine is of an overall tusk-form, cut out of creamy coloured shell, stands 91 mm tall, and weighs just over 97 g. Face and arms are clearly depicted. In addition to the eyes, nose, mouth, and some sort of headdress or hair arrangement, there are four small nubbins around the face, perhaps representing ear and cheek studs. In the bottom of the same set of steps, there were also deposited five greenstone beads (B1194–B1198; Figure 3.16 right). This association is interesting as an expression of the important relationship observed in other and later contexts between anthropomorphic figurines and greenstone.[30] The depositions are also important as being the first in a series of figurine and other offerings made in the entranceways to successive ceremonial platform with the likely purpose of empowering those approaches.

Also in Episode 6, post-dating the creation of the stepped entrance to 12570 and cut into the outer face of the bottom step, 12625 was a small hole containing a simple tuff tusk

(B1199) that had been buried upright, probably facing northeast (Figures 3.17a, 3.18 left). There is no detailing of features, but the overall form and dimensions of the piece suggest that it is an equivalent of the more explicitly anthropomorphic tusk-shaped figurines. 164 mm tall, and weighing 349 g, it is distinguished by the application of red paint to the flat top of its head. The lower tip of the figure is flattened. The figurine was encircled by 34 beads (B1200), each of the same greenstone, set in the soil at about waist height (Figure 3.18 right).[31]

In Episode 7, a tusk-shaped figurine of white and orange spondylus shell (CT789) was set upright and facing northeast in a small hole (12662) cut into the centre of the ramp giving access to platform 12482, about 1.40 m out from the entranceway (Figures 3.10c, 3.19 left). Laid flat above the top of the figurine was part of a white tuff disc (B1205; Figure 3.19 right). The shell figurine itself lacks any explicit anthropomorphic detail. It stands 94 mm tall and weighs 145 g. Its surface is polished all over, but still bears very evident traces of tunnelling by shell-boring clams. The stone disc fragment suggests a finished

---

[30] The material of the top and bottom steps was not of a single deposit, but it seems likely that the upper and lower walls that comprised those steps were created as part of a single design.

[31] The beads do not appear to have been directly attached to the figurine.

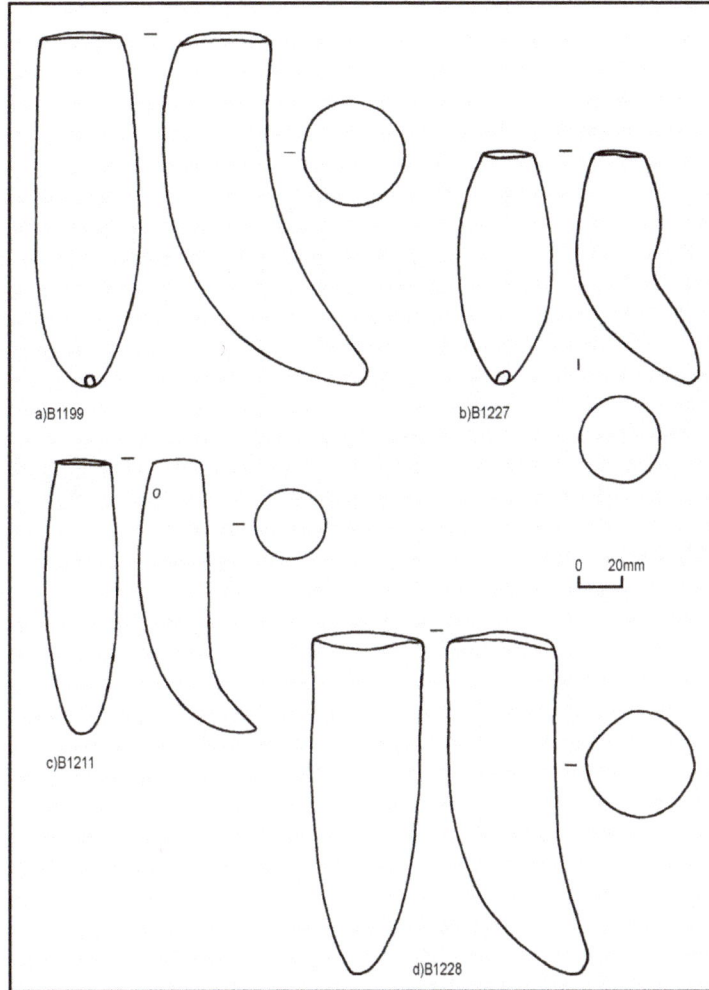

Figure 3.17. Simple tusk-shaped stone figurines: a) tuff figure buried in a hole at the foot of the Episode 6 stairway; b) tuff figure deposited in pit cut by the Episode 8 wall; c) marble pendant buried upright in pit 12681 outside the Episode 7 wall; and d) tuff figure set upright and visible in a hole outside the Episode 8 wall.

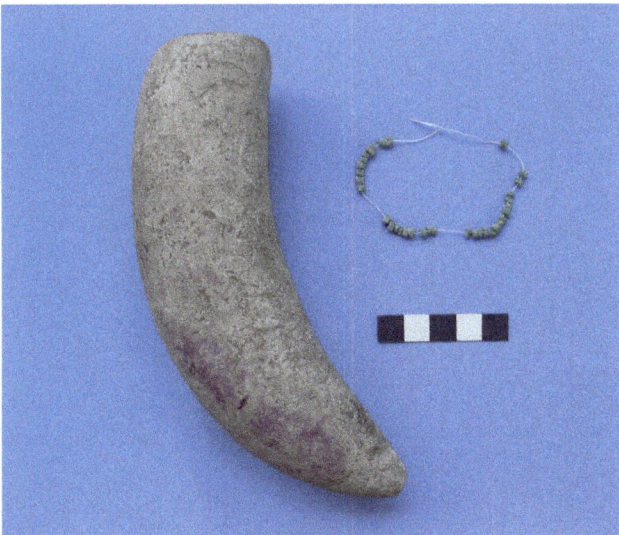

Figure 3.18. Tuff figurine B1199 and 34 greenstone beads B1200, deposited in a hole cut at the base of the Episode 6 stairway. Reprinted from Late Formative Shamans of the Ecuadorian Coast: Architectural, Mortuary, and Artifactual Evidence from Salango in the Middle and Late Engoroy Phases (600–100 BC), by R. Lunniss, Ñawpa Pacha 41(2), 2021, by permission of Taylor & Francis Ltd, http://www. tandfonline.com.

Figure 3.19. Figurine of *Spondylus calcifer* CT789 and half of a tuff disc B1201, buried in the centre of the Episode 7 ramp.

artefact of oval outline, biconvex, and with a flattened edge, measuring a minimum of 107 mm across, and 16 mm thick at the centre point. A smaller fragment of tuff disc was associated and perhaps also incorporated in the capping of the figurine. This piece, however, appears to have been part of an originally uniconvex disc of smaller dimensions.

Located in the entranceway itself, against the end of the wall 12501 and cut into the upper part of the ramp, were two features that contained figurine parts in their fill. 12526 came first, and was a larger, irregular shaped pit with a mixed fill of a few largish pottery sherds, some pieces of stone and a few shells and shell fragments. There was also the lower half of a small tuff figurine, measuring 34 mm tall (B1181; Figures 3.20c, 3.21). Although the head is missing, there is clear depiction of the arms and hand (at least on the right side). Though not a dedicated figurine

deposition, it seems likely that the figurine fragment was an important element of the offering.

A little later, a smaller pit, 12503, was cut through a small patch of soil that covered feature 12526. This time, in addition to ten small pottery sherds and a few unidentified fish bones, there was an incomplete and eroded tuff figurine measuring 183 mm tall and weighing 459 g (B1179: Figures 3.20b, 3.22). Little remains of detail, but the outline of the neck or face on the left side is clear. Given the size of the artefact and the size and shape of the feature, it is possible that the hole was designed to accommodate and support the figurine in an upright position.

The final depositions incorporated in the entranceway belong to Episode 8. 12845 and 12991 were two small holes, about 70 cm apart, cut into the floor 2.20 m out from the entrance through wall 12348 prior to the construction

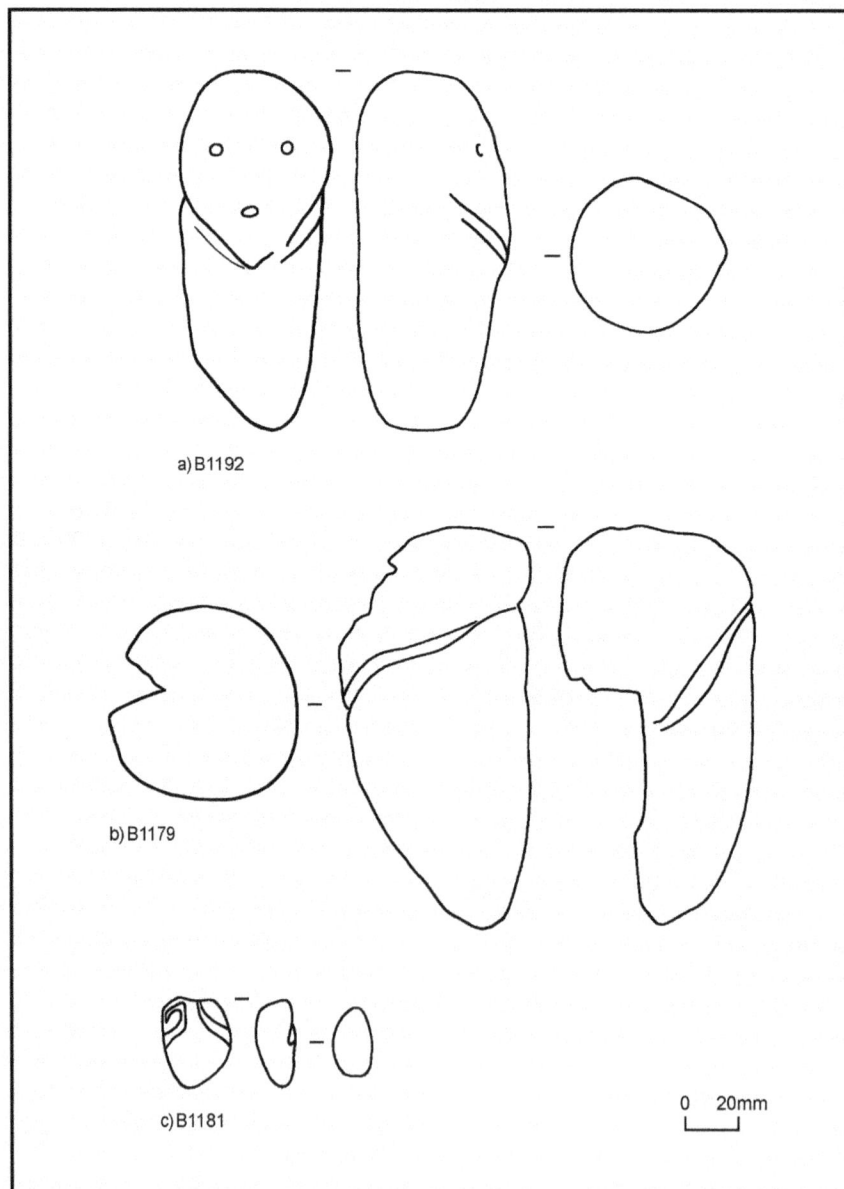

Figure 3.20. a) Tuff figurine from the Episode 6 platform; b) incomplete and eroded tuff figurine and c) lower half of unusual, small tuff figurine, from pits cut into the Episode 7 ramp.

Figure 3.21. Incomplete tuff figurine B1181, deposited in the Episode 7 ramp.

Figure 3.22. Incomplete tuff figurine B1179, deposited in the Episode 7 ramp.

of the ramp (12398 etc). Set and buried in each of the holes was a complete and unworn straight-backed tusk-shaped anthropomorphic figurine, B1223 and B1247 (Figures 3.23, 3.24).[32] The stones are of the same light green or greyish green tuff and of identical style. Attention is paid to the head, including a pair of bands across the forehead, eyes, ears, nose, mouth, and lower jaw. There is also a stylized representation of the arms crossed over the stomach. In cross section, the backs are rounded while the fronts are pointed. The first is slightly larger, at 191 mm tall and 394 g, than the other, at 180 mm and 338 g.

A further three stone figurines were set in small holes cut into the floor around the outside of the platform. Features 12477 and 12926 probably belong to Episode 8. They lay outside the east corner of the platform. In each case, the figurine was set upright facing northeast and, at least in the second instance, with the head level with or proud of the top of the hole. In 12477, the figurine (B1176), of greenish white volcanic tuff, was not of the normal tusk shape, but more of a rectangular block, with a flat base, parallel sides, a rounded top, and a front and back that taper slightly from top to bottom (Figures 3.25, 3.26). Again, though, emphasis is placed on the face, where eyes, nose, mouth, lower jaw, and head bands are detailed. Also prominent are the arms, folded across the stomach, the hands not quite reaching each other. 194 mm tall, the piece weighs 1431 g, substantially more than any of the others so far described. Though mostly complete, it had suffered some light damage to either side of the front of the head. In 12926, the figurine (B1228), also of tuff, was a simple tusk shape, with no detail of features (Figures 3.17d, 3.27). At 158 mm tall, it weighs 314 g. Though complete, it had suffered light erosion over its entire surface.[33]

The third dedicated deposition, 12052, post-dated and lay just to the southeast of the base of the ramps of Episode 8. Again, the tuff figurine (B1159) was set upright and facing northeast, and the head protruded over the top of the hole enough that its own top was damaged and broken off. The figure is relatively large, at 252 mm tall, and weighs 1191 g (Figures 3.28, 3.29). Its shape is unusual, but the anthropomorphic details of the face and arms are unmistakable. And again, the arms reach across the stomach, with the hands not quite meeting.

Feature 12681 belongs to Episode 7. It lay outside the front wall of 12501, to the southeast of the entranceway. It was recorded as an irregular oval pit, 1.10 m long and about 50 cm wide, oriented on a northwest-southeast axis, with a depth of about 60 cm. Floating, as it were, in the very middle of the pit, was an upright figurine pendant of light brown marble (B1211), tusk-shaped but lacking detail, 127 mm tall and weighing 213 g (Figures 3.17c,

---

[32] No indication is made in the register of the direction faced by the figurines.
[33] The field notes indicate that the lower half of the figurine had been painted, though the colour is not specified. No paint, however, was visible to my inspection more than 15 years after excavation of the object.

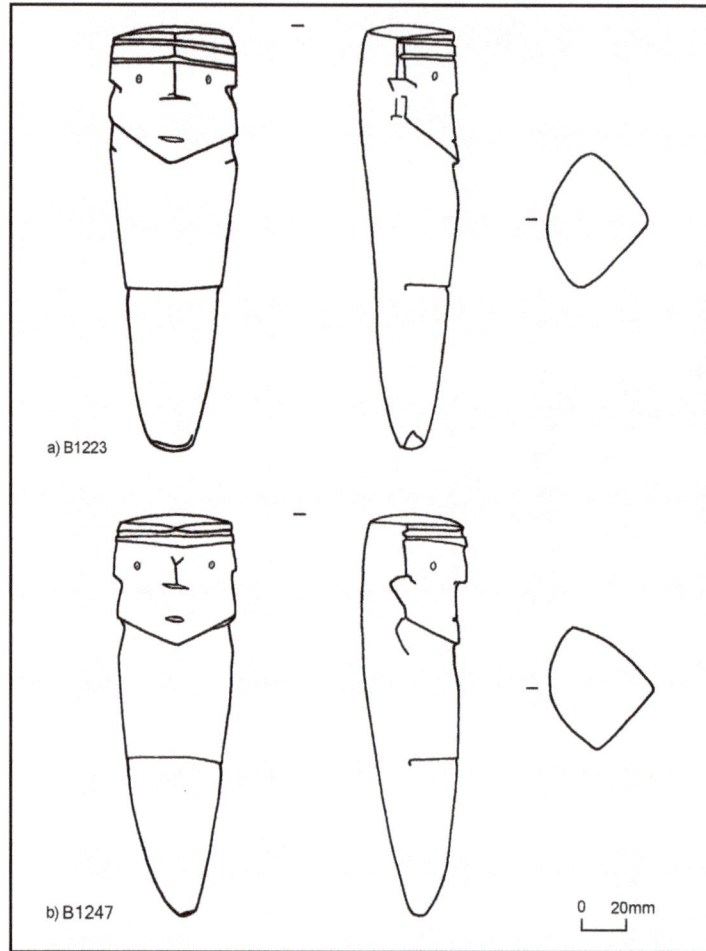

Figure 3.23. Pair of matching stone figurines from beneath the Episode 8 ramp.

Figure 3.24. Tuff figurines a) B1247 and b) B1223, buried beneath the Episode 8 ramp, either side of the central axis. Reprinted by permission from Springer Nature Customer Service Centre GmbH: Springer, Pre-Columbian Landscapes of Creation and Origin, by J. Staller, ed. © (2008).

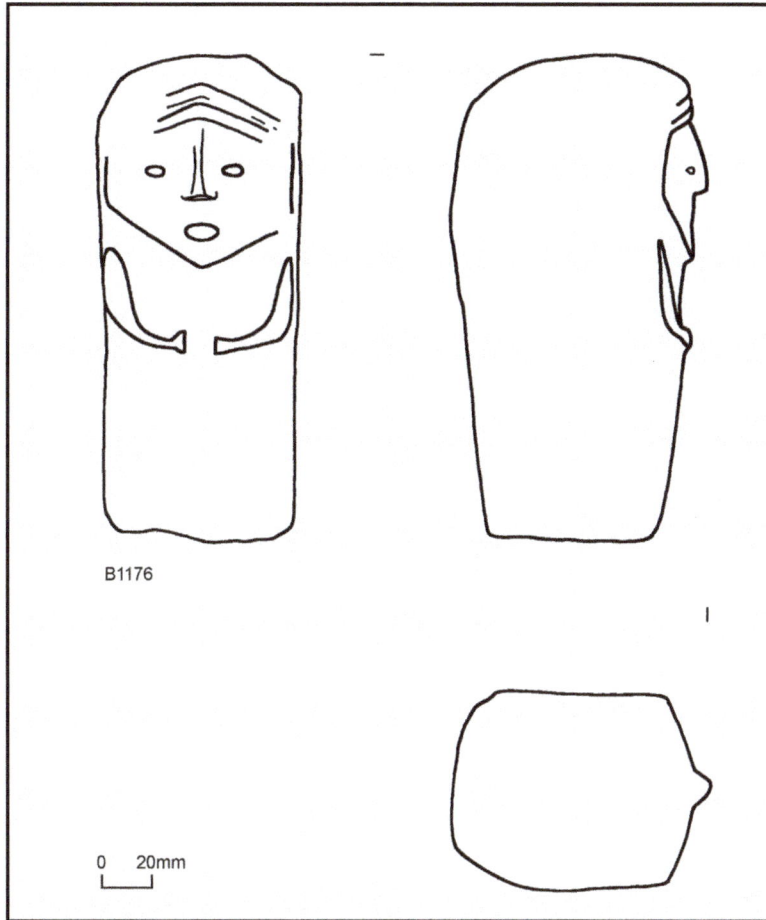

Figure 3.25. Large stone figurine from the Episode 8 exterior floor.

Figure 3.26. Tuff figurine B1176, deposited in the floor outside the Episode 8 wall. Reprinted by permission from Springer Nature Customer Service Centre GmbH: Springer, Pre-Columbian Landscapes of Creation and Origin, by J. Staller, ed. © (2008).

Figure 3.27. Tuff figurine B1228, deposited in the floor outside the Episode 8 wall. Reprinted from Los ancestros y el mito de emergencia: una interpretación de los figurines de piedra asociados con una plataforma funeraria del Engoroy Tardío en el Sitio Salango, Provincia de Manabí, Ecuador, by R. Lunniss, Ñawpa Pacha 31(2), 2011, by permission of Taylor & Francis Ltd, http://www.tandfonline.com.

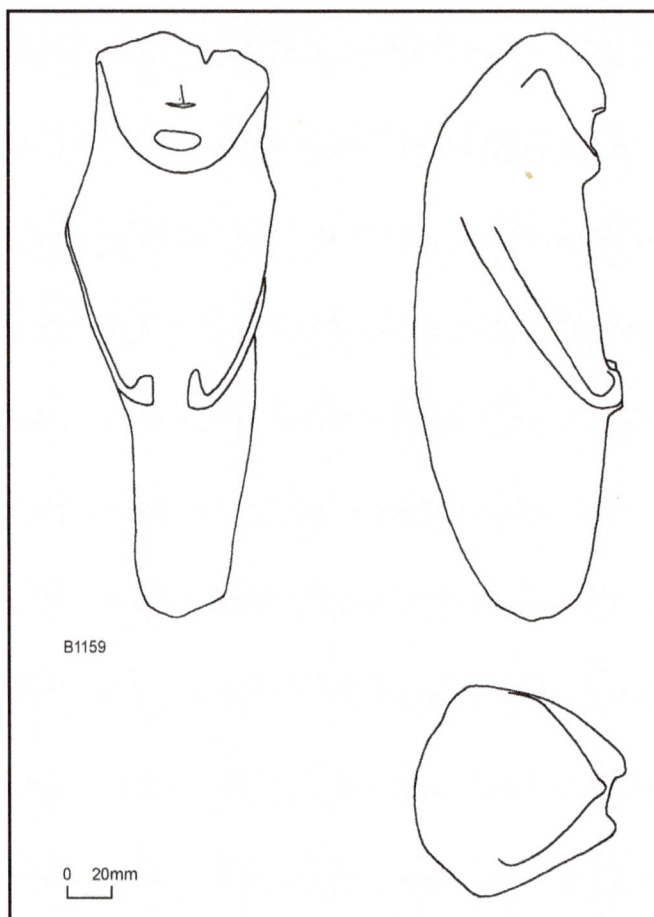

Figure 3.28. Large stone figurine from the Episode 8 exterior floor.

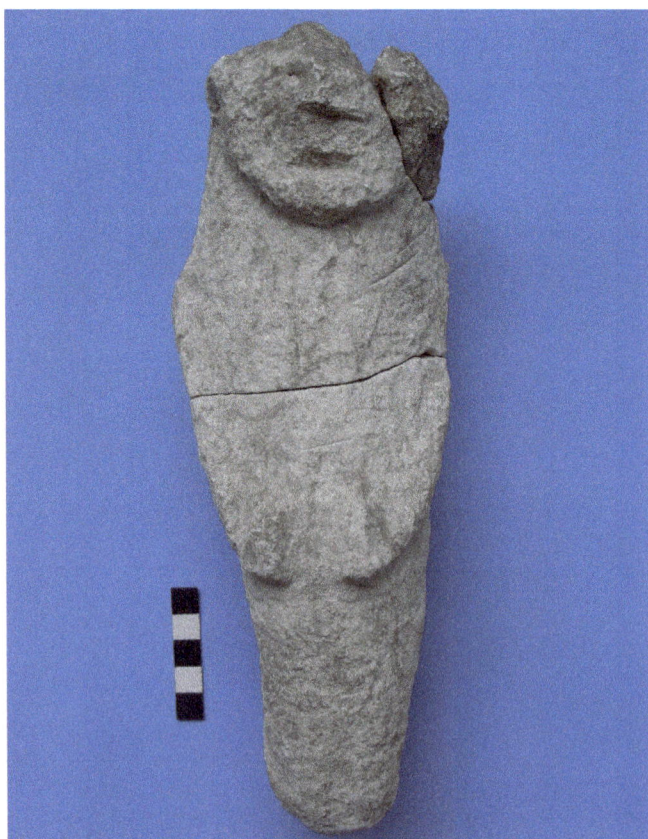

Figure 3.29. Tuff figurine B1159, deposited in the floor outside the Episode 8 wall.

Figure 3.30. Marble pendant B1211, miniature pottery bowl B1209, three greenstone beads B1212, and tuff disc B1210, all deposited in feature 12681 outside the Episode 7 wall. Reprinted from Late Formative Shamans of the Ecuadorian Coast: Architectural, Mortuary, and Artifactual Evidence from Salango in the Middle and Late Engoroy Phases (600–100 BC), by R. Lunniss, Ñawpa Pacha 41(2), 2021, by permission of Taylor & Francis Ltd, http://www.tandfonline.com.

3.30 left).[34] The pendant is flat topped, but sharp tipped, and of very fine workmanship. Around its waist, regularly set and all at the same level, were three rectangular greenstone beads (B1212; Figure 3.30 top right). Also in the fill, as well as shell (including 78 *Cerithium* sp.), pottery sherds, lithics, and fish bone, but with no record of their specific location, were a disc of white tuff (B1210) and part of a small ceramic lime pot (B1209; Figure 3.30 bottom right, top centre). It is not clear whether these artefacts were all of the same deposition, or whether the figurine and beads were elements of a feature perhaps intrusive into an earlier pit containing the disc and lime pot. It may be that we are faced here with a combined set of different materials that relate to a relatively complex ritual sequence centring on or ending with the burial of the figurine.

Feature 12951 was recorded as a possible rubbish pit, partially truncated from above by the foundation trench for wall 12348 of Episode 7 but also partially sealed by a layer (12849) of Episode 4.[35] In the feature there was a simple tusk-shaped figure of tuff (B1227), 108 mm tall and weighing 127 g (Figures 3.17b, 3.31). Like the larger simple tusk form of B1191, it had a flat top to its head and a flattened lower tip. Unlike the other simple tusk forms,

Figure 3.31. Tuff figurine B1227, of uncertain context within T4.

---

[34] It is not stated which direction the figurine faced.
[35] What, in this case, is uncertain, is whether the figurine belonged to a feature 12951 once entirely capped by layer 12849, or whether it was set in a smaller, unrecognized pit that cut into 12951 but pre-dated wall 12348.

however, there is a suggestion of a waist rendered by the frontal swelling of the upper part of the figure.

There are then three more figurines whose contexts are only loosely defined. The first (B1192) was recovered during excavation of layer 12579, over platform cap 12570, and would belong to Episode 6 (Figures 3.20a, 3.32). It is of grey volcanic tuff and has roughly the shape of a straight tusk. It is worn, especially over the face, but its details remain visible, including eyes, nose, mouth, and lower jaw. Measuring 138 mm tall, it weighs 382 g.

The remaining two figurines were not excavated in context but recovered during the excavation of T4 having fallen out of their original sites of deposition. One (B1161) is of greenish white tuff and has a distinctive flattened form (Figures 3.12d, 3.33). With a truncated pear-shaped outline, its incised detail depicts arms, legs, and some sort of headdress. Feet are also suggested. It stands 104 mm tall and weighs 102 g. The other is an exquisitely made red spondylus pendant (CT785; Figures 3.12e, 3.34). Only 21 mm tall, 7.8 mm wide, and 3.8 mm thick (5.5 mm at the nose), and weighing just 1.4 g, it nevertheless carries more detail than any of the other figurines so far described. The head and face, with eyes, nose, mouth, and hair are all evident, as are the arms and legs. The suspension hole is drilled transversally through the head just above the level of the mouth. As with B1161, feet are also suggested.

And across its lower section is a pair of parallel lines also carried by the other figurine. In short, these two appear to be related stylistically, though of differing scale and material.

Figure 3.33. Tuff figurine B1161, of unknown context within T4.

Figure 3.32. Tuff figurine B1192, from the Episode 6 platform.

Figure 3.34. Anthropomorphic pendant of *Spondylus princeps* CT785, of unknown context within T4.

3.2.2 Human Burials

Three human burials were found in long pit graves cut into the platform cap 12482, and these may belong to Episode 7, Episode 8, or even to some moment of transition after Episode 8 but before the ceremonial centre was transformed into the funerary precinct of the Bahía II occupation of Salango.[36] Towards the centre of the platform, grave 10755 contained a primary, extended burial on a southeast-northwest axis. The grave being severely truncated, only the head, upper body, and upper arms were preserved, and then poorly. The individual, an infant, lay supine, arms by either side and with the head, looking up, to the northwest. A rectangular greenstone bead (B1027), 20 mm long by 5 mm wide, was found lying across the chin (Figure 3.35).

The other graves were along the northwest side of the platform, close to the wall 12501. Grave 10933, near the north corner, oriented south-southwest to north-northeast, also much truncated from above and to the southwest, contained the very poorly preserved remains of an extended burial, perhaps of a child, probably with the head lying to the north-northeast. No grave goods were found.

The final burial lay in grave 10877, about halfway down the northwest side of the platform. The pit, on a north-northeast to south-southwest axis, was 1.20 m long, up to 80 cm wide, and about 50 cm deep, with vertical sides and a flat bottom. There was some disturbance to one side of the southwest end, where a later feature had intruded, and the preservation of the bones was poor, but the skeleton appeared to be complete. The individual, a young child, lay extended, supine, with the head to the southwest and turned to the right (facing east-southeast), and with the arms by the sides. Grave goods included: over 950 black ceramic beads (CT639); the shoulder, neck, and rim of a polished black jar that was set behind the head; and a *Vasum caestus* conch, partly stripped of its exterior, which was set between the upper legs (Figure 3.36). The beads were reported as two separate strands, one at the neck and over the right shoulder, the other over the pelvis and near the left wrist, i.e., a necklace and a bracelet. However, it seems likely that there was in fact just one single very long, looped strand that extended from the neck to the level of the waist.[37]

In addition to these three features, there was a fourth pit cut into the top of the platform cap 12482 that shares several features of Late Engoroy graves at Salango, though there were no associated human bones or even bone fragments. Pit 10708 was 1.70 m long, 0.60 m wide,

Figure 3.35. Greenstone bead B1027, deposited in grave 10755.

and 0.22 m deep, though it was likely originally deeper. Had it once contained a body that was subsequently removed, it seems likely that at least one or two bones or bone fragments would have been left behind, since skeletons always lie on the bottom of the grave, for the most part occupying just the lower 10 to 20 cm of fill, and thus it may be that there never was a body present in the pit. Alternatively, the body was recovered after interment but before decomposition. Apart from a very few pottery sherds and fish bones, the pit contained a greenstone bead (B1019) and an incomplete zoomorphic whistling bottle (B1036; Figure 3.37). The pit was located about 2 m in from the entranceway, slightly to left of centre, and was oriented along the main axis of the platform, i.e., southwest-northeast, and though truncated from above, along two sides and at its southwest end, it conforms to the shape and dimensions of Late Engoroy adult graves at Salango (Lunniss 2001:111). Likewise, the artefacts are also matched by goods in other graves: greenstone beads are typically found (Lunniss 2001:Table 5), and one grave contained both a greenstone bead and a zoomorphic bottle similar to that found in 10708 (Lunniss 2001:117, 229, Figs. 31, 120).

3.2.3. Stone Discs, Beads, Lime Containers, and a Zoomorphic Bottle

The presence of discs of different stone types, and of beads of greenstone, shell, and ceramic, has been indicated for various contexts, including figurine depositions, human burials, and floors. A review of these findings is now in order so that we can more fully appreciate 1) the range of materials and forms employed in the creation of these artefacts, and 2) the pattern of their distribution, in particular their relation to structures and to structured depositions of all sorts. A small sample of lime pots is also described, as well as the zoomorphic bottle of feature 10708.

---

[36] A further three graves sharing characteristics typical of Late Engoroy burials at Salango were also found, but these post-date early Bahía II period wall construction.

[37] The plan suggests that the beads, though massed at the two points described, extended across the body. Also, the great majority of beads were not visible at the time of planning, having disappeared perhaps into the chest and stomach cavity.

Figure 3.36. Neck of a ceramic jar, necklace of ceramic beads CT639, and a modified *Vasum caestus*, all deposited in grave 10877.

Figure 3.37. Zoomorphic whistling bottle B1036, deposited in grave-like feature 10708.

Stone Discs. Stone discs were found in association with two postholes, two figurine depositions, and six layers.

From two postholes (13390, 13387) underlying the floor of Episode 1, one disc (B1264) was of brownish grey shale, sub-circular, with flat top and bottom but the top bevelled to meet the vertical edge, and 16 mm across by 4 mm thick (Figure 3.38a). The other (B1262) was of light blue green tuff, flat, with both surfaces smoothly polished and measuring 36 mm across by 5 mm thick (Figure 3.38b).

From Episode 2 were two discs of greenstone, recovered from the central floor (13316) and an overlying ash layer (13324). The discs were each of a fine-grained muted grey

Figure 3.38. a) Shale disc B1264 and b) tuff disc B1262, both from Episode 2 postholes; and tuff discs c) B1230, from the Episode 3 platform, d) B1187, from outside the Episode 7/8 platform, e) B1218, from outside the Episode 6/7 entrance, and f) B1210, from the Episode 7 figurine deposition 12681.

green tuff that was quite distinct from any of those stones used for bead manufacture (Figure 3.39). They were also of similar form to each other, being slightly irregularly made with flat sides not quite parallel, and the edges only roughly rounded. One (B1258) was slightly larger, at 12 mm diameter by 10 mm thick, than the other (B1259), which measured 8 mm across by 6 mm.

From the Episode 3 platform (12593), are two more or less identical discs of white tuff (B1229 and B1230) of oval form, biconvex, with flat edges, and both sides smooth (Figure 3.38c). They measure 53 mm by 47 mm by 14 mm, and 52 mm by 47 mm by 10 mm.

From the Episode 6 platform (12570), one disc of white tuff (B1190) was of the same form as the previous two mentioned, but larger, at 73 mm by 65 mm by 17 mm. Another (B1191), incomplete, also of white tuff, was oval but uniconvex, with an original long dimension of about 60 mm, 50 mm wide and 8 mm thick.

From a layer (12673) outside the entrance to the Episode 6 or 7 platform, came a single disc (B1218) of white tuff (Figure 3.38e). With a sub-square or sub-circular outline, it is biconvex and flat-edged. One side is smooth, the other not. It measures 89 mm by 86 mm by 18 mm.

The final two discs (B1187, B1188) from layers came from a layer outside the east corner of the Episode 7/8 platform (Figure 3.38d). Again, they were of identical material, a grey white tuff, and similar form, being oval,

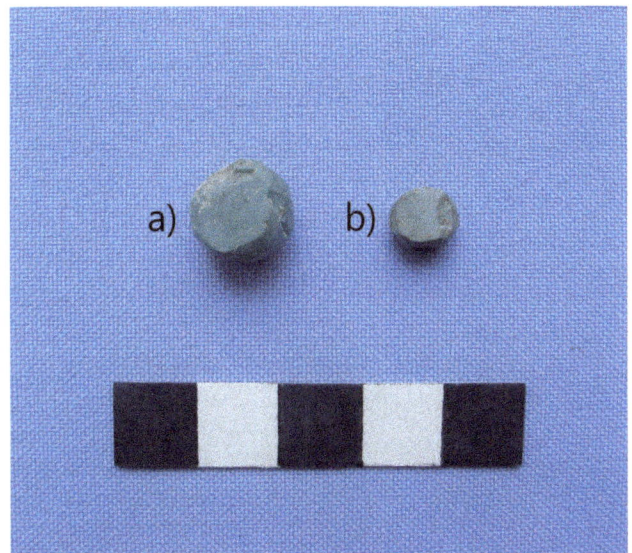

Figure 3.39. Greenstone discs a) B1258 and b) B1259, from the Episode 2 ceremonial house floor.

biconvex, and with flattened edges. The first measures 70 mm by 54 mm by 14 mm, and the second 85 mm by 73 mm by 22 mm.

A disc fragment (B1205) and a complete disc (B1210) associated with the figurine depositions (12662, 12681) of Episodes 7/8 were of white and grey white tuff, both of them oval and biconvex, and of approximately the same dimensions, the first originally measuring perhaps 116 mm

Figure 3.40. Stones from the offering of pit 13155 in the north corner of the Episode 2 ceremonial house. Reprinted by permission from Springer Nature Customer Service Centre GmbH: Springer, Pre-Columbian Landscapes of Creation and Origin, by J. Staller, ed. © (2008).

by 107 mm by 16 mm, and the second 105 mm by 96 mm by 17 mm (Figures 3.19 right, 3.38f).

In addition to these manufactured discs, there were thirty-one stones recovered from a shallow pit (13155) cut into the wall gully of the Episode 2 house (Figure 3.40). Twenty-seven of these were coloured, polished pebbles, measuring about 1 cm across, two were larger, unpolished flat oval pebbles, 3 cm and 4 cm long, and two were chert flakes. None of these stone types occur naturally at the site, and these were obviously selected elsewhere and then deliberately buried in the pit. It is notable that the small pebbles are of similar size and shape to the small shale discs with bevelled edges and the small greenstone discs, while the larger pebbles compare with the flat discs of tuff. This suggests that the pebbles and the carved discs may have been analogous, the latter being crafted equivalents of the other, "natural" objects.

Beads. There was just one instance of ceramic beads (CT639), and they were associated with a human burial (10887) set in the Episode 7/8 platform (Figure 3.36). All of them (950 complete beads and 25 fragments) appear to have been made as a single batch, sharing the same fine very dark grey to black paste. They were made by rolling a long strip of clay round a thread, and then cutting the individual bead lengths when the clay was dry enough to hold its shape but still wet enough that the ends of the beads taper somewhat because of the pressure brought to bear on them by the knife. They are from 2 mm to 5 mm long, and up to 2 mm across at the centre point, while the hole through them may be from 0.75 mm to 1.5 mm thick.

The beads, then, are not perfectly cylindrical, but taper slightly at the ends, and show some variability in size.[38]

Shell beads are not very common (n=77), and all are made with locally available species. None were found either with figurine depositions or with human burials. The largest group (n=68) was a set (CT794) made, unusually, of *Protothaca beili* shell, that was associated with a layer (12673) at the entrance to the Episode 6/7 platform (Figures 3.41, 3.42j). Additionally, they are of an unusual shape, perhaps determined by the nature of the shell, being roughly squared in cross-section with no attempt made to round them, and are variable in size, measuring from 4 mm to 8 mm across, and from 2 mm to 5 mm in thickness. The ribbed outer surface of the shell lends the beads a distinctive appearance.

Otherwise, seven beads came from soil layers of the Episode 8 ramp (Figure 3.42). Of these, five are of polished red shell, perhaps *Spondylus princeps*. Two (CT760, CT766) are of rounded tubular form, measuring 9 mm long by 3.5 mm across and 11 mm long by 5 mm across (the latter being a half bead, split longitudinally), while three (CT761, CT763, CT765) are polished flat discs, measuring 6.5 mm across and 3.5 mm thick, 4 mm across and 1.5 mm thick, and 5.5 mm across by 3 mm thick. One bead (CT787) is a flat white disc, measuring 4.5 mm across by 1.5 mm thick, while the final bead (CT770) is a modified specimen of *Fisurella* sp., in

---

[38] They are easily differentiated from the more regular segmented ceramic beads of Manteño date (Currie 1995:518, Fig. 9).

Figure 3.41. Beads of *Protothaca beili* CT794, from outside the entrance to the Episode 6/7 platform.

which the top has been cut off, and the body exterior and edges are polished. Two other beads were both regular, polished discs of white shell: one (CT774, 4 mm across by 2 mm thick) came from a layer (12450) outside the platform with no precise stratigraphic position determined; and one (CT782, 3.5 mm across by 2 mm thick) came from the clay floor outside the Episode 8 front wall.

Almost as common as shell beads are those of greenstone (n=60). All but one, found with a human burial, came from figurine depositions and/or contexts related to the entrance to the platforms. First were the five beads (B1194–B1198) set in the bottom step at the entrance to the Episode 6 platform and matched by the shell pendant figurine (CT786) at the top (Figure 3.16 right) They were all of the same greenstone, of similar irregular globular form, and presumably derived from the same workshop. With rounded edges and flattened sides, they measured from 9.5 mm by 8 mm across and 6 mm wide, to 13 mm by 11.5 mm across and 8 mm wide.

In a hole (12625) cut into the front edge of the same step, a tuff figurine (B1192) was surrounded at waist level by a set of 34 irregular disc beads (B1200) of light greenstone

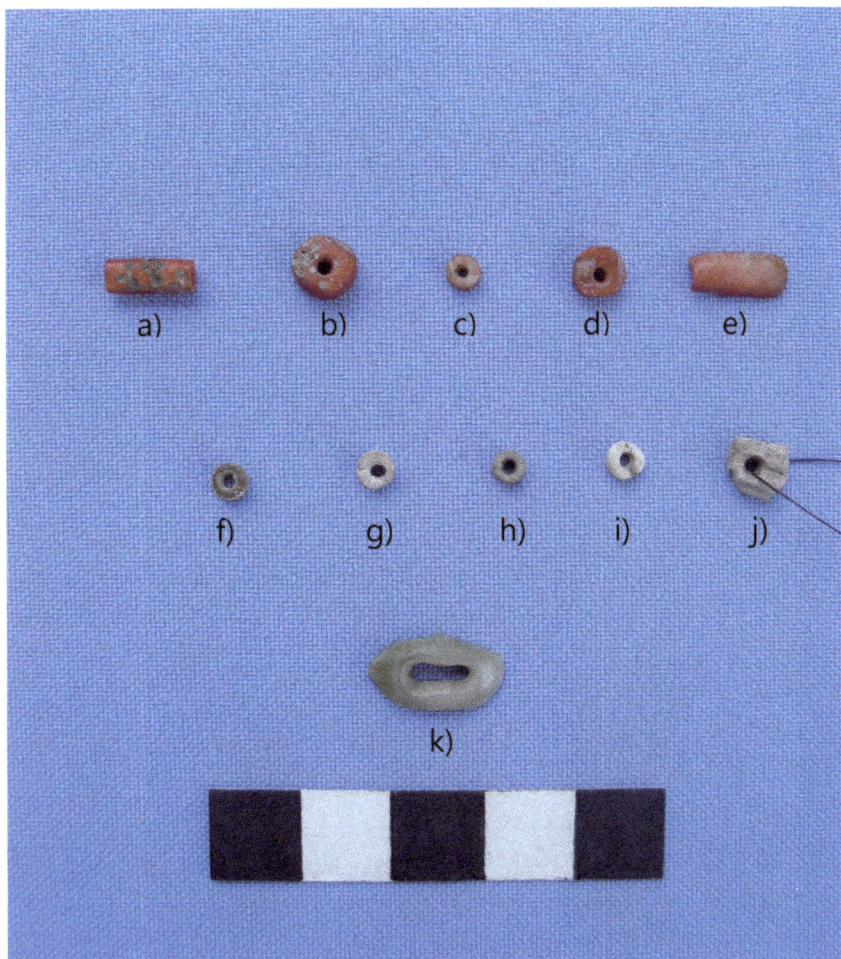

Figure 3.42. Beads of *Spondylus princeps*: a) CT760, b) CT761, c) CT763, d) CT765, e) CT766, of white shell f) CT754, g) CT774, h) CT782, i) CT787, j) CT794, and of *Fisurella* sp.: k) CT770, all from contexts of Episode 8.

(Figure 3.18 right). They measure from 2.5 mm to 4 mm across and 1.5 mm to 2.5 mm thick.

And set around the waist of the marble pendant (B1211) in the pit (12681) outside the front wall of Episode 6 or 7, were three beads (B1212) of rectangular form and roughly similar dimensions (14 mm by 7.5 mm by 6.5 mm; 14.5 mm by 6 mm by 5.5 mm; and 15.5 mm by 6.5 mm by 5.5 mm; Figure 3.30 top right). Each appears to be of a different material, and each subject to different treatment in its manufacture. Thus the second bead, of a fine grain and an unusually pure and intense green, has markedly sharp edges, though it is not perfectly rectangular in overall form, and each side is composed of two or three flat planes, each of these having been produced by a separate movement or set of movements, rather than being a smooth single convex surface as in the other two cases.

From the entrance to the platform, the largest set of greenstone beads is from layer 12673 of Episode 6 or 7. Of these, one group of ten are regularly formed discs (B1208A) of a distinctive, laminar, glassy material, and measure 7 mm to 8 mm across, and 2.5 mm to 4 mm in thickness (Figure 3.43a). In addition, there are two fat cylindrical beads (B1207) of greenstone marbled with brown (Figure 3.43b left and right). Very regularly made, they have a circular cross-section, and the sides are straight save where they taper slightly to meet the flat ends. They measure 14 mm long by 9 mm across, and 16.5 mm long by 11.5 mm by 10 mm across. And then, from the same layer, a final disc bead (B1208B) is of brownish grey quartz, and measures 5 mm across and 2 mm thick (Figure 3.43b centre).

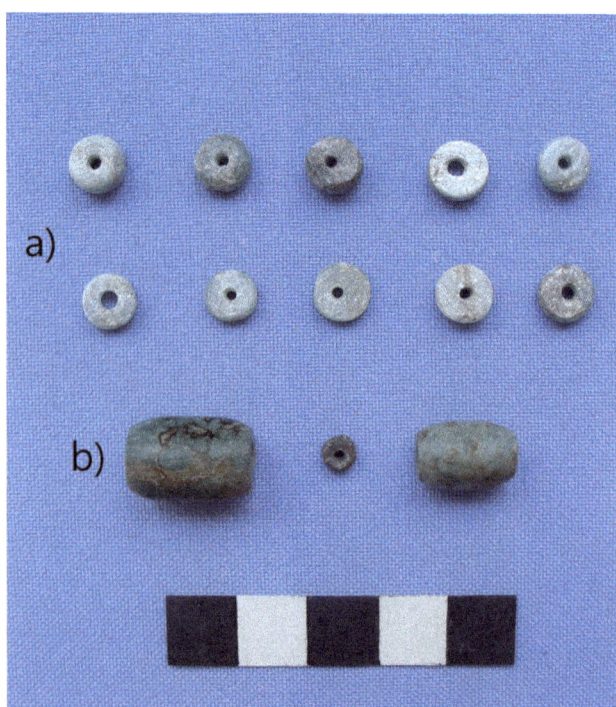

Figure 3.43. Greenstone beads a) B1208 and b) B1207, from outside the entrance to the Episode 6/7 platform.

Figure 3.44. Greenstone beads a) B1203 and b) B1204, from the Episode 7 ramp.

Three stone beads come from layers of the Episode 7 ramp. From 12659, one (B1203) is of malachite (Figure 3.44 left). It is very irregularly disc-shaped, with incompletely rounded edge and uneven ends, measuring 6 mm by 5 mm across and 7 mm thick. From the same layer, another bead (B1204) is of a more standard greenstone and regular disc shape, measuring 4 mm by 4.5 mm across and 3.5 mm thick (Figure 3.44 right). Third, from layer 12656, there is a half bead (B1202) of light greenish grey tuff. Of oblong form with flat sides meeting at rounded edges, it suggests original complete measurements of 15 mm long by 10.5 mm across.

A single greenstone bead (B1019) came from the empty grave (10708) cut into the Episode 7/8 platform (12482). This was an irregular discoid shape, measuring 9 mm to 10 mm across by 6.7 mm thick. Finally, there was a single oblong greenstone bead (B1027) set at the chin of the individual buried in the grave (10755) also cut into the Episode 7/8 platform (12482; Figure 3.35). The bead measures 20.5 mm long by 6.5 mm by 5.5 mm across.

Lime Containers. Associated with the Episode 3 platform (12953) was a complete, if slightly worn, pottery vessel (B1232) in the shape of a tree snail (*Strophocheilus popelairianus*; Figure 3.45). Measuring 73 mm long and 43 mm across, its exterior is brown and roughly polished, and the spiral from mouth to apex is delineated by a groove up to 4 mm wide and 3 mm deep. Vessels like this (e.g., Lathrap et al. 1975:458) are interpreted as lime containers, and Ledergerber (1992) has confirmed this function through identification of lime residues on the vessel interiors.

A small carinated vessel with everted rim (B1209), by analogy with similar sized vessels (Lathrap et al. 1975:No. 455) also a lime container, was found in the Episode 6/7

Figure 3.45. Pottery lime container in the form of a tree snail (*Strophocheilus popelairianus*) B1232, from the clay of the Episode 3 platform. Reprinted by permission from Springer Nature Customer Service Centre GmbH: Springer, Pre-Columbian Landscapes of Creation and Origin, by J. Staller, ed. © (2008).

pit (12681) in association, direct or indirect, with a marble pendant (B1211) and other artefacts (Figure 3.30 centre top). The pot is incomplete, of fine fabric, with a very dark grey core and brown interior and exterior surfaces. The exterior upper body and interior rim are polished, the exterior lower body is incompletely polished. Standing 42 mm tall, it has a rim diameter of about 36 mm.

Zoomorphic Bottle. One zoomorphic bottle (B1036) was found in the empty grave (10708) of Episode 7 or 8 (Figure 3.37). The figure of a quadruped is incomplete and lacks most of the head, though the lower neck and whistle and one ear survive. The right foreleg, as well as part of the right shoulder, is also missing. The body is of tubular form (145 mm long), flattened at top and bottom so that it is wider (84 mm) than deep (62 mm). There is a short, pointed tail that curves upwards. The legs are short and stubby, and each has three appliqué pellets at the foot, with two pellets to the front and sides and one to the centre rear. The spout, 52 mm tall and with a rim diameter of 24 mm, leans forward slightly, with the strap handle extending towards the rear of the neck. Overall, the bottle is 128 mm tall and survives to 178 mm long. It has a fine fabric, with a grey core and light red or reddish brown interior and exterior.

Around the base each of the tail and of the neck is a pair of incised lines, 3 mm to 4.5 mm apart. Pairs of incised lines also decorated the head. Bands of iridescent paint run across the body and handle. Post-fire yellow paint decorates both the lower part of the tail and the lower neck. The rest

of the body is a polished dark brown, save the underside which is not polished. The head and tail were also left unpolished. The one ear has a 2 mm hole through its tip, with an unfinished hole just to the side of that. Although there are differences in form and decoration, the bottle is likely an equivalent of a complete example excavated from an Episode 7/8 grave in T3 (Lunniss 2001:Fig. 120).

4

The Complete Configurations of the Late Formative Ceremonial Structures at OMJPLP–141B

Abstract: The Late Formative ceremonial structures at OMJLP–141B comprise eight main episodes. Episodes 1 to 6 are of Middle Engoroy and date to 600–300 BC, while Episodes 7 and 8 are of Late Engoroy, dating to 300–100 BC.

Episode 1 consisted of a yellow clay floor and central hearth. In Episode 2, over a larger yellow clay floor was raised a northeast-facing rectangular house with interior roof supports and an outer wall of narrow posts set in a shallow gully. Offerings were placed in the two rearmost postholes of each of the three central files of roof supports. There were internal partitions and fixtures, a central fire pit, and other open hearths. The outer wall was later dismantled, and a fence set up outside the front, and five human individuals were buried to the rear. The interior house floor surface was mostly clean of artefacts, but discard and debris accumulated around the exterior. For Episode 3, yellow clay was added to create a ramped rectangular northeast-facing platform. A small wooden structure stood at the rear, and the central area had open hearths and ash scatters. A dense artefact scatter surrounded the platform. For Episode 4, a low clay wall was set around the old platform. More yellow clay was added, creating a square ramped platform. A fence of narrow posts was set all along the clay wall, and a clay floor was laid around the outside. There was continued use of the summit for open hearths. Two dogs and a pair of great curassows were buried at the rear and to the left of the central axis. More artefact discard accumulated all around. Episode 5 is uncertain, but likely saw new low walls along the front and back and more yellow clay added to the platform edges. At the rear, next to the central axis, were two offering pits. There was continued use of the platform for open hearths. In Episode 6, a new platform was created with a small proscenium at the entrance. A narrow clay wall along the front served as the bottom of an elaborate clay stairway that incorporated shell and stone figurines and greenstone beads. The exterior clay floor was resurfaced and extended. There was no evidence for hearths, but an arc of four posts was set across the centre of the platform.

For Episode 7, a massive clay wall was set around the earlier platform, creating a square enclosure. More yellow clay was added to create a raised platform to the front of the enclosure. A new ramped approach and stepped entranceway was made, with offerings of figurines and other artefacts. Offering pits were also sited outside the entrance and at the rear. In Episode 8, the exterior clay wall was widened, and a new ramped approach added, with upright stone figurines buried under the ramp and rear wall, and a gateway was erected with a central large post. The platform and area to the rear were used, as during Episode 7, for primary extended human burials, mainly of adult males and females, along with associated fire pits and rubbish pits. Stone figurines were set upright in small open holes all around the platform. The end of Late Engoroy use of the platform is marked by a layer of volcanic ash.

Resumen: Las estructuras ceremoniales Formativo Tardío en OMJLP–141B constan de ocho episodios principales. Los Episodios 1 a 6 son de Engoroy Medio (600–300 a.C.) y los Episodios 7 y 8 son de Engoroy Tardío (300–100 a.C.).

El Episodio 1 consistió en un piso de arcilla amarilla y un hogar central. En el Episodio 2, sobre un piso de arcilla amarilla más grande se levantó una casa rectangular orientada al noreste con soportes de techo interiores y una pared exterior de postes angostos colocados en una zanja poco profunda. Hubo ofrendas en los dos hoyos de poste más traseros de cada una de las tres filas centrales de soportes de techo. Había particiones e instalaciones interiores, un pozo de fuego central, y otros hogares abiertos. Más tarde se desmanteló el muro exterior y se colocó una valla en el exterior de frente, y cinco individuos humanos fueron enterrados en la parte trasera. La superficie del piso interior de la casa estaba mayormente limpia de artefactos, pero desechos se acumularon alrededor del exterior. Para el Episodio 3, se agregó arcilla amarilla para crear una plataforma rectangular con rampa orientada al noreste. Una pequeña estructura de madera se encontraba en la parte trasera, y el área central tenía hogares abiertos y capas de ceniza esparcida. Artefactos desechados rodeaban la plataforma. Para el Episodio 4, se colocó un muro bajo de arcilla alrededor de la antigua plataforma. Con más arcilla amarilla se creó una plataforma cuadrada con rampa. Se colocó una cerca de postes angostos a lo largo del muro de arcilla, y un piso de arcilla alrededor. Hubo uso continuado de la cumbre para hogares abiertos. Dos perros y un par de pavones grandes fueron enterrados por el eje central en la parte trasera. Más artefactos descartados se acumularon por todas partes alrededor. El Episodio 5 vio nuevos muros bajos a lo largo de la parte delantera y trasera y se agregó más arcilla amarilla a los bordes de la plataforma. En la parte trasera, junto al eje central, había dos pozos de ofrenda. Continuó el uso de la plataforma para hogares abiertos. En el Episodio 6, se creó una nueva plataforma con un pequeño proscenio por la entrada. Un estrecho muro de arcilla de frente servía como base de una elaborada escalera de arcilla que incorporaba figurines y cuentas de piedra verde. El piso exterior de arcilla fue repavimentado y extendido. No había evidencia de hogares, pero se colocó un arco de cuatro postes en el centro de la plataforma.

Para el Episodio 7, se colocó un enorme muro de arcilla alrededor de la plataforma anterior, creando un recinto cuadrado. Se agregó más arcilla amarilla para crear una plataforma elevada al frente del recinto. Se hizo una nueva rampa con escalera, con ofrendas de figurines y otros artefactos. Pozos de ofrenda también se ubicaron fuera de la entrada y en la parte trasera. En el Episodio 8, se amplió el muro de arcilla exterior y se agregó una nueva rampa, con figurines de piedra verticales enterrados debajo de la rampa y la pared trasera, y un portón fue elevado con un gran poste central por la entrada. La plataforma y el área en la parte trasera se usaron, como durante el Episodio 7, para entierros humanos primarios extendidos, principalmente de hombres y mujeres adultos, junto con pozos de fuego y pozos de basura asociados. Figurines de piedra se colocaron en posición vertical en pequeños hoyos abiertos alrededor de la plataforma. El final del uso Engoroy Tardío de la plataforma está marcado por una capa de ceniza volcánica.

4.1. Introduction

In this chapter the data from sectors T4 and T3 of OMJPLP–141B are brought together to reconstruct, as far as possible, complete profiles as well as ground plans of the structures for each of the episodes identified (Figures 4.1 & 4.2). The details for T4 have been presented in the previous chapter, while those for T3 are to be found in Lunniss (2001). Now, the aim is to focus on the overall configuration of the structures themselves, and the relationships to be had between them and their associated features.

Though twelve radiocarbon dates were obtained for T3, the results were generally unsatisfactory for excessive standards of deviation and internal inconsistency (Lunniss 2001:288–290, Table 24). Thus the chronology established for T3 is based on correlation of the pottery with ceramic sequences dated with radiocarbon elsewhere (Lunniss 2001:288–292), and this chronology can be applied to site OMJPLP–141B in general. Accordingly, Episodes 1 to 6, which correspond to Middle Engoroy, and Episodes 7 and 8, which correspond to Late Engoroy, date to approximately 600–300 BC and 300–100 BC respectively.[39] However, it should also be remembered that the transition from Middle

to Late Engoroy in ceramic terms involved a staggered sequence of events as different vessel forms changed in turn (Lunniss 2001:267–270).

In the following account, the structures themselves are described first, along with all secondary features incorporated in them. Afterwards, attention is brought to the two principal feature sets associated with the later episodes, i.e., human graves and figurine depositions.

4.2. Episode 1

The first constructed setting for ritual practice for which there is clear evidence consisted of a 3 cm thick yellow clay floor (13360) with a central hearth (13361; Figure 4.3). The original shape and extent of the floor is uncertain. None of the layer was uncovered in T3, there was extensive truncation in T4, and we cannot tell how much of the edges of the floor, as revealed, may have been worn away. However, the hearth was roughly equidistant from each of the northeast and northwest corners of the floor as it survived, suggesting that it lay at the centre. If then, we assume that the north side of the floor survived more or less as originally created, an original rectangular outline could have measured approximately 5.10 m by 5.40 m, with its longer axis from north to south. Alternatively, if we posit an originally circular floor, then a minimum diameter would have been 7.20 m.

---

[39] See Zeidler (2003:499–501) for comment on some of the radiocarbon dates from T3 and their implications in his survey of coastal Ecuadorian Formative chronology.

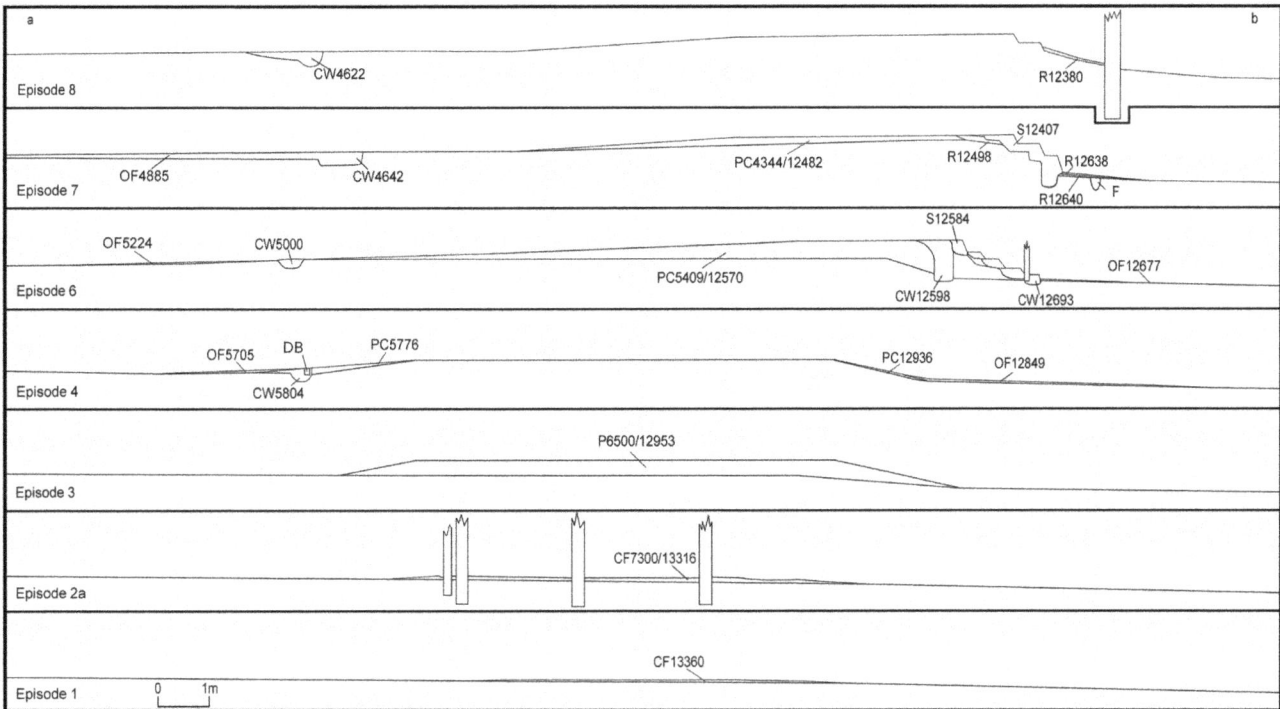

Figure 4.1. OMJPLP–141B: Reconstructed profiles along the central axes. Adapted by permission from Springer Nature Customer Service Centre GmbH: Springer, Pre-Columbian Landscapes of Creation and Origin, by J. Staller, ed. © (2008).

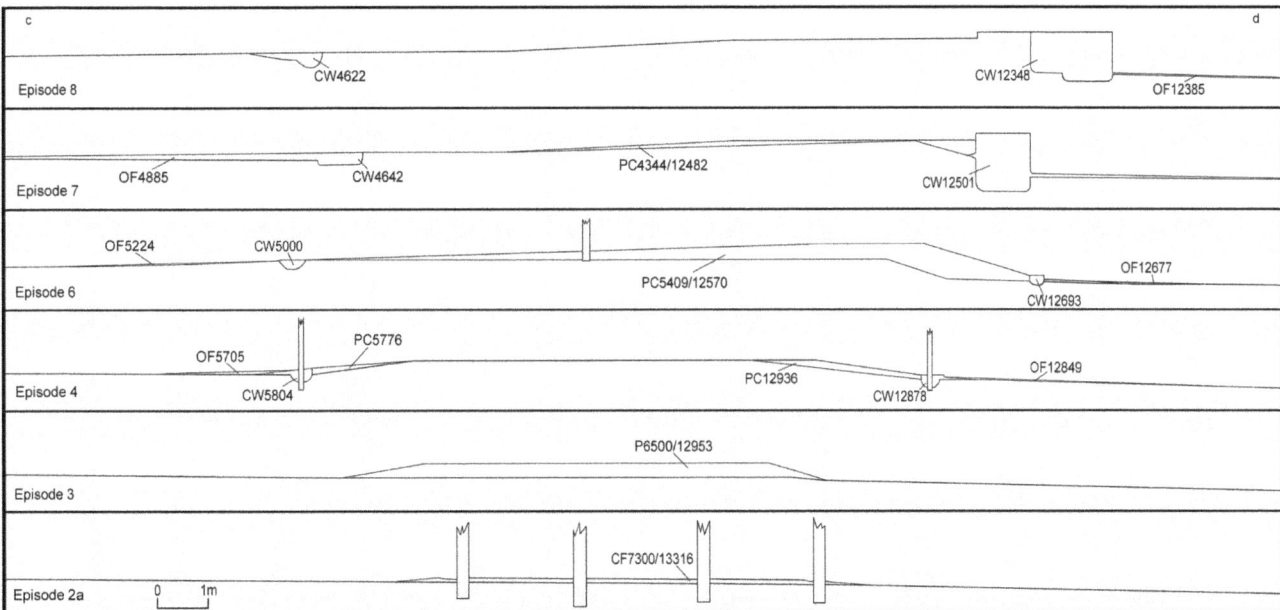

Figure 4.2. OMJPLP–141B: Reconstructed profiles to northwest of central axes. Adapted by permission from Springer Nature Customer Service Centre GmbH: Springer, Pre-Columbian Landscapes of Creation and Origin, by J. Staller, ed. © (2008).

No associated postholes, other features, or artefacts are recorded. Allowing, however, for the incompleteness of the evidence, the hearth was both in the open air and the focus of activity on or around the floor.

4.3. Episode 2

The 10 cm to 15 cm thick yellow clay layer 13316 of T4 correlates with layer 7300 of T3 (Lunniss 2001:74–77,

Figs 8, 9; Lunniss and Mudd 1987), and the combined data from Trenches 3 and 4 can be used to estimate the original form and dimensions of both the floor and the rectangular northeast-facing wooden house that was set over it, even though the east corner was largely destroyed and the south corner was left unexcavated. The floor measured about 11.20 m (northwest-southeast) by 9.60 m (northeast-southwest), with a general thickness of about 10 cm (Figure 4.4). The house itself measured approximately

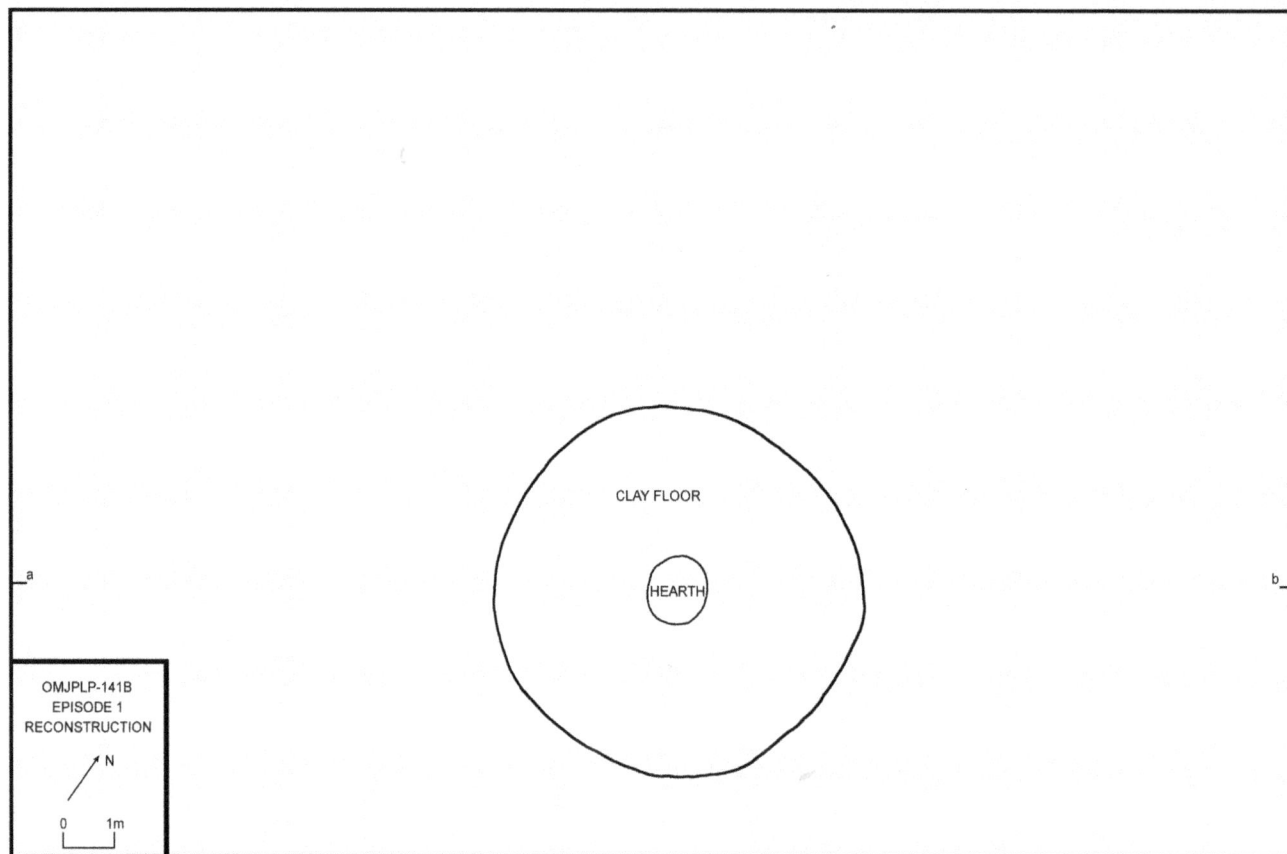

Figure 4.3. OMJPLP–141B: Reconstructed plan of the Episode 1 floor and hearth. The circular form of the floor is conjectural. Reprinted by permission from Springer Nature Customer Service Centre GmbH: Springer, Pre-Columbian Landscapes of Creation and Origin, by J. Staller, ed. © (2008).

10.10 m by 7.40 m. Around the edge of the house was a skirt of clay that sloped down to the edges of the floor. This skirt was up to 1.50 m wide along the front, 0.70 m along the back, and 0.50 m along the sides.[40]

The data from T3 had earlier suggested a sequence with two principal episodes of construction, Phases 1 and 2, within a larger four-part scheme, and in reconstructing the overall design of the house, that model and the posthole patterns identified by that analysis were initially used as a base line for interpretation of the features of T4. First, the main feature of the Phase 1 structure in T3 was seen to have been a perimeter wall, represented by a series of postholes, 15 to 20 cm wide and 11 to 45 cm deep. These were found mainly along the southwest side, spaced at up 50 cm apart, with a cluster of holes at the west corner. Secondly, a line of holes perpendicular to the southwest wall suggested an internal wall, 2.50 m in from the northwest side, while two shallow gullies further to the southeast may each have also represented some sort of internal partition. Additionally, there was an arc of four postholes across the interior of the floor, with two to the northwest of the end of the smaller internal gully, the other to the southeast.

For Phase 2, the outer wall posts were dismantled, and a set of substantial roof supports were erected. Seven postholes were found in two rows running northwest-southeast, the holes and rows spaced at intervals of 2.30 to 2.50 m. The holes were up to 40 cm across at the surface, and up to 70 cm deep, tapering as they descended, with rather narrower moulds for the posts. While four postholes were found in the row along the southwest side of the floor, only three were found in the next row up, while the fourth, against the northwest side, had been destroyed by a later feature. A perimeter gully was considered to be associated with this second phase, as were five human burials and the deposition of a stone disc with a greenstone bead.

The evidence from T4, however, suggested the need for significant modifications as well as additions to the model just outlined. First, those main posts which had originally been identified as roof supports belonging to the second phase would have formed part of the original infrastructure of the house.[41] And given the position of the holes with relation to the outline of the floor and to the location of the entrance as evidenced by T4, originally there would have been space for five files of posts running northeast-southwest, with the central file on the same axis as the

---

[40] The floor was built on ground that dropped about 10 cm from southwest to northeast, and maybe as much also from southeast to northwest. Though this slope was largely compensated for in the laying of the floor, there seems to have persisted a slight drop from southeast to northwest.

[41] Indeed, this was suggested as a possibility in the original analysis (Lunniss and Mudd 1987).

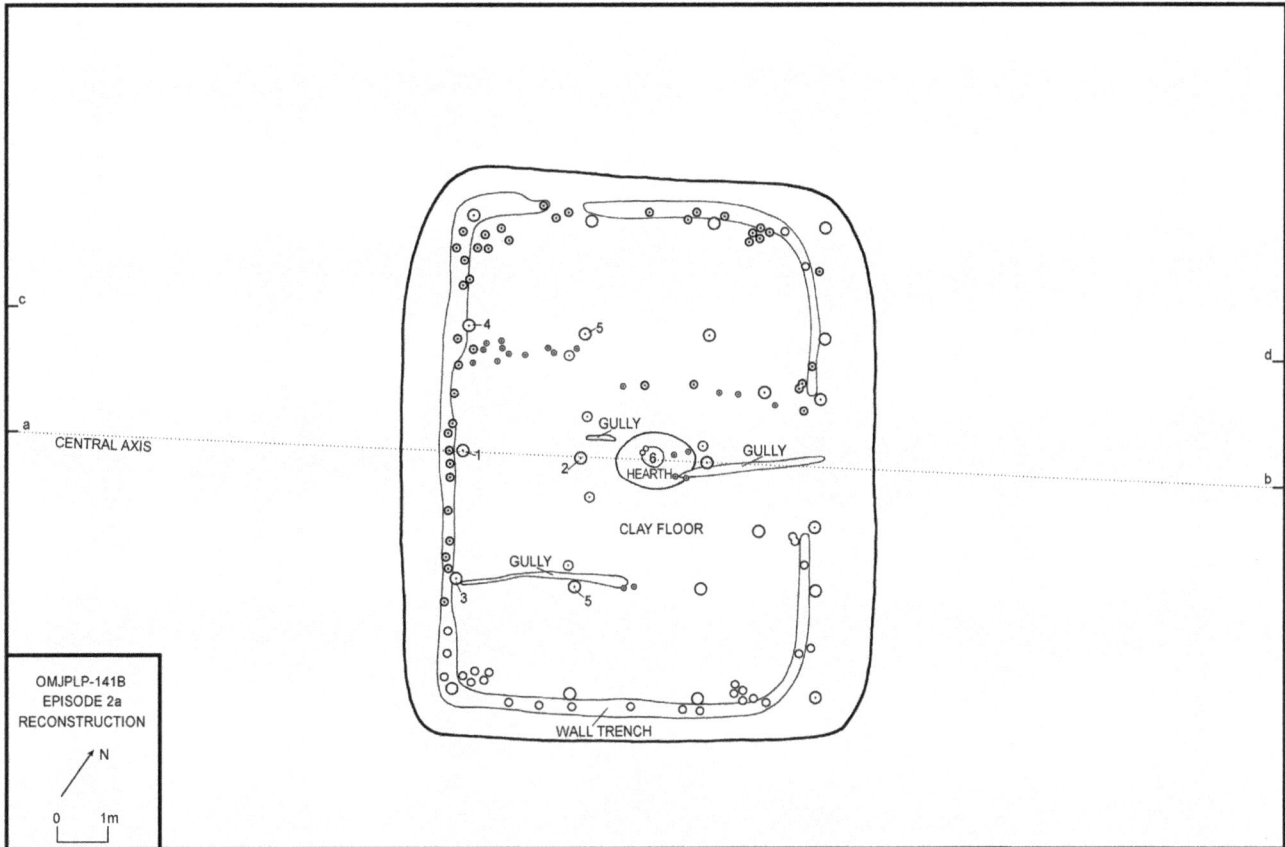

Figure 4.4. OMJPLP–141B: Reconstructed plan of the main elements of the Episode 2a house, with the entrance to the northeast. Buried offerings in the postholes of roof supports included: (1) two tuff discs at the base, and a juvenile *Spondylus princeps* in the packing; (2) a tuff disc at the base and a *Vasum caestus* in the packing; (3) a shale disc in the base and three copper flakes in the packing; (4) probably as (3); (5) a shale disc. (6) was a small ash pit. Reprinted by permission from Springer Nature Customer Service Centre GmbH: Springer, Pre-Columbian Landscapes of Creation and Origin, by J. Staller, ed. © (2008).

centre line of the entranceway. Second, the perimeter gully was integral to the construction of the wall indicated by the line of postholes around the inside of the edge of the floor.

In T4, just two holes of a third row were found to match the distribution pattern of the holes for the presumed roof supports of T3.[42] One (13145) lay in the central file, while the other (13102) occupied the northwest-centre file. No hole was found in the expected position of the northwest file, even though the floor in that area was undisturbed. It may be that the hole was simply missed during the excavation. The relevant area of the southeast-centre file had been previously destroyed. Further to the northeast was the fourth, front row. At the east corner, there were two holes (13328, 13326), either of which might have supported a main post, though one (13328) seems more congruent with the established pattern. Evidence, however, for the north corner had been lost. While evidence for a southeast-centre file posthole was also lost, there was no sign of any in the northwest-centre file, but this may have been overlooked. However, a 2.50 m wide entranceway is defined by a hole either side of the central axis on this

leading row (13151, 13319), perhaps with a second pair of holes on either side 1.25 m to the southwest (13097), the corresponding hole on the southeast side having been destroyed.

The overall pattern of those larger holes of T3 interpreted as roof supports, when combined with data from T4, represents an infrastructure founded on square units measuring about 2.50 m in each direction. The southwest and the next two rows would have had five posts each. Along the northeast front of the building, there was a post at each corner, and a post either side of the entranceway, probably also with a post at the end of the northwest-centre and southeast-centre files. The 2.50 m wide entranceway was perhaps further defined by a pair of posts 1.25 m back in from the front row.

The holes for these main posts were themselves constructed with more care and intent than has been mentioned. The clay packing of the holes of the three central files of the back two rows each contained one or more surviving offerings (Lunniss 2001:142, 143). On the central file and main axis of the building, the rearmost hole (7322) contained two flat discs of blue green tuff (see B1262, Figure 3.38b) at its base, and a juvenile *Spondylus princeps* part way up from

---

[42] Though in each case only the top of the post mould was identified and excavated.

Figure 4.5. The rear left quarter of the yellow clay floor of the Episode 2 house. Bamboo posts indicate the rear wall. The yellow clays of the platforms of subsequent Middle and Late Engoroy episodes are visible in the profile behind, and above them the deposits of Early and Middle Regional Development episodes. View to the northeast. The scaling rod measures 100 cm.

the bottom. The next hole (6584) to the northeast in that file contained a similar tuff disc at its base, and a *Vasum caestus*, a small conch, in the packing. Meanwhile in the southeast-central file, the rearmost hole (7247) contained a small grey shale disc (see B1264, Figure 3.38a) at its base, and three small flakes of copper in the packing; and the next hole to the northeast (7092) had another shale disc at its base. Thirdly, in the northwest-centre file, while the rearmost hole (7192) was mostly destroyed, the second hole (7276) also had a small shale disc at the base. In other words, while the holes of the central axis are marked by shells and tuff discs, those of the files immediately to either side are marked by shale discs and copper.[43]

The main posts having been erected, the perimeter wall was then added (Figure 4.5). In T4, evidence for this wall is provided by three more individual holes (13395, 13397, 13399) along the northwest side, with a cluster of five (13165, 13171, 13181, 13358, 13356) somewhat to the southwest of where the north corner, destroyed by later features, would have lain. On the northeast front, there were

two possibly relevant holes northwest from the entrance: one (13334) lay in the gully, while the other (13348) lay slightly outside it. Southeast from the entrance, most of the evidence for the front wall was lost, as was all evidence for the wall on the southeast side.

Thus, there was indeed a line of posts around the exterior in the initial phase of building, and there seem to have been more posts along the back than along the sides, and fewest along the front. Now it is necessary to consider the external gully. The initial idea, that the gully post-dated the postholes, was based on the observation that the fill of the gully overlay most of the posthole fills. It was also suggested that the gully might have been caused by water dripping off the roof. This interpretation now seems to be wrong. Rather, I would suggest that the gully and the postholes were contemporary and of related function, and that the gully supported some sort of wall infill that stretched between and was held upright by the exterior posts.[44] This infill may have been some sort of woven panelling, or a series of removable upright posts such as are used to consolidate the walls of Achuar houses (Zeidler 1983:Foto 3; Descola 1996:111). While the wall mostly ran outside the main posts, along the front, it ran inside

---

[43] It is unfortunate that we cannot know what may have been contained by hole 7192. Nothing was found in the incompletely preserved hole, 6779, at the northwest end of the rearmost row. It is also unfortunate that the main postholes of T4 were not fully excavated. It may however be that offerings were limited to the rearmost rows only, and then only to the central three files. This area seems to have been of especial interest.

---

[44] It is worth noting here that no daub was found with this or any of the subsequent structures.

them. Furthermore, the gully appears to make the turn from the northwest side to the northeast front well inside the position where the north corner roof support would be expected to lie. On the northwest side, near the west corner, a gap in the gully may represent a side door. And when the wall of embedded posts came to be dismantled, the moulds were deliberately backfilled first, and after that the gully itself filled with silt.

Additionally, the interior of the building in the first phase was furnished with a variety of partitions and other fittings, and the different areas defined by these features became the settings for a variety of different activities. In the first place, there are the shallow internal gullies. Although it is not known exactly how the gullies were used, it seems likely that they each represent the base of some sort of partition that was connected to one or other of the main posts. One gully (13191) ran down the forward half of the building along its main northeast-southwest axis, leading from the entrance to the central fireplace (13331). Here it is notable that the gully is slightly skew of the axis, as it had to run to one side of the central post (13145) of the third row. Furthermore, any partition supported by the gully would have split the central area into two parts. A short section of gully registered in T3 could then be seen as having supported an extension, albeit laterally displaced, of the main central partition to the southwest of the central hearth, running past the opposite side of the central post of the second row. In terms of relative chronology, it seems that the main central gully, since it partially overlaps the area of the hearth, would have post-dated it, in which case the hearth would represent one of the earliest events, if not the first, conducted in the building.

In the rear south quadrant of the house, one other gully, also running northeast-southwest, extended from the rearmost post of the southeast-centre file to the corresponding post of the second row. Two holes (13170, 13168) that lie immediately to the northeast of the end of the gully may have been related to it.

If there were gullies sectioning off the interior along the central and southeast-centre files of main posts, was there any such equivalent for the northwest-centre file? Although much of the floor was destroyed, there was no indication of any gully in the substantial area that remained. When we consider the posthole patterns, however, the evidence does suggest an internal wall or fence along the rear section of the file. In T3, a row of postholes ran between the positions of the rearmost and second posts. These, like the holes of the external wall, were all emptied of posts at one stage, though it is possible that other holes represent a subsequent replacement partition. In T4, while several holes lay between the second and third posts of the file, they do not stand out, amongst other features in that general area, as forming a discrete set that could have been an extension of the row in T3.

Rather more notable is a line of holes (13085, 13083, 13087, 13077, 13149, 13110) that run midway between the centre and northwest-centre files from just north of the

second row as far as the rearmost (13097) of the posts to the northeast of the entrance. This line is striking because it appears to define the southeast limit of the scatter of postholes occupying the northwest half of the front of the building, though there is also a deep posthole (13343) next to the central main post of the third row.

There is also evidence for an important division running transversally across part of the rear of the building in T3. This consisted of an arc of four similarly sized holes, 30 cm to 40 cm deep, with two to either side of the central axis. The two middle holes lay just to the northeast of the line of the second row of main posts, while the outer holes lay slightly to the southwest, one lying next to the southeast gully, the other next to the line of posts along the northwest-centre file. The symmetry of their position with respect to the main structural elements is too close for coincidence, and they can be interpreted as having held posts that marked off the central rear portion of the house. The original analysis of the building placed the holes in the first phase and suggested that they were possibly dismantled for the second, in which case they would have been in use at the same time as those other early partitions.[45]

This review has considered just the more obvious internal posthole patterns. It must be remembered, however, that there were very many more features encountered than have been mentioned specifically here. For example, three holes (13318, 13320, 13330) just inside the northwest side of the entrance probably represent some part of the structure of the doorway. A full analysis of their distribution would perhaps render much interesting further information on internal structuring and activity but is beyond the scope of this report.[46]

We now turn to look at the data concerning the locations of the open hearths. We have seen that the central hearth, which measured 1.50 m by 1.10 m, was in place from the start of the building, and that it lay at one end of the gully leading from the entrance way. At the centre of the hearth, close to the centre of the building, there was a circular pit (13230), 40 cm across and 8 cm deep, with a pure ash fill. In the west side of the pit were two narrow postholes (13239, 13241). Secondly, immediately to the northeast of the pit, there were two pairs of narrow postholes (13333, 13337 and 13339, 13341), about 15 cm deep, lying either side of the central northeast-southwest axis. The symmetry of their position with respect to the main plan and to the pit is striking. These posts appear to represent some sort of ancillary structure associated with the main hearth.

---

[45] This, in turn, would suggest that any central partition would not have extended right across the rear half of the floor, a view that is confirmed by the fact that the short section of gully leading back from the central fireplace ends at the line of the arc.

[46] Secure interpretation is hampered by the loss of large areas of the floor through later intrusive activity. But for the east quadrant of the building there is record of numerous postholes cutting a yellow clay floor that may correlate with 13316/7300. This floor and the holes were found during excavation in 1982 of unit L82-Level 12.

Figure 4.6. The rear left quarter of the Episode 2 floor showing light grey ash scatters and very dark red burnt patches contrasting with the yellow of the clay as originally laid. The gully of the rear wall and its later silt fill is visible just inside the edge of the floor to the left. View to the northwest. The scaling rods measure 50 cm and 100 cm.

Within the front half of the interior a second area of burnt floor (13309) with overlying ash lay 3 m to the northwest of the central hearth, though there was no evidence of an ash pit within it. However, there was a relatively dense concentration of postholes around the patch of burning, and these might suggest the presence both of associated fixtures and of a partition or screen. Other areas of burnt floor were recorded for the rear of the interior (Figure 4.6). In all cases, there was evidence not only of repeated use of the hearth sites, but also of regular resurfacing of the affected areas, and this pattern appears to have continued through both main phases of use of the house.

In sum, the interior of the building was characterised by the presence of internal partitions, furniture and fixtures, a central fire pit, other open hearths, layers of ash and layers of yellow clay repair to the original floor. There was also just a very sparse artefact scatter, though this was mainly limited to the very final moments after the dismantling of the structure prior to the creation of the following platform (Episode 3), when a *Strombus peruvianus* conch, and various elements of two tripod bowls and a bottle spout

were left in or close to the emptied holes of three roof posts. However, a white spondylus pendant (CT831) and a small greenstone disc (B1258) were embedded in the house floor, and a number of armadillo scutes were placed over an ash scatter, prior to the laying of a patch of yellow clay floor repair.

As we move outside the building and off the clay floor, we find that the approach to the entranceway was itself defined and controlled by further fencing, and all this probably belongs to the second phase, Episode 2b (Figure 4.7). First, 1 m out from the entrance through the front wall, and just beyond the edge of the floor as it was preserved, there was a row of three postholes (13033, 13042, 13037), 28 cm deep, and 18 cm to 20 cm in diameter. The meter long southwest-northeast line formed by the holes suggests a set of posts bisecting the approach to the doorway. This line, moreover, corresponds on the outside of the building to the division represented by the main central gully on the interior. Secondly, there was a posthole (13027), 27 cm deep and 15 cm diameter, situated to the northwest of the first hole of this row and a meter out from the main

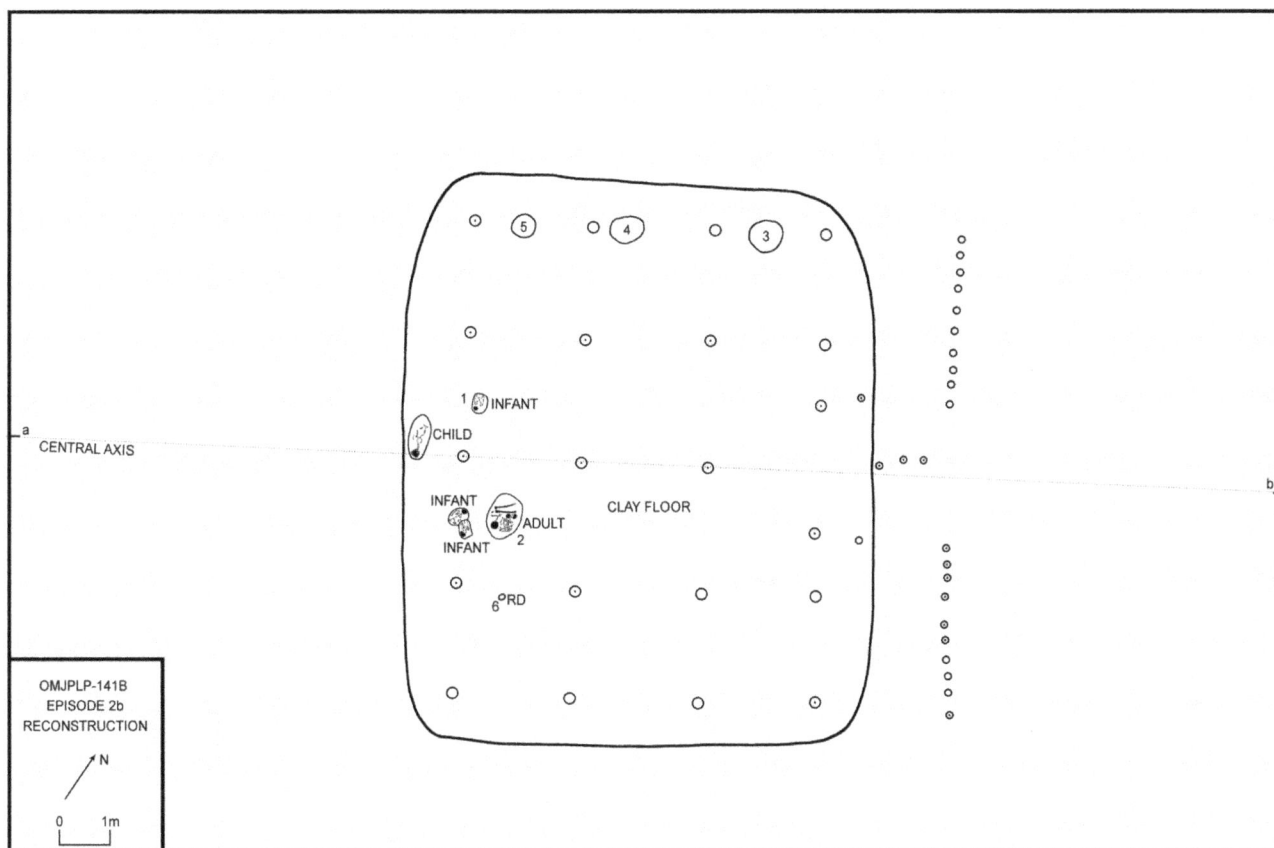

Figure 4.7. OMJPLP–141B: Reconstructed plan of the main elements of the Episode 2b house, with the five human burials. Accompanying one infant burial (1) was a string of shell beads, and with the adult burial (2) there was a string of shell beads and a pottery tripod bowl. Pits contained offerings of stones (3), ash (4 and 5), and a stone disc and greenstone bead (6). Reprinted by permission from Springer Nature Customer Service Centre GmbH: Springer, Pre-Columbian Landscapes of Creation and Origin, by J. Staller, ed. © (2008).

northeast entrance post of the doorway, suggesting further elaboration of the approach, particularly if there was a corresponding post on the southeast side.

Thirdly, and moving 50 cm beyond the end of the row of posts dividing the approach, there was another line of posts, this time running northwest to southeast. Seven holes, up to 33 cm deep, with diameters of around 10 cm were found (13058, 13047, 13049, 13051, 13053, 13055, 13060), the last of them lying 5 m southeast from the line of the central axis. These posts constituted, then, the southeast section of an outer fence that corresponded to and lay 2.50 m from the line of the front wall of the building. Whether or not the fence went right round the building is not clear. Fourteen relatively deep (mostly 25–40 cm) postholes (13062, 13250, 13254, 13256, 13258, 13260, 13264, 13068, 13070, 13252, 13262, 13266, 13272, 13274), lay beyond the presumed southeast edge of the clay floor. Two (13070, 13272) could be read potentially as the only encountered elements of a northeast-southwest row, but that is probably to stretch the evidence too far. The others mostly lay between those two and the edge of the house and suggest at the very least that this area was not empty but included some sort of minor structure associated with the main house.

The general chronology of the building of the house therefore will have been as follows. First, for Episode 2a the roof support was erected, and the external wall and doorway were put in place. The partitions as represented by the internal gullies and postholes were next constructed. After some period, Episode 2b saw the external wall dismantled, along with the original internal partitions, and a new fence set outside the front of the building either side of the approach to the door, the approach itself also being divided by a short row of posts.

Regarding the other features associated with the house, we have seen that the central hearth was established at the start. Three other features all belong to Episode 2b, each being cut into the line of the original wall trench along the northwest side. First, there were two pits with ash fills: 13243 (in T4) lay towards the west corner, and 6687 (in T3) was set at the west corner. The third feature was a shallow pit, 13155 (in T4), with a ritual offering of polished pebbles and other stones, that was placed at the north corner.

The five human burials and the offering of the stone disc and bead also belong to the Episode 2b and were situated at the centre rear of the house (T3). It is notable that all the

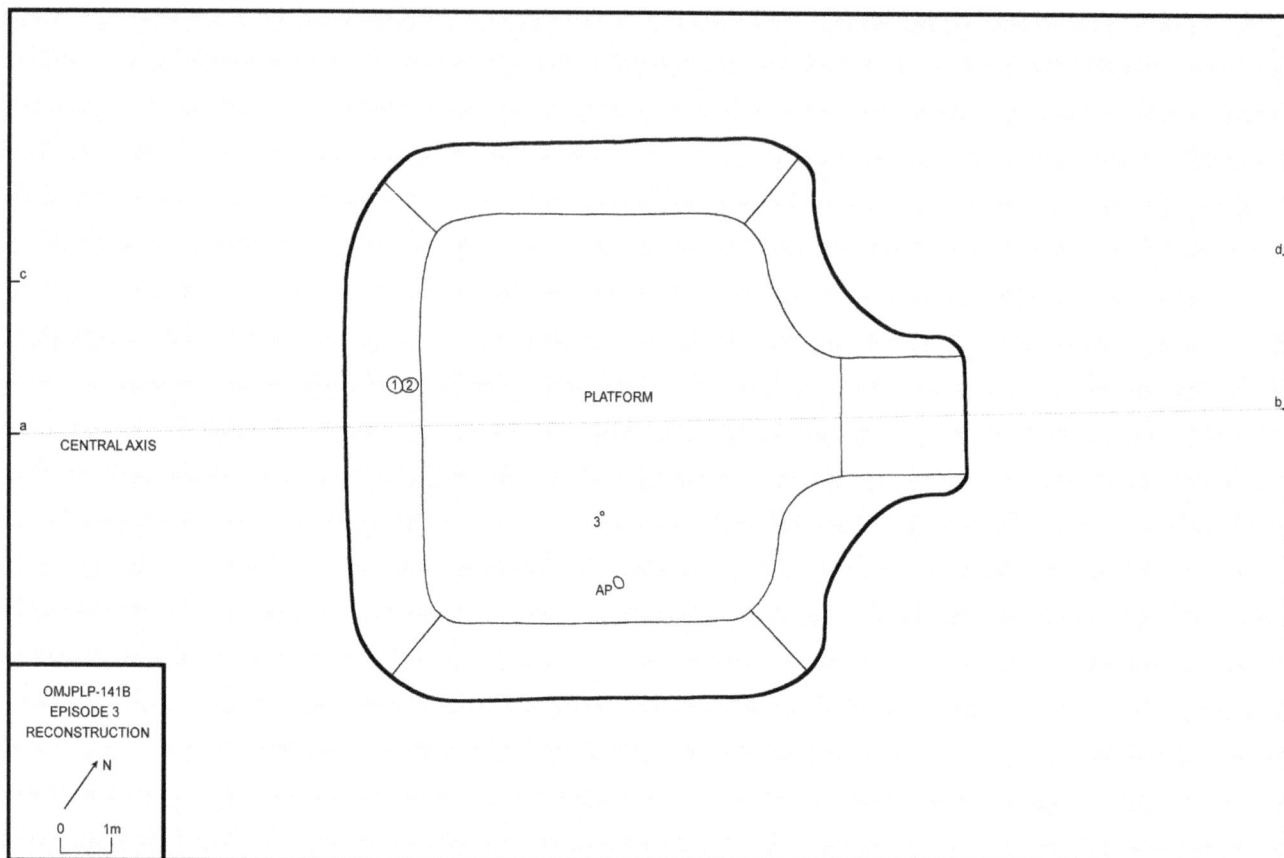

Figure 4.8. OMJPLP–141B: Reconstructed plan of the Episode 3 platform, with offerings of (1) armadillo scutes, a red *Spondyus princeps* bead, and three greenstone beads, (2) a tuff disc fragment, a white shell bead, and six greenstone beads, (3) a ring of gold wire, and an ash pit. Adapted by permission from Springer Nature Customer Service Centre GmbH: Springer, Pre-Columbian Landscapes of Creation and Origin, by J. Staller, ed. © (2008).

burials lay not only at the back of the house, but within the area previously marked off in front by the arc of four postholes that crossed the rear sector. The adult (6855) and one of the infants (6807) lay a little away from the wall, but one infant (6792) was immediately adjacent to the wall, while the third infant lay in a grave (6803) that cut the wall gully. The child (6681) uniquely, lay outside the line of the wall but still within the area of the clay floor. It is probably no coincidence either that the head of this child lay on the main northeast-oriented axis of the house. The offering (7175) of flat tuff disc and bead was placed not far to the southeast of the adult burial.

Throughout the occupation of the structure, there was significant accumulation of artefacts and other debris around the exterior, this material encroaching over the edge of the floor itself, and finally resulting in a layer up to 6 cm thick.

4.4. Episode 3

The yellow gravelly clay layer 12953 of T4 correlates directly with layer 6500 of T3 (Lunniss 2001:78, 79, Fig. 10), and the combined data from each sector can be used to suggest the complete outline, profile, and dimensions of the original structure, though it must be noted that, once again, the southeast side was not recovered. Episode 3 saw

the creation of a low, four-sided platform that covered the area occupied by the previous building (Figures 4.8, 4.9). The platform was about 11.00 m wide and measured 9.40 m from front to back.[47] Access to the platform was via a 2.40 m. long ramp, about 3.10 m wide, which projected forwards from the centre of the northeast side, such that the overall dimension along the main axis was 12.30 m. Since the slope down to the edges around the sides was up to 1.50 m wide, the top was significantly smaller than the base and covered an area that may have been as little as 8.00 m by 7.00 m. However, the top of the platform seems to have projected forwards at the centre, so forming a sort of small proscenium at the top of the ramp.

The layer of clay itself was not more than 35 cm thick in any one place. But it also lay over the raised surface of the earlier floor, and the centre of the platform was about 45 cm higher than the ground immediately off the edge

---

[47] The surviving outlines of the northwest side and southwest rear may suggest a trapezoidal form, with a slightly wider back than front. But none of the other Late Formative structures at Salango have such a form, nor is it otherwise documented for the coast, and it seems more likely that a rectangular outline is correct. In the reconstruction of the outline, the rear edge was taken as a base line for determining the perpendicular orientation of the central northeast-southwest axis and that of the sides. It should be remembered, however, that the outline shown, and the measurements given, are not based on exact data, but rather serve as a general guide.

Figure 4.9. The rear left quarter of the Episode 3 yellow clay platform. View to the northeast. The scaling rods measure 50 cm and 100 cm.

of the ramp to the northeast. However, the ground round the platform also sloped up from northeast to southwest, so that the centre was only 30 cm higher than the exterior surface to the rear.

Embedded in the clay were greenstone beads (B878, B864, B862, B861, B860, B855) and shell beads, stone discs (B1229, B1230, B869), a stylized stone human figurine (B1231), and a lime container (B1232) in the form of a tree snail. There were also several artefacts deposited in small pits cut into the clay surface. On the rear southwest slope, just to the northwest of the central axis, were two pits, one cut by the other. The first (5875) contained armadillo scutes, a red spondylus bead and three greenstone beads, while the second (5873) had a stone disc and a disc fragment, a white shell bead and six greenstone beads (Lunniss 2001:148, 149). And a gold ring was buried in a small hole (6176) cut into the floor southeast of the centre of the platform (Lunniss 2001:147).[48]

The platform was the site of some new sort of wooden structure. There were a relatively large number of features (n=159) found to the rear (in T3), though some of these may have belonged to later episodes of platform construction and use. Towards the front, only a very few

(n=11) features were found in T4. In both areas, there was heavy intrusion from later features with subsequent loss of the platform surface and any holes that may have lain there. The evidence is uncertain but suggests that any new building would have been significantly different from that of Episode 2. First, the rear of the platform, including the downward slope at the edge, was apparently more intensively built upon than the front. Second, there is no obvious evidence for any sort of systematic grid of roof supports as was found earlier. It may be that building was limited to a less substantial structure, or series of structures, that were themselves clustered to the rear, leaving the forward area more open.

As with Episode 2, the central area was heavily marked with red fire-staining, ash, and patches of clay repair over these hearths, and one of these areas included a small ash pit (5694), located near the southeast side of the platform top. Likewise, the area around the platform was covered with artefact scatter, though even more thickly than in Episode 2.

4.5. Episode 4

The wall 12878 of T4 is the same as wall 5804 of T3. Additionally, platform cap 12936 and exterior clay surface 12849 of T4 were obviously designed to fulfil the same roles at the same moments in the sequence as platform cap 5776 and clay layer 5705 respectively of T3 (Lunniss

---

[48] Though it is possible that these three features belonged to a later episode.

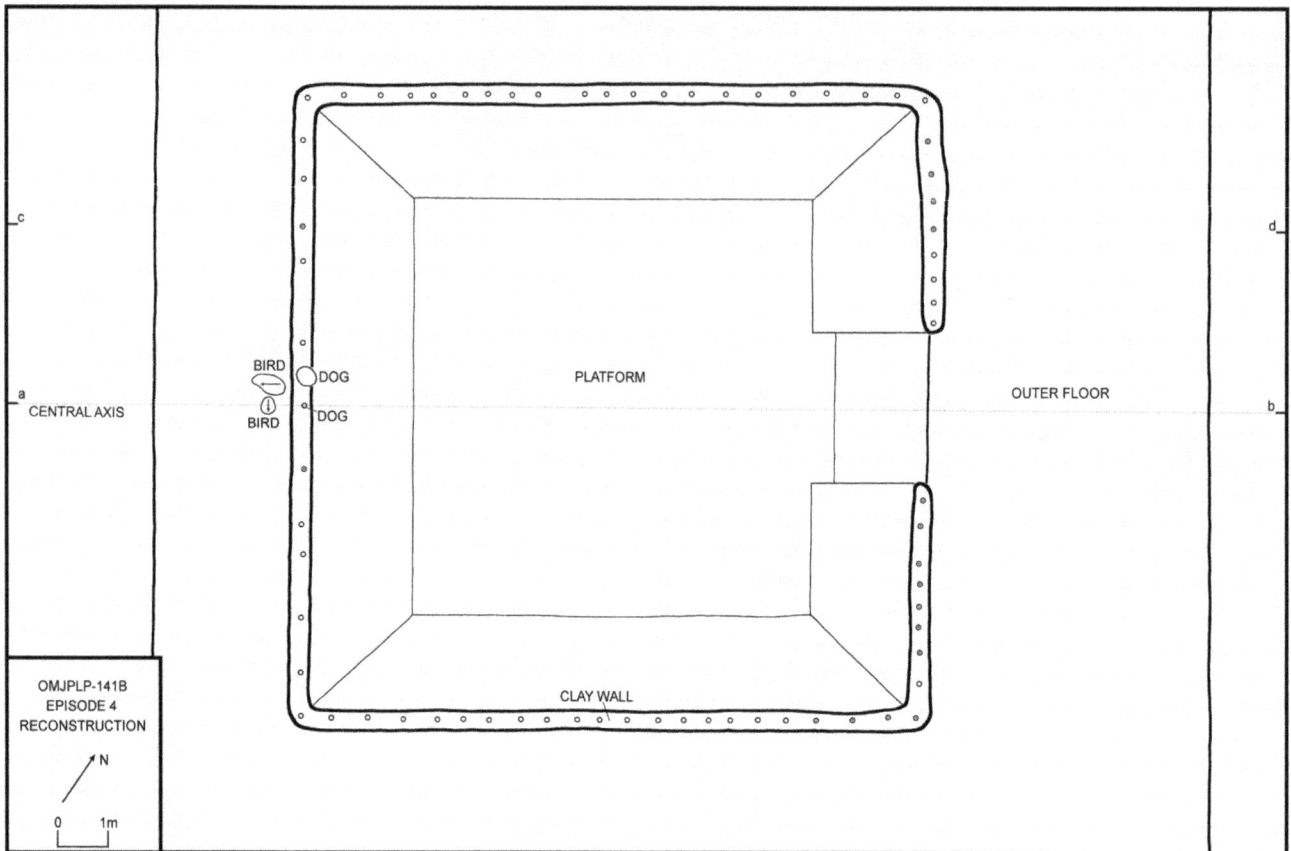

Figure 4.10. OMJPLP–141B: Reconstructed plan of the Episode 4 platform, with surrounding clay wall and its postholes and two dog and two bird burials to the rear. Adapted by permission from Springer Nature Customer Service Centre GmbH: Springer, Pre-Columbian Landscapes of Creation and Origin, by J. Staller, ed. © (2008).

2001:79, 80, Fig. 11). Reconstruction of the overall form of the perimeter wall and platform of Episode 4 is based on data recovered from the front, including the entrance and east corner, along with the forward section of the southeast side and part of the back side.

First, a shallow trench, 30 to 40 cm deep and up to 40 cm wide, was cut all round the outside of the Episode 3 mound (Figure 4.10). The trench was next filled with hard, yellow brown clay that both rose as a low wall 10 to 15 cm higher than the top of the trench and extended as a shallow layer to between 60 and 80 cm away from the trench's outer edge. The wall formed a square enclosure of approximately 12.80 m along each side, with a 3 m wide gap in the centre of the northeast front spanning the ramp of the earlier platform.

The wall served to contain a layer of gravelly yellow clay that was then deposited around the earlier platform, reaching up its sides as far as the top edges. Although the new platform was larger than the old one in extent, no clay was added to the summit, save perhaps where the edges needed redefinition. By this stage, the platform top measured about 8 m each way, though it might have been wider than long. There appears this time also to have been a slight projection of the top towards the entrance before reaching the slope of the newly resurfaced ramp. The ramp now measured about 1.85 m in length, ending at the line of the perimeter retaining wall.

Additionally, the wall served as a foundation for a row of narrow posts, set in holes up to 35 cm deep and from 10 to 15 cm in diameter, at intervals of 40 to 70 cm, that extended along the northeast front and northwest and southeast sides. Several postholes were also recovered along the back, southwest side, though few of them matched closely the pattern established by the other sides. It may be that the posts of the back were less closely spaced, as is shown on the plan, or that there was some rather different arrangement.[49]

Not long after these first stages in the reconstruction of the platform, a new clay floor was laid around the outside of the platform. This floor covered the clay that had originally extended out from the wall and reached out to at least 6 m away along the northeast side, but perhaps only 2.70 m away to the southwest.

The back side of the wall appears to have been about 15 cm higher than the front side, while, outside the wall, there was as much as a 30 cm fall in ground level from back to front. The centre of the platform, while perhaps standing only 15 cm higher than the exterior floor to the rear, was

---

[49] The holes found along the back lay directly on the wall or to either side of it. In addition to the smaller holes, there were also, towards the west corner, some wider and deeper postholes. The back seems to have had a more complicated history at this stage than the front and sides.

over 40 cm higher than the ground immediately outside the entrance. Moreover, the clay floor continued to fall away lightly towards the northeast, dropping 12 cm over a distance of almost 6 m.

It is not yet clear whether there was any sort of wooden building erected on the platform during this episode. There are possible postholes and other features cut into the material added to the edges of the platform, but they present no obvious pattern to suggest a superstructure, and they may rather represent several smaller fixtures, in particular towards the rear. What is certain, however, is that the base of the platform was now doubly defined, both by the perimeter clay wall and by the posts set into the wall. Around the centre of the platform top, while there may have been no building as such, there was continuation from previous episodes of the practices involving open hearths and ash scatter.

Four animal and bird burials were set on or next to the centre of the rear wall. First, there is the dog (*Canis familiaris*) whose incomplete but at least partially articulated skeleton was found buried vertically in a small hole (5624) cut precisely into the centre of the rear southwest side of the wall.[50] Then just to the northwest, a second dog was buried in a pit (5600) cut into the inner edge of the rear wall.[51] Also on the main axis of the structure, though set 60 cm to the southwest of the first dog and somewhat later than the main construction event itself, there was the burial (5324) of a male great curassow (*Crax rubra*), which lay on its left side on an overall northwest-southeast axis, though its back was curved and its neck bent so that the head pointed round towards its pelvis. Two beads of greenstone and shell accompanied the bird. Immediately to the northwest of this offering, there was a female of the same species (5462).[52] This time, the bird lay on its back, head to the southwest, tail to the northeast. Within the area of the body there were 35 polished and rounded chert flakes, while a broken greenstone bead lay elsewhere in the fill.

Around the platform, there was continued accumulation of discarded rubbish.

4.6. Episode 5

The nature of the overall configuration created during Episode 5 is not clear. In the first place, the evidence for the "wall" 12899 of T4 is incomplete. If it is assumed though that some sort of clay boundary did extend around the entire platform, then, on grounds of stratigraphic order, wall 5092 (Lunniss 2001:81, 82, Fig. 12) is the most likely context of T3 to correlate with 12899. However, 12899 and 5092 were of different clays, one being dark yellow brown, the other darkish red brown; and 5092 was set in a U-shaped trench and not simply laid over the earlier platform edge. Importantly also, there is no corner preserved anywhere, and as evidence for the entranceway there are just two partially preserved fragments of what may have been walls successively marking the southeast side of the ramp. It is not, therefore, possible to produce any well-supported definition of the entire platform perimeter, and it may be that the elements from T4 and T3 currently grouped for this episode do not, in fact, belong with each other.

There are several points worth noting, however, regarding the different components brought together here. First, along the northeast side, there was addition of yellow clay to the platform, initially (12876) filling the ground between the platform edge and the new perimeter as defined by 12899, and then (12791) extending the range of the platform to cover 12899 as well. To what extent the rear half of the platform was re-laid is uncertain, but activity may have been limited there to the northwest and southeast sides. Nor is it clear which of the two yellow clay layers of T4 corresponds to 5766 in T3. Secondly, wall 5092 at the rear may have supported a fence of narrow posts, as is suggested by two holes, a meter apart, cut into the centre of the wall along its best-preserved section. Third, the rear wall, close to the central axis, is again the site for important offerings. This time, cutting the inside edge of wall 5092, one pit (6659) contained the deposition of a figurine pendant, an anthropomorphic figurine of fossil wood, a malachite bar and two greenstone beads (Lunniss 2001:128, 129). And directly over that, there was another pit (5113) with offerings that included shell beads, a greenstone bead, a broken stone disc and part of a shell rattle (Lunniss 2001:149). Fourth, the exterior area to the rear the platform was twice resurfaced with clay (5364, 5224) prior to Episode 7, and the first of these rearward clay surfaces may be associated with Episode 5. Fifth, the wall fragments bounding the southeast side of the entranceway (12855, 12632) indicate the use of a new concept for the definition of the approach to the platform, one that is more clearly presented in Episode 6. And finally, the burning of fires in open hearths and the spreading of the ash produced by those fires, is once more indicated for the platform surface itself.

4.7. Episode 6

For Episode 6, platform cap 12570 of T4 is equivalent to cap 5409 of T3 (Lunniss 2001: 83, 84, Fig. 14). Together, these contexts indicate the construction of a new yellow gravel clay platform that completely buried the surfaces of the earlier version (Figure 4.11).[53] The northwest

---

[50] This animal was originally reported as an ocelot (Lunniss 2001:145–7). Subsequent identification as a dog was made by Dr. Patrick Gay. While the field records indicate that the remains of the dog were buried in a vertical position, it is not clear which way up the remains were set.

[51] 5600 was severely truncated by later features, and apart from three ribs, only leg bones survived excavation. Vertebrae, however, are reported in the field notes, which also describe the skeletal remains in general as unarticulated. However, the survival of the leg elements and the location of the pit suggest that the animal may have been laid down along a northwest-southeast axis, with its back to the southwest, though there is no indication as to which end the head lay at.

[52] The birds were originally reported as perhaps herons (Lunniss 2001:145–147). Subsequent identification as a male-female pair of *Crax rubra* was made by Dr. Francisco Sornoza.

[53] Following reconsideration of the evidence, the original plan and description, as published (Lunniss 2008) not long after the original manuscript of the present study was submitted to the Banco Central, have been altered.

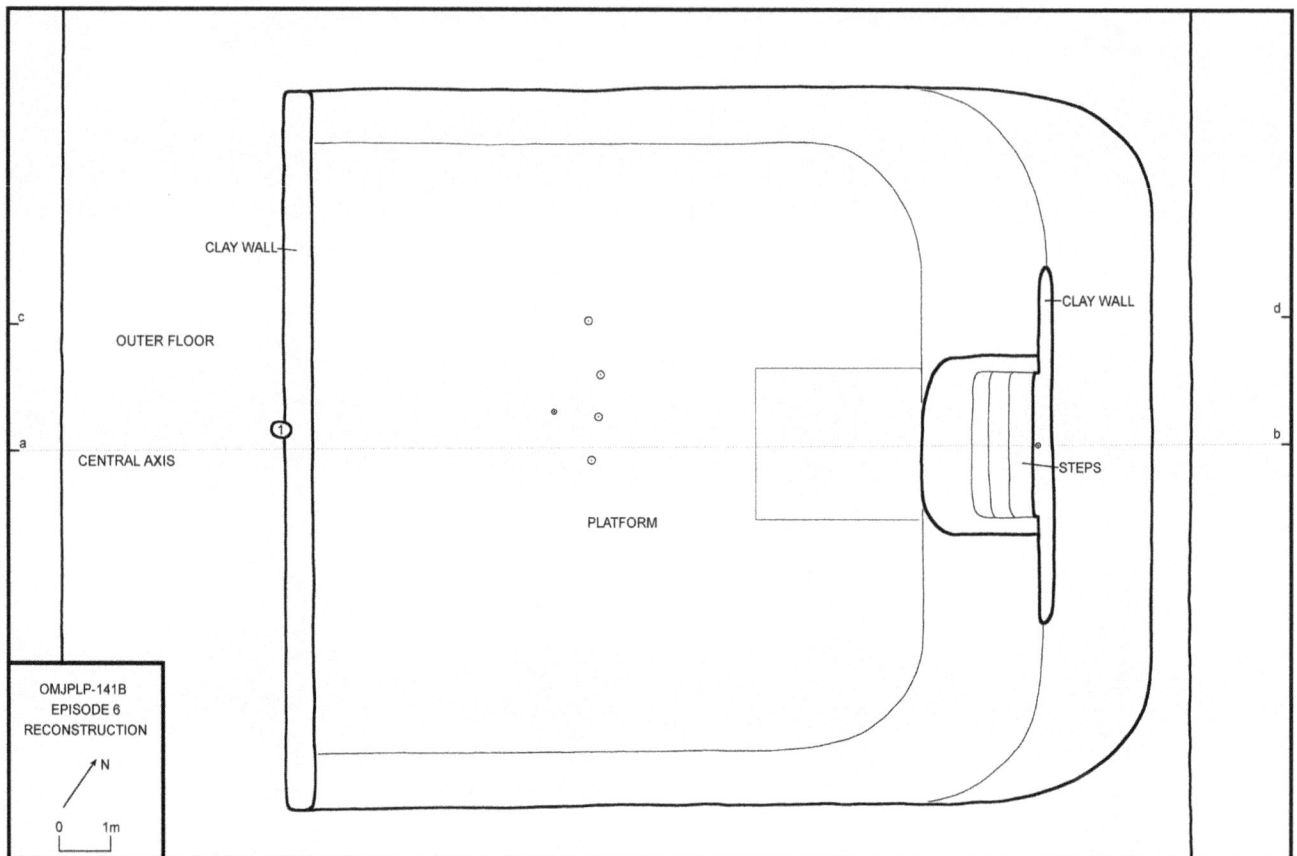

Figure 4.11. OMJPLP–141B: Reconstructed plan of the Episode 6 platform, showing the stepped entrance with small central pit in the bottom step, the approximate extent of the proscenium, the arc of postholes across the centre, and the rear clay wall with an offering pit (1) containing stone tools and other artefacts. Adapted by permission from Springer Nature Customer Service Centre GmbH: Springer, Pre-Columbian Landscapes of Creation and Origin, by J. Staller, ed. © (2008).

and southeast sides of the platform, however, were not preserved, and much of the northeast front, to either side of the entrance, was lost to later intrusion. The overall dimensions and exact form of this new structure are therefore estimated with some guesswork, and the front corners are especially conjectural. But it can be presumed that the length from front to back was around 14.30 m, while its width was between 12 m and 14 m.

From its ground level rear edge, the platform surface rose gradually for 9 m to the northeast, then, at the centre, levelled off to form a small proscenium about 3 m square just inside what was to be the entrance. The high point so reached was about 35 cm higher than the back and 70 cm higher than the ground outside the entrance. To either side of the proscenium, the forward top edge was a few centimetres lower. The new yellow clay then sloped down to the forward base of the platform from which point it then extended, as a shallow, slightly sloping layer, a further 2 m or more out to the northeast.

Along the base of the front slope of the platform, a narrow clay wall was next constructed. This wall extended only along the main, central section of the front, such that its total length would have been about 7 m. It rose around 12 cm over the top of its foundation trench and the

ground outside it and served as a low step that marked the edge of the platform proper from the floor beyond it. Its own central section also served as the bottom step to an elaborate 3.50 m wide approach to the top of the platform. This consisted of a series of clay steps laid between the arms of a U-shaped wall of clay set in a trench that bracketed the approach. More clay was laid over the surface at their head and perhaps also to either side of the steps. These steps, their surround, and the low wall at the base of the platform were all made of hard brown clay that would have contrasted in terms of both colour and texture with the gravelly yellow substance of the platform itself.

Importantly, the top and bottom steps of the added stairway were both endowed with offerings. In the material of the top step was buried an anthropomorphic shell figurine pendant (CT786). In the material of the bottom step were buried five greenstone beads (B1194-B1198). Echoing these depositions, a stone figurine (B1199) was buried upright, facing northeast, its waist encircled by 34 greenstone beads (B1200), in a small hole later cut into the edge of the base of the stairway. Several features cut into the steps suggest further activity in the entranceway. One well defined small hole was cut into the middle of the base wall, perhaps to support a post, else to contain some offering that has since perished.

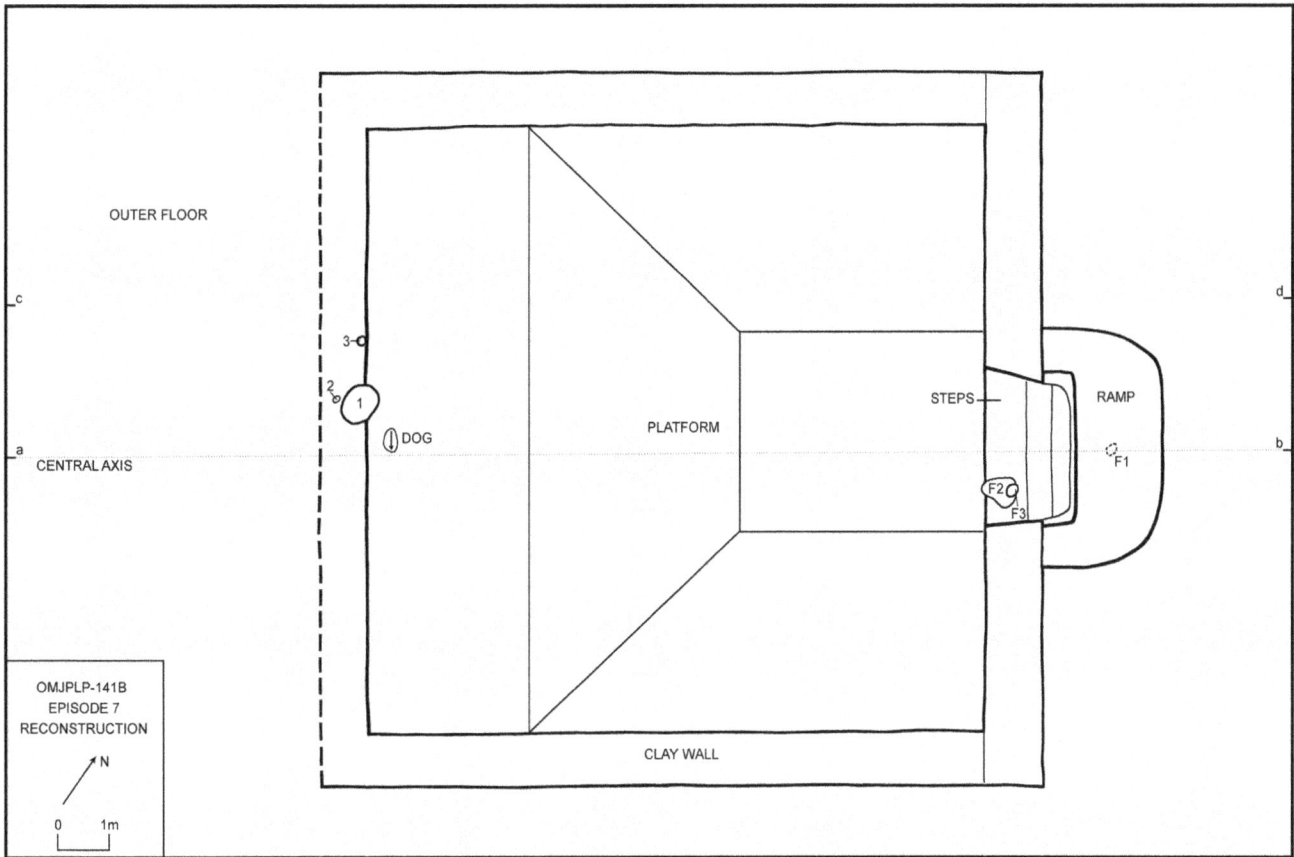

Figure 4.12. OMJPLP–141B: Reconstructed plan of the Episode 7 platform, with the surrounding clay wall and entrance with ramp and steps during one stage of elaboration. Cut into the ramp, one offering pit (F1) contained a spondylus tusk figurine with a broken tuff disc, while two others to one side of the top step (F2 and F3) each contained an incomplete tuff figurine. Three offering pits in the rear wall contained (1) a malachite disc, (2) a modified *Muricanthus* sp. conch over 472 chert flakes, and (3) pottery sherds, a broken net weight, two chert lumps, and two pebbles, while a dog lay buried just inside the rear wall. Adapted by permission from Springer Nature Customer Service Centre GmbH: Springer, Pre-Columbian Landscapes of Creation and Origin, by J. Staller, ed. © (2008).

The nature of the sides and rear of the platform is less certain, as is the way the front met the sides. But along the back, there may well have been another low wall (5000; Lunniss 2001:81, Fig. 13), no higher than the ground beyond. However, the clay of this wall differed from that of the entrance walls, being of a reddish brown colour. Neither was either of the ends reached by the excavation of T3. It cannot be said, then, whether this wall turned round the back corners of the platform base to its northwest and southeast sides, or whether, alternatively, the sides of the platform were left without walling. If, however, we take the rear wall as a guide, then there was still a drop of 25 cm or more in the exterior ground level from the back edge to the front of the platform.

At some stage there was resurfacing with yellow brown clay of the area to the northeast of the platform, extending the floor there to at least 2.70 m away; and there may also have been resurfacing of the southwest exterior with hard brown clay (5224), taking the floor to 4 m or more away from the rear wall.

Once more, there was an artefact deposition made into a pit (4721; Lunniss 2001:149) cut into the rear of the

platform, this time slightly northwest of the centre line. The offering included two stone hammers, flaked tools, and rough chert nuclei, as well as a fragment of tuff disc and a disc of *Pinctada mazatlanica*.

The top of the platform seems to have been generally bare of any sort of wooden superstructure, and one human grave (5734), located towards its rear, probably belonged to this episode. However, just into the rear half of the platform, slightly northwest from the central axis, there was a series of four postholes, 12 to 15 cm in diameter and up to 18 cm deep, set in an arc curving out towards the entrance, with a fifth hole, 10 cm wide and 15 cm deep, 90 cm inside and to the southwest of the arc. Whether these holes represent the original entire set of posts is not clear, as much of the platform surface was destroyed by later features. However, the arc of holes indicates the presence of a small fence that separated off the centre rear section of the platform. Second, it replicates, though at a slightly reduced scale, the arc of postholes found marking off the rear of the Episode 2a structure. Third, it seems likely that there was a direct connection between the positioning of the fence and the fact that the main group of Late Engoroy graves was located to its southwest.

Figure 4.13. The rear left corner of the enclosure wall of Episode 7. The two scales (30 cm and 100 cm) lie across the rear (southwest) section of the wall, which is darker after dampening and already exposed along its outer edge by excavation of the Episode 8 wall. In the top left of the image is the trench already exposed by removal of the wall of the left (northwest) side of the enclosure. The floor in the foreground is marked by the excavation of firepits, rubbish pits, human graves, a shallow circular clay-lined pit, and the small holes of stone figurine depositions. View to the north.

With this stage, use of the platform as a setting for open hearths, ash scatters, and the associated practices of earlier episodes came to an end.

4.8. Episode 7

In Episode 7, wall 12501 of T4 correlates with walls 4632 and 4642 of T3 (Lunniss 2001:83–89, Fig.14), as does platform cap 12482 with context 4344 of T3 (Lunniss 2001:83, 86, 87, Fig.15). Most of the front wall, including the entrance and east corner, the northwest side and the forward section of the southeast side, and part of the back wall, were available for reconstruction of the overall form (Figures 4.12, 4.13, 4.14).

The new structure was begun by setting a massive wall of hard clay in a U-shaped trench around the earlier platform. The overall shape of the enclosure so created was roughly square, measuring about 14 m in each direction. The wall, with vertical sides, was up to 1.20 m wide along the front, but narrower along the sides. Along the front, with a total dimension from top to bottom of at least 1.10 m, it rose 80 cm above the trench top and outer floor. At the front corners, there was a drop of about 30 cm down to the northwest and southeast sides, though the top along the sides remained higher than the outer ground level. However, as the sides approached the rear, the difference between the top of the wall and the outer floor diminished, such that along the rear, the top was level with the newly created outer floor (see below). This was since, although the wall along the back and sides was horizontal, the ground surrounding the platform sloped down from its southwest rear to its northeast front.

Along the rear side of the enclosure, the clay of the wall was spread thickly also over the area to the southwest. The new clay was not simply laid over the old floor but set in a specially made extension cut out from the side of the wall trench, so that the wall and floor (4885) comprised a single unit, indistinguishable at the surface.[54] It is likely that this surface would have continued all around the enclosure, but it was only at the rear that it was level with the wall. Nevertheless, the floor, as it extended to the southwest, dropped away slightly, falling perhaps 10 cm over 5 m. In sum, it appears that the new enclosure was surrounded by ground that fell away both to the front and to the back, though the situation along the sides is not clear.

---

[54] Though there may have been some difference in the make-up of the clay used. Small grains of yellow clay, visible in the matrix of the floor, were not found in the material of the wall.

Figure 4.14. The wall trench along the rear of the Episode 7 platform after excavation of the clay walling. To its left is the narrower trench of the enclosure wall of Episode 8. View to the northwest. The scales measure 30 cm and 50 cm.

The entrance through the wall was not exactly centred over the main axis of the enclosure but lay slightly to the southeast of that line. This was because rather than construct an entirely new ramp or stairway, the design incorporated the old stairway as constructed in the previous episode. However, there were several changes to the entrance which followed the next stage in Episode 7.

After the wall had been built, there was a new layer of yellow, gravelly clay laid over the top of the earlier platform. The main effort was directed to recapping the central and forward sections of the platform, the rear perhaps being left unaltered. The yellow clay, then, extended from side to side and all along the front, sitting on the lip of clay that protruded inwards from the base of the wall. With this new clay, the top of the platform and the top of the front wall were probably now level with each other. But just as the sides and rear of the wall were lower than the front, so they must have been lower than the platform top. Furthermore, the evidence suggests that the high part of the platform was limited to a proscenium, measuring around 4.80 m long by 4 m wide, immediately

behind the entrance, and that the platform surface sloped down from this area both towards the back and to the two sides.

Once the new yellow clay was in place, there was alteration made to the entrance. Firstly, there was a series of surfaces laid down from the old steps of Episode 6 out towards the northeast, in effect creating a ramped approach that extended up to 2.30 m out from the wall. The ramps themselves were endowed with various offerings that were cast over their surfaces or included in their matrix. These offerings included shell beads (CT794), coloured stone beads (B1203, B1204, B1207, B1208), a stone disc (B1218), and a broken tuff bead (B1202). Additionally, however, there were various pits cut into the entrance at different stages. Two of these (12526, 12503), towards the top and to the southeast, contained broken tuff figurines (B1181, B1179). At the very centre of the ramp, and just outside the entrance through the walls, a third feature (12662) contained a tusk-shaped figurine of shell (CT789), over which had been laid a part of a tuff disc (B1201).

Figure 4.15. A dog buried, head to the southeast, in a grave (5533) just inside the rear wall of the Episode 7 platform. The scale measures 10 cm.

Next, a series of steps was cut into the ramp from the top of the entranceway, and a trench was dug along the outside of the walls at the entranceway. The trench and steps were then used to support a thick clay fill that was itself shaped to create a series of three new steps reaching up to the platform top. Thus, the approach through the walls was first via what remained of the earlier ramp, and then up the newly created clay steps (12407). The top step, in turn, led directly to the high central and forward area of the platform.

Features were recorded along the rear of the wall. Just to the northwest of the central axis was the site for two features containing offerings. One of these pits (4327; Lunniss 2001:149f, 150) had a malachite disc in its base, while the other (4645; Lunniss 2001:147, 148) had an offering of 472 chert flakes and a modified conch (*Muricanthus* sp.). A little to the northwest again, a third pit (4098; Lunniss 2001:149) cut into the inside edge of the wall contained pottery sherds, a broken net weight, two lumps of chert and two pebbles that might have served as hammers. Meanwhile, inside the wall, lying immediately to the northwest of the main southwest-northeast axis, there was a dog burial (3353; Lunniss 2001:145–7), the animal lying on its left side, back to the northeast, head to the southeast and tail to the northwest, i.e., perpendicular to the main axis (Figure 4.15).

In addition, there were several postholes along the rear of the wall, indicating the presence of some sort of secondary structure or structures in this area. No features have been recorded along either the front or the side arms of the wall. It may be that the holes along the back supported posts that acted as a vertical boundary marker in this area where the wall was at the same level as the ground outside it. However, the intensity of depositional and other ritual activity (to be described below) over and to either side of this rear section of the wall makes it at least as likely that the holes may represent temporary structures put up in association with these rites.

While there is no obvious evidence for any sort of structure on the top of the platform, it is to be noted that there is evidence from T3 for internal division along its central northwest side. This consists of two truncated linear features (4131, 4140; Lunniss 2001:84, 85, Fig. 14). One ran parallel to and about 1.50 m in from the northwest side, incidentally or otherwise overlying a pit (4425; Lunniss 2001:149, 150) that contained a malachite disc in its lower fill, while the other, 4.20 m long, at right angles to and extending from the northwest side wall itself, probably met the former before passing beyond it towards the centre line of the platform. In each case, the linear feature consists of a shallow trench filled with hard brown clay. No sign of the first feature was identified in T4. Neither seems to have supported posts, and they were possibly designed to mark out boundaries between different areas of the platform through their difference in colour and texture.

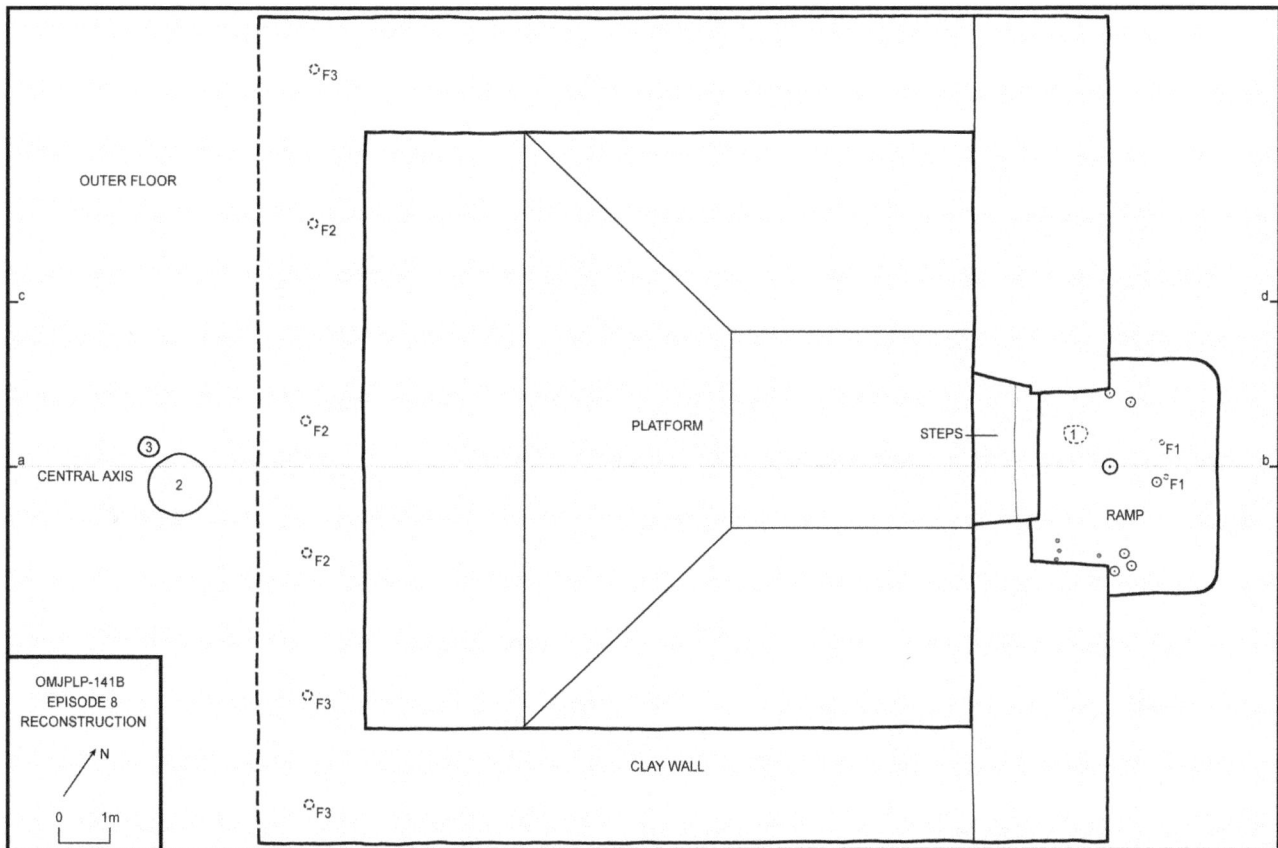

Figure 4.16. OMJPLP–141B: Reconstructed plan of the Episode 8 platform, with the surrounding wall and entrance with ramp, steps, and the postholes of the large central post and other gateway elements. Two tusk-shaped tuff figurines (F1) were buried upright under the ramp, and a bird (1) was buried in the top of the ramp. Three large tuff figurines (F2) were found under the rear wall, and a further three (F3) are postulated. Outside the rear wall there was a large circular pit lined with different coloured clays (2), and a smaller pit (3) with a modified *Muricanthus* sp. conch upright over the neck of a pottery jar, with two *Pinctada mazatlanica* valves to either side. Reprinted by permission from Springer Nature Customer Service Centre GmbH: Springer, Pre-Columbian Landscapes of Creation and Origin, by J. Staller, ed. © (2008).

4.9. Episode 8

For this episode, wall 12348 of T4 correlates with wall 4622 of T3 (Lunniss 2001:83–89, Fig. 16). Reconstruction of the complete outline of the wall is based on evidence for most of the front section, including the entrance and east corner, and part of the back.

The principal event of Episode 8 was the addition of a new clay wall that completely enclosed the wall of Episode 7, so creating a structure that overall measured 17.10 m from front to back and about 16.40 m from side to side (Figure 4.16).[55] This new wall was of the same hard brown clay as the earlier one, and the two elements formed a single, massive boundary to the platform measuring almost 3 m across along the front and perhaps 2.30 m along the sides, and standing 70 to 80 cm above the ground outside the front.[56]

Along the front of the platform, a clay floor extended directly out from the foot of the wall, sloping gently away to the northeast and dropping almost 15 cm over a distance of 2.50 m. Along the back of the platform, the new wall lay flush with the old wall and the outer clay floor associated with it, not disturbing the gentle slope away to the southwest. It is likely that along the sides, the wall will have stayed roughly horizontal, as in the previous episode, perhaps rising gently from southwest to northeast, with a relatively abrupt rise of 20 to 25 cm at the north and east corners of the front.

With the new wall, the entrance became more complicated than ever before. Firstly, the new opening was wider than the old one, and its sides narrowed rather than widened as one moved inside. Secondly, it was not centred in line with the old opening, but slightly to the southeast. Thus, even though the northwest side was roughly in the same position as that of the old entrance, on the southeast side the approach ran into an 80 cm wide block of clay presented by the outer face of the old wall.

The approach to the new entrance was built as a series of superimposed ramps that ultimately led from about 2.50

---

[55] None of the northwest side of the wall was recovered, as it lay beyond the excavation areas. But it is assumed that just as the front, back, and southeast sides were all set outside the Episode 7 wall, so on the northwest side the new wall will have enclosed the earlier, and in the same manner as suggested for the southeast side.

[56] The top of the new outer wall as recorded was about 10 cm lower than that of the inner wall, but this may represent differential preservation rather than any original difference in levels.

Figure 4.17. Oblique view, looking west, of the entrance to the Episode 8 platform showing the two clay steps (12407, originally part of the Episode 7 stepped entrance) at the top and the clay ramp (in its second version, 12380) sloping down from them. The scale measures 100 cm.

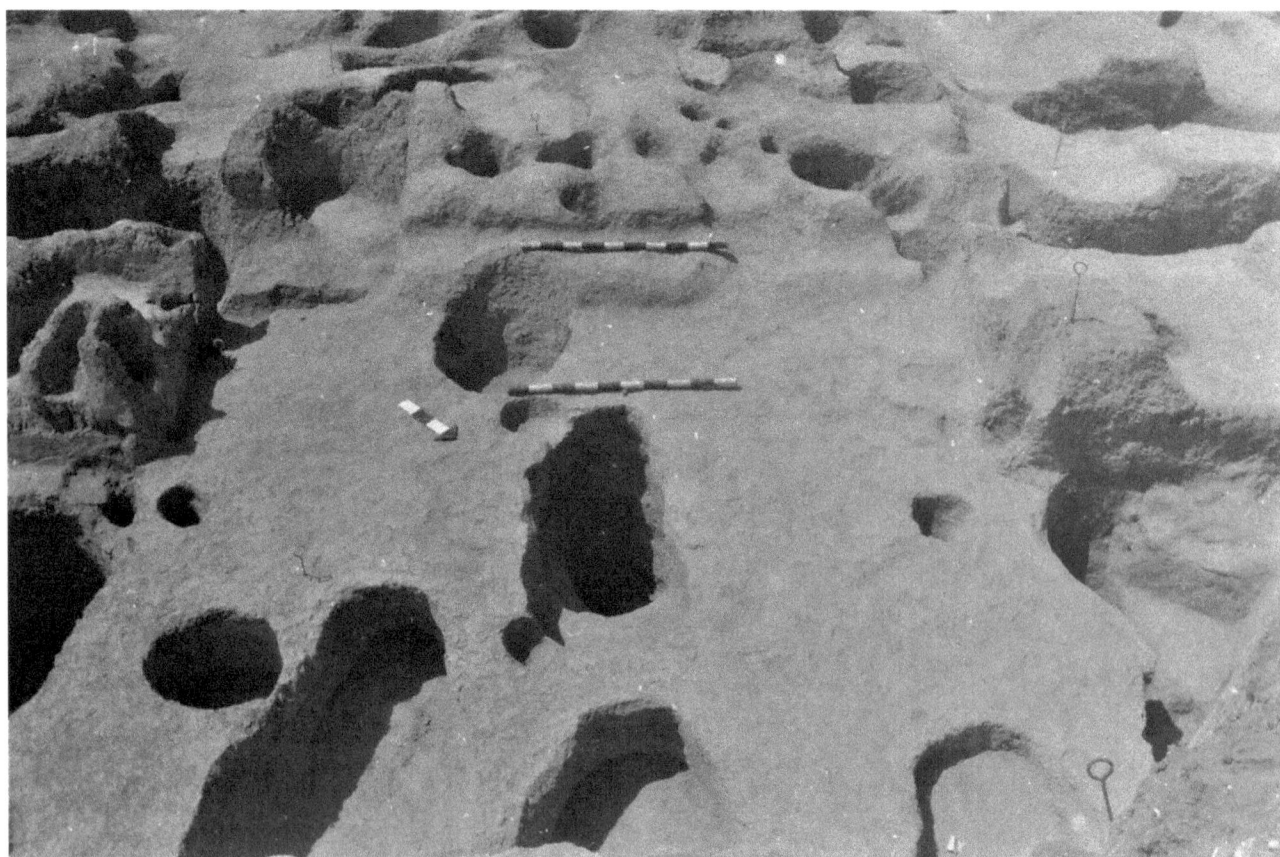

Figure 4.18. View up the ramp and steps at the entrance to the Episode 8 platform. Visible are the large posthole (12365) of the central post and smaller holes of other elements of the gateway (see Figure 3.9). The scales measure 100 cm.

m out from the wall to the base of the second step down the old stairway (Figures 4.17, 4.18). The final ramp was about 3.50 m long and 4.70 m wide, as it extended to either side of the opening, and seems to have risen in two stages, more gently as far as the outer edge of the wall (20 cm over 2 m) and then more steeply as far as the step (40 cm over 1.50 m). There would then have been a step of 10 cm, and then another of about 15 cm to reach the top of the entrance.

The construction of the ramp has been described earlier but should be summarized here. First, two anthropomorphic stone figurines (B1223, B1247) were set in holes either side of the central axis as defined by the earlier entrance, a meter outside the new wall. Various layers of soil were then put down, creating a slope that gradually rose above the bottom step of the old stairway. These layers contained various artefacts and materials that were probably offerings, including complete and broken shell beads (CT760, CT761, CT763, CT765, CT766, CT770), broken shell rattles (CT762, 764), broken fishhooks (CT768, CT769), ash, fish bones and bird bones. One layer was cut by a pit containing a bird skeleton.

In addition, there is clear evidence for some sort of gateway set up in the entrance towards the top of the ramp, between the ends of the new wall. A large post, perhaps 30 cm wide, with its base set over a meter deep into the ground, that could have stood several metres tall, marked the central division of the entrance at one stage, with smaller posts set to either side, close to the edges of the entrance. Several stakes in the alcove formed by the protruding block of the old wall on the southeast side represent some other minor fixture.

The entrance, however, was not the only area of the new structure to be endowed with dedicatory offerings. Along the back side, three stone figurines were found buried beneath the base of the new wall (Lunniss 2001:85, 86, 129, Fig. 15). Their relative locations suggest that there may have been originally six along the back. No features under the wall trench were identified along the excavated front and southeast sections. However, the base of the trench lay lower than the lowermost layers excavated in T4, and it could be that the entire wall rested over a continuous row of similar figures that were simply not reached by the excavators. At the very least, however, there were stone figurines both beneath the ramp at the front and beneath the wall at the rear.

In addition, just outside the rear wall, on or close to the central axis as suggested by the main post in the entranceway, there was a shallow circular clay-lined pit (4336; Lunniss 2001:168f, Figs. 15, 40) and a smaller pit (3806; Lunniss 2001:148, Figs. 15, 36c) with an offering of a jar neck, a modified *Muricanthus* sp. conch, and two *Pinctada mazatlanica* valves.

No alteration was made to the yellow clay of the platform interior. During Episodes 6 and especially 7 and 8,

however, the platform was the setting for a variety of activities related to human funerary rites. The evidence, principally from T3, consists of human graves, pottery-rich rubbish pits, and fire pits. Additionally, the area outside the Episode 8 wall was the setting for many anthropomorphic stone figurine depositions, again mainly encountered in T3. Each of these sets of features will now be reviewed. But it is important to conclude this section noting that the platform summit as recorded for T3 and the ramp and exterior floor to the front in T4 were covered by a layer up to 3 cm thick of volcanic ash, and that this layer of volcanic ash marked the end of the sequence of construction of Late Formative ceremonial structures at 141B.

4.10. Human Burials of Episodes 6, 7, and 8

A total of 28 primary, articulated human burials of Episodes 6 to 8 were recovered from T3 (n=25) and T4 (n=3).[57] Since there are a few but important differences between the graves of T3 (Lunniss 2001:109–123) and those of T4, they are here first considered as separate groups, and then later compared. Additionally, associated with the graves in T3 were a like number of rubbish pits (Lunniss 2001:159–162) and fire pits (Lunniss 2001:172–166). Similar rubbish pits and fire pits may also have present in T4, but none have yet been specifically identified. These associated features are briefly summarized also.

The graves from T3 were of single individuals, save one instance of a double burial involving an adult female and infant. They were also all oriented on a northwest-southeast axis, with 13 headed to the northwest and 12 to the southeast, while the infant of the double burial lay perpendicular to this axis, across the abdomen of the woman. A total of 21 burials were extended (or probably extended) and supine (Figure 4.19). Three, perhaps four, were semi-flexed on the back, i.e., with the knees raised. One was fully flexed on the back, and one had the individual twisted onto his left side. The population included three infants, one sub-adult and twenty-two adults. Of the adults, eight each were identifiable as male and female. There was no correlation between orientation and sex.

While not all the graves were completely preserved, it is possible to suggest that adults tended to be accompanied by at least one artefact out of a wide range of possible materials and forms. Though the emphasis was on pottery vessels, greenstone ornaments, and obsidian blades, other goods included shell artefacts, complete or incomplete unworked shells, antler points, and a fish bone point. One grave included a unique and elaborate container made from a modified deer skull (*Odocoileus virginianus*) with a *Pinctada mazatlanica* lid. Goods were sited next to, over, or under different parts of the body, but with a preference for the area of the head.

---

[57] Two of the T3 graves may immediately post-date Episode 8 but conform to the general pattern of the other burials.

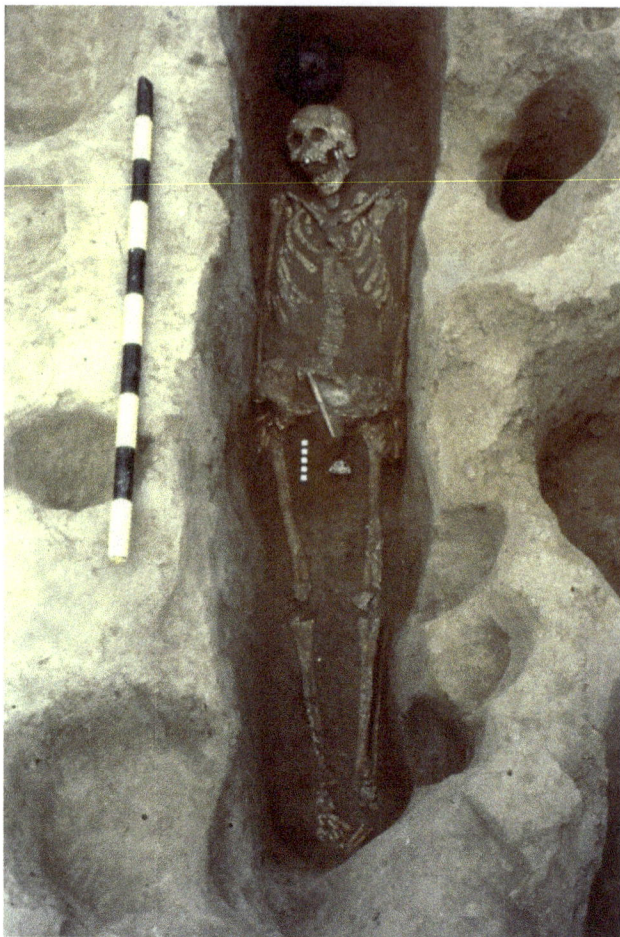

Figure 4.19. The extended burial (4429) of an adult male of Episode 7 or 8, head to the southeast. Accompanying goods were a whistling bottle behind the head, a greenstone bead in the left ear, a shell (*Fasciolaria princeps*) baton over the pelvis, and a *Spondylus calcifer* and a *Lyropecten subnudosus* set upright over the knees. The scales measure 100 cm and 10 cm.

These graves were all situated together in an area that covered the rear of the platform, the perimeter clay wall, and the immediate exterior surface. Amongst them, to the rear of the platform was a dog burial. The graves all lie behind, i.e., southwest from, the position of the arc of posts associated earlier with the Episode 6 platform cap. In Episode 2, all the graves were also sited at the rear of the house, southwest of a similar arc of posts earlier set across the central axis. It can be suggested then not only that the location of the Episode 6, 7, and 8 graves was determined in accordance with some strict conceptualization of the space of the platform, i.e., that they should be limited to the rear, southwest side, but also that the arc of posts made an explicit statement as to the forward boundary of that appropriate rearward space, even though the posts would have been dismantled before the majority of burials occurred.

The spatial distribution of these northwest-southeast oriented graves is more striking when compared with the burials, excavated as part of T4, that were found further to the northeast. Though these three graves match the general internal characteristics of the main set, the infant

on the central axis and the two children on the northwest side all lay well ahead of the other group. Furthermore, the two children were both aligned according to a different, north northeast-south southwest orientation. While then, they do not form an entirely coherent set or subset, they do indicate that the concepts of space and death were linked in a more complex relationship than would be suggested by the main group alone.

This complexity is further suggested by the bone-free but grave-like feature located just to the northeast of the infant burial just mentioned. Its unique southwest-northeast orientation, though perpendicular to the general burial axis, was instead aligned with the main building axis, though lying slightly northwest from that line. This feature, then, perhaps mediated between the building and the majority set of graves.

Associated with the group of rearward graves were a similar number of rubbish pits and fire pits (Figures 4.20, 4.21). Their direct relation with funerary rites is indicated by their close physical proximity to the graves and their contemporaneity. Like the graves, they also lie in an area that covers the rear of the platform, the rear wall, and the immediately outlying floor. However, it is notable that they lie over a rather larger area than the graves, surrounding them to the southwest and northwest. Indeed, they also transgress the line, imaginary or otherwise, that marks the forward extent of the main group.[58]

4.11. Anthropomorphic Stone and Shell Figurines and Pendants

The stone and shell figurines and pendants for T4 have been described above in detail. That set is now combined with the data from T3 (Lunniss 2001:128–141, Figs 41–69) to demonstrate the general pattern of deposition across the site through time.[59] The artefacts present a sequence of change in terms of both form and depositional context, such that one can also postulate changes in symbolic meaning, about which more will be said in the following chapter.

The sequence begins with the slender white spondylus tusk-shaped pendant (CT831) from the floor of the Episode 2 house. Although it has no details that might represent human features, the form, at a reduced scale, is that of the anthropomorphic figurine pendants found in later contexts. The small purple spondylus pendant (CT822) from the midden layer outside the house, an interesting and rare form, may perhaps represent a small tooth, but is not otherwise related to the more clearly tusk-shaped pendants.

---

[58] See Lunniss 2001:Fig. 16 for a plan of the relevant graves, rubbish pits and fire pits of T3.

[59] The pottery figurines are omitted from this discussion as they all belong to a different set of ritual activities and are likely to have had quite different meanings.

Figure 4.20. A rubbish pit (3185) associated with the funerary rituals of Episode 8. The scale measures 30 cm.

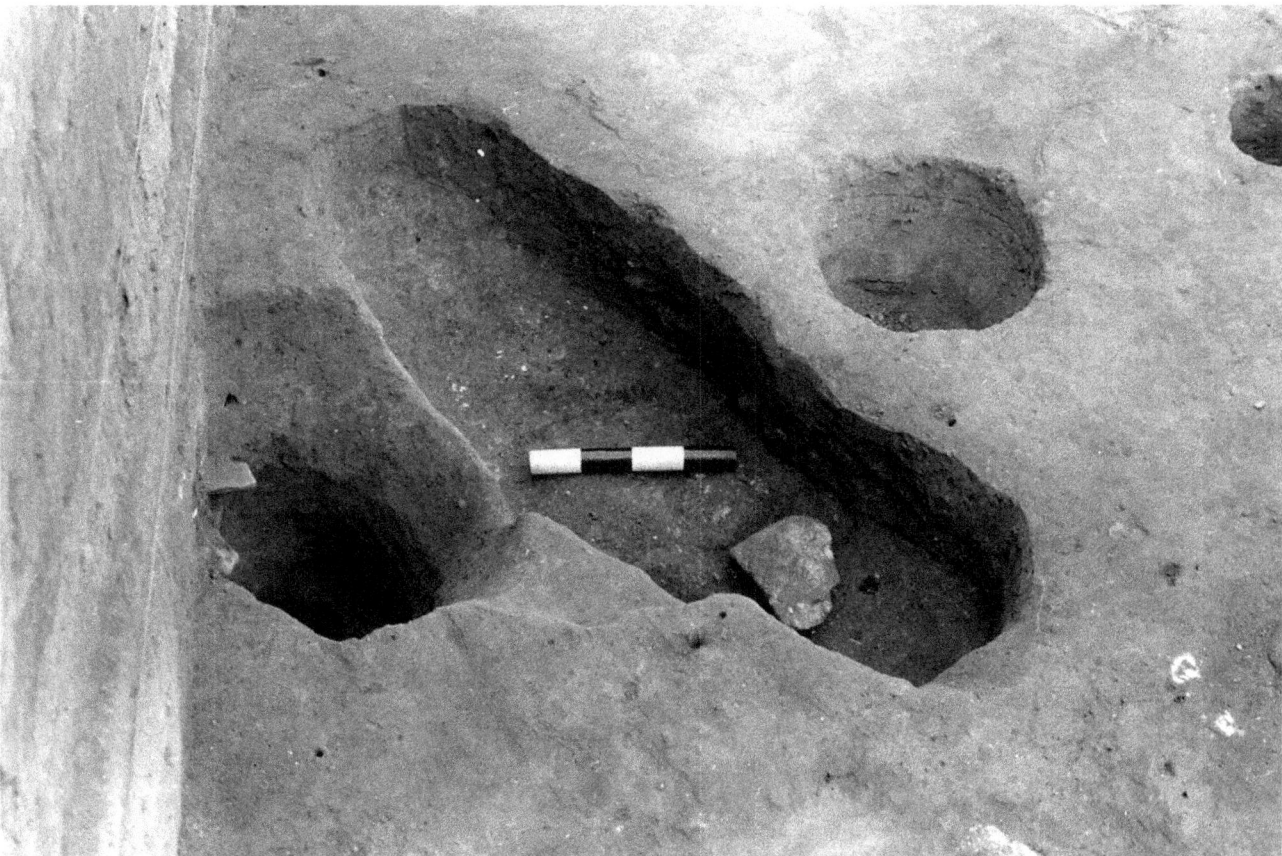

Figure 4.21. A fire pit (3455) associated with funerary rituals of Episode 8. It lay outside and parallel to the rear enclosing wall of the platform. The scale measures 40 cm.

The first relevant artefact of stone is the white tuff proto-figurine (B1231) from the platform layer of Episode 3. Again, while there is no detailing of features, the shape and general dimensions suggest that it is a representation of the human form. Both this and the Episode 2 tusk-shaped pendant seem to have been deliberately deposited in the material of the floors from which they were excavated.

The first deliberate deposition of a figurine in a hole came in Episode 5, with a feature (6559; Lunniss 2001: 128, Figs. 41a, b, 70b, 72k, l) cut into the inside edge of the rear wall of the platform. Carefully arranged and buried in the pit were an anthropomorphic pendant carved out of a large tusk (B933), along with a large proto-figurine of fossil wood (B919), a cut and polished malachite bar (B893) and two greenstone beads (B899, B900). This deposition is significant both for its internal complexity and for its position. The fossil wood was set upright, to one side of the hole, facing northeast, with the pendant just in front, suggesting that the pendant was literally or symbolically worn by the other piece. The malachite bar was at the bottom of the pit, while the two beads lay flat, side by side, 2 cm above the top of the figurine. While the full meaning of the organization of the offering is yet to be explored, it is important that the two figurines were associated with artefacts of greenstone, a conjunction to be repeated frequently later in the sequence. Furthermore, while copper flakes were associated with the Episode 2 structure, this was the earliest context found to have contained malachite.[60] Finally, it is notable that the offering as a whole was oriented to the northeast, respecting the orientation of the platform itself, and that it was situated to the rear of the structure, close to, though perhaps slightly northwest from, its central axis.

With the following Episode 6, there was another structured figurine pendant deposition in association with greenstone beads. But this time it was at the front of the platform, incorporated in the material of the entrance stairway. The cream-coloured shell figurine pendant (CT786) was set in the top clay step of the stairway, while five greenstone beads (B1194–B1198) were set in the clay of the bottom step. In this expression of the association between figurines and greenstone, the materials are placed in separate locations such that they bind the stairway together and express its essential wholeness. The separate location of figurine and beads, however, also points to a dialectical aspect of association, in which their relative positions, at top and bottom, reflect simultaneous opposition and complementarity. There is furthermore a striking similarity of shape and size between the figurine and the pendant of the Episode 5 deposition, although there are also important differences, such as the placing of the four nubbins on the shell pendant's face. The pendants, most likely deriving from different sources, appear to represent two visions of a single being.

Cut into the bottom of the same stairway, and thus post-dating its construction, was a second figurine deposition. This was a simple tuff tusk with no carved details (B1199), but with a red-painted top to its head, the only instance of figurine decoration with this colour. The figurine was buried upright, facing northeast, with 34 greenstone beads (B1200) around its waist.

Also associated with Episode 6 was a worn anthropomorphic tuff figurine (B1192) from layer 12579 over platform cap 12570. This was notable as the only instance in which a tuff figurine was found within the area of the platform itself. It also appears to be the earliest example of an explicitly anthropomorphic tuff figurine. However, both of these facts suggest an anomaly, and it may be that the recorded data do not entirely reflect the original context of deposition.

With Episode 7, the approach to the platform was once more the focus of activity involving shell and tuff figurines. This time, there was an orange and white spondylus tusk-shaped figure (CT789), wholly lacking in incised details, buried upright and facing northeast, in a small pit cut into the centre of the ramp just outside the entrance through the wall. Over the head of the figurine was laid, horizontally, part of a small tuff disc (B1201). Two further pits contained figurines. One larger hole, cut to the southeast side of the upper section of the ramp, contained, amongst other material, the worn lower half of a small and unusual tuff figurine (B1181), while a smaller hole, cut down into the top of the other, contained, again amongst other material, an incomplete and eroded tuff figure (B1179). Details of the exact location and posture of the artefacts were not recorded, but it is notable that in each case the figurine was both eroded and incomplete, and that the pits containing them were not placed in the centre of the approach. These were not, then, primary figurine depositions, nor of the same order as the others previously described for the entrance, even though they occupy an important position within the entranceway.

Outside the Episode 7 platform, not far southeast from the entrance, a plain tusk-shaped pendant of brown marble (B1211) was found upright in the middle of a pit, with three greenstone beads (B1212) around its waist. There were other artefacts too, including a tuff disc (B1210), and a miniature lime pot (B1209), as well as 78 *Cerithium* sp. and other shells, lithics, sherds, and fish bone, though it is not clear whether they are, in fact, directly related to the pendant and the beads.

Episode 8 saw a great number of figurines deployed around the platform. First, large flat-based tuff figures (anticipated by the fossil wood proto-figurine B919 of Episode 5) were buried in holes cut into the base of the foundation trench for the main wall (Lunniss 2001: 129, Figs. 42–44). Three figures (B801, B802, B803) were found in such depositions along the rear wall, and there were probably three more along that section. Whether they ran around the entire wall is not known. One (B803) was painted green, and had

---

[60] As malachite is a green carbonate of copper from which the metal can itself be extracted, it is likely that it and copper carried closely related cosmic meanings.

a shallow hole cut into the top of its head. It also stood over a green-painted stone disc (B807). Another (B802) had a purple spondylus bead in the fill with it. The figures faced southwest, north northeast, and west. In parallel, two matching tusk-shaped figures (B1223, B1247) were buried in a pair of small holes cut into the ground beneath the site of the ramp that was to give access to the new platform. The holes straddled the centre line of the entranceway as defined by the wall of Episode 7.[61]

After platform construction, the exterior clay floor became the general setting for a new type of figurine deposition. In these cases, small holes were dug to accommodate anything from one to 14 figures. Most importantly, the figures were left standing upright but unburied, their heads protruding slightly over the tops of the holes. Thirty-seven such depositions were recorded for T3 (Lunniss 2001:129–141, Figs. 45–69) and T4 (B1176, B1228, B1159), and there were certainly many more that were removed by later, intrusive features. Figurine depositions of this type were recorded also at 141A and 141C, large figurines with shell inlaid eyes were found 80 m south from 141B, and one imagines that others lay in the intermediate areas.[62]

The Episode 8 primary figurine depositions at 141B included 74 figurines or figurine equivalents, in a wide variety of forms and materials, but with two main types. First, there are the tusk-shaped figures, deriving their form from tusk or tusk-shaped pendants designed to be worn around the neck. This type is generally characterized by their shape and consequent inability to stand unsupported, and their smaller size (mostly 100 mm to 200 m tall), lightness (140 g to 500 g), and consequent portability. On the other hand, there is a smaller group of larger (195 mm to 250 mm), heavier (1400 g to 5050 g), flat-based sculptures, not so readily carried, which can often stand unaided. Both the tusk-shaped and flat-based forms are explicitly or implicitly anthropomorphic. In addition, there are carved anthropomorphic figures of other shapes, carved ichthyomorphs, a disc with carved geometric design, and carefully selected but unmodified river stones. The range of carved material includes white or light-coloured volcanic tuff (most commonly), creamy brown marble (n=1), and coral (n=1). Figures from multiple depositions tended to share a slightly distinct style of crafting and raw material, suggesting that they were made as lots. Four tuff figures were painted green. Four figurines were each associated with a greenstone bead or pendant, while one of these was also associated with two obsidian flakes and a red spondylus bead and stood over a *Pinctada mazatlanica* valve, and the disc was also associated with a greenstone bead.

None of these primary figurine depositions were located inside the perimeter line as defined by the Episode 8 wall.

However, there were two mutilated figurines, lacking lower halves, which were buried at the head of a grave sited on the platform in T3. In addition, there were six disturbed or secondary depositions of individual pieces, and three of these also lay within the area of the platform itself. In terms of alignment of the figurines, it is notable that the most favoured orientation was to the northeast - outside the front of the platform the three single figurines all faced northeast - followed by the southwest, with lesser numbers of depositions facing other directions.[63]

The full extent and composition of these Episode 8 depositions are unknown. But the primary depositions were clearly conceived as being necessarily excluded from the platform proper, save under the exceptional circumstances of the grave offering, and in that instance the figures were broken. It is also suggested that the primary depositions were first placed close to the wall, and as time went by, they were placed further and further away. However, while the figurines were restricted to the area exterior to the platform, they nonetheless overlapped the area of human graves and the area of fire and rubbish pits associated with those graves.

Finally, there were the two unique and highly unusual pieces from T4, both recovered out of context, but most probably belonging to Episode 7 or 8. One (CT785) is a relatively naturalistic miniature portrayal of a standing human made from red spondylus. The other (B1161) is a highly stylized representation on a plaque-like piece of white tuff. While the tuff figure may perhaps have been set, uncovered, in a dedicated figurine deposition of the Episode 8 type, the pendant is likely to have been a buried offering.

---

[61] As previously noted, the figures may have been associated with the earlier episode, but in that case would have had to be buried in front of the Episode 7 ramp.

[62] Kurc 1984:34 mentions 19 recovered during the cleaning of the 141C profile.

[63] In multiple depositions, individual figurines could face one direction, while there was a collective orientation in another direction. In such cases, it is the collective orientation that is considered primary.

5

Discussion of the Late Formative Ceremonial Structures at Salango

Abstract: The central ceremonial area at OMJPLP–141B Salango and its surrounds went through a complex history of successive construction, use, and termination. Beginning with the simple Episode 1 open floor and central hearth, and the elaborate house of Episode 2, by Episode 8 the original configuration and use of the site had undergone many significant changes. The idea of a roofed and walled house, in which rites would be conducted out of the view of non-participants, had long been replaced by that of a raised platform from which a watching crowd could be addressed and included. A rectangular form with a northwest-southeast aligned long axis had been transformed into a similar form but with a northeast-southwest aligned long axis. And an initial focus on fire-related rituals had been replaced by two linked concerns represented by burial of the human dead and the visible placement of stone figurines. The final platform itself covered 280 m^2 but, including the exterior clay floor, the area of constructed space would by Episode 8 have grown to more than 720 m^2, while ceremonial activity extended far beyond.

Underlying the changes just outlined, there were several important principles of spatial organisation embodied directly in the structures themselves and suggested by the differential use of the structures and the areas around them. These principles relate to three interconnected concepts: the horizontal northeast-oriented central axis, the vertical axis, and concentric space radiating from a central point.

Salango was initially identified as a place of value for its access to the natural and spiritual power of the ocean waters and the island. After the purification and renewal of the site in Episode 1, Episode 2 saw the construction of a house aligned with and thus harnessed to the forces of the sky and underworld, acting both as a model of the cosmos and a place that could be identified as the cosmos itself. The design of later structures, with their use of different media for the differentiation of space, put increasing emphasis on the demarcation of the sacred centre. Sacred objects and substances contributed extra cosmic power to the overall building design. With each episode, the new structure was validated by its incorporation of and foundation upon what had preceded it. And while the human dead endowed the site with proximate ancestral power, the incorporation of shell and stone figurines saw the addition also of original ancestral power. Eventually, Salango was explicitly configured as an origin site and was linked to coastal communities from the Santa Elena Peninsula to the south to Manta in the north.

Resumen: El área ceremonial central de OMJPLP–141B Salango y sus alrededores pasaron por una compleja historia de sucesivas construcciones, usos, y terminaciones. Comenzando con el piso abierto y el hogar central simple del Episodio 1, y la casa elaborada del Episodio 2, para el Episodio 8 la configuración original y el uso del sitio habían pasado por muchos cambios significativos. La idea de una casa techada con pared exterior, en la que los ritos se llevarían a cabo fuera de la vista de los que no participaban, había sido reemplazada durante mucho tiempo por la de una plataforma elevada desde la cual se podía dirigir e incluir a una multitud que observaba desde afuera. Una forma rectangular con un eje largo alineado de noroeste a sureste se había transformado en una forma similar, pero con un eje largo alineado de noreste a suroeste. Y un enfoque inicial en los rituales relacionados con el fuego había sido reemplazado por dos preocupaciones vinculadas representadas por el entierro de los muertos humanos y la colocación visible de figurines de piedra. La plataforma final en sí misma cubría 280 m^2, pero, incluido el piso de arcilla exterior, el área de espacio construido habría crecido a más de 720 m^2 para el Episodio 8, mientras que la actividad ceremonial se extendió mucho más allá.

Detrás de los cambios esbozados, había varios principios importantes de organización espacial tanto incorporados directamente en las estructuras mismas como sugeridos por el uso diferencial de las estructuras y las áreas a su alrededor. Estos principios se relacionan con tres conceptos interconectados: el eje central horizontal orientado al noreste, el eje vertical, y el espacio concéntrico que irradia desde un punto central.

Salango fue identificado inicialmente como un lugar de valor por su acceso al poder natural y espiritual de las aguas del océano y la isla. Después de la purificación y renovación del sitio en el Episodio 1, el Episodio 2 vio la construcción de una casa alineada y, por lo tanto, unida a las fuerzas del cielo y el inframundo, actuando como un modelo del cosmos y un lugar que podría identificarse como el cosmos mismo. El diseño de estructuras posteriores, con su uso de diferentes medios para la diferenciación del espacio, hizo un énfasis creciente en la demarcación del centro sagrado. Los objetos y las sustancias sagradas contribuyeron con un poder cósmico adicional al diseño general del edificio. Con cada episodio, la nueva estructura fue validada por su incorporación de y fundamento sobre lo que la había precedido. Y si bien los muertos humanos dotaron al sitio de un poder ancestral próximo, la incorporación de figurines de concha y piedra supuso la adición también del poder ancestral original. Eventualmente, Salango se configuró explícitamente como un sitio de origen y fue ligado a comunidades costeras desde la Península de Santa Elena al sur hasta Manta al norte.

Having established the Late Formative structure plans most likely suggested by the various archaeological data recovered from OMJPLP–141B, we can now stand back and consider how the buildings and spaces may have appeared, how they were used, and what they may have signified. In this we will necessarily refer to ceremonial spaces and religious beliefs as indicated by other archaeological data and by ethnography. However, we should also bear in mind the fact that these structures comprise the first substantial evidence for ceremonial buildings of the Ecuadorian Late Formative. The quantity and quality of information they offer is such that we can use this sequence as a new model for understanding of the evolution of local concepts of ritual space during this period.

5.1. Site Configuration and Use

The purpose of the Episode 1 hearth was ceremonial. This is argued on the joint grounds that there was no evidence for any obviously domestic activity on the floor in association with the hearth, and that the floor and hearth were subsequently overlain by a house, itself of clear ceremonial function, which was composed of a similar yellow clay floor and was also built as a setting for rituals involving fire. Open hearths and scatters of ash over the central ceremonial floors were found through the following three episodes also. Here, then, in Episode 1, the floor and the hearth were fundamental to the character of the site as subsequently understood by those who created its successive structures. The floor, differentiated from the ground around it using carefully selected and laid clay brought from outside the site, was a clean, presumably sacred space, while the hearth was the central focus of ritual practice.[64]

With Episode 2, the earlier yellow clay was overlain by a more extensive layer which, in turn, served as the

floor for the wooden house that was raised over it. This complex structure presents a dramatic contrast to the simple setting created in the previous episode. The careful and elaborate construction of the house, the presence of hearths, ash scatters, and floor repairs, and the absence of casual discard, all indicate that the building was a sacred space used for ceremonial purposes rather than a domestic habitation.

In its first phase, fire was the principal focus of much of the activity in the house. It is likely that the ceremonies were attended by just a small number of people, and that they were at least partially hidden from the view of any non-participants who may have been gathered outside. The internal divisions would have imposed restrictions on movement and may have served to direct movement through the house. They may also have served to define separate spaces that were each appropriate for very different specific activities. The various fixtures or furniture suggested by other postholes would have been used in the ceremonies but would have also reduced the available space for any movement around the house.

In the second phase, a different set of activities was introduced, focusing on the burial of offerings and of the human dead. Within the area of recovered floor, there were two general settings for these events. Firstly, the line of the dismantled northwest wall was selected for the creation of two pits for the burial of ash and a third pit, towards the north corner, for the burial of specially selected stones. Secondly, the rear central section of the house, either side of and over the old wall line, was the site chosen for the five graves. The small offering of a stone disc and a green stone bead was also set in the rear of the house, slightly southeast from the graves. However, apart from the creation of the ash pits, there is evidence, in the form of more ash scatters and burning of the floor, that the earlier fire-related rituals continued to be of importance. In this later stage, the house itself consisted principally of the roof with secondary elements or fixtures at various locations across its interior. It seems to have been completely open

---

[64] Yellow clay of the sort used for this and for later floors is found on all the hills slopes surrounding the site.

around the sides, and more spacious within the area under the roof. However, the outer fence would have controlled access and would have impeded direct observation, from the outside, of the ceremonies conducted within the interior.

More will be said later of certain principles of spatial structuring that recur throughout the sequence, but meanwhile it should be noted just how organized were the spaces created by and in this building. Specifically, organization within the building is shown in terms not only of the location of the roof supports and wall, but also in the offerings made when the roof posts were erected, in the creation of spaces though the use of internal divisions, in the precise location of the central pit, in the use of the side wall for three offering pits, and in the selection of the rear area for human burial.

Meanwhile, an interpretation of the relation between the house and the space around it would depend on an adequate knowledge of just how that external space was configured. We know that the building sat towards the base of the headland, on ground that sloped gently away to the northeast, about 100 m in from the high tide line, and about 3.50 m above sea level. There is evidence that the building and its front, outer fence, did not stand in complete isolation, but that some sort of structure lay close to the southeast side. The floor was surrounded by a layer of accumulated artefact discard in a notably organic matrix. The contemporary settlement extended no more than 200 m along the beach to the northeast, and 100 m to the east of the house.

No other structures, however, have been identified, either habitational or ceremonial, and we cannot say for the moment what the overall settlement configuration will have been, how many houses they were, or where and how they were situated with respect to the house we are considering. Above all, we cannot be certain how the space immediately surrounding the house was composed, and whether, for example, it, and any ancillary structures, were located within some sort of plaza generally reserved for public meetings or ceremonies. The fact that the floor of the Episode 2 house was surrounded by discard scatter might suggest that the area around it was not considered sacred. However, floors of undoubted ceremonial function around later central structures were also subject to artefact discard and were not maintained as perfectly clean spaces. In other words, the immediate exterior area, though differentiated from the immaculate central space, could, potentially, be both dedicated to ceremonial practice and a place in which rubbish might be strewn, and I would suggest that the rubbish around the later structures probably derived from ceremonial events carried out either in the central space of the platform, or in the immediate periphery where the material was discarded.

In the case of Episode 2, then, it can be argued that the area immediately around the house floor, though not differentiated materially from what lay further away, in the sense that no artificial surface was created there, was conceived as a space intermediary between the sacred centre and the mundane ground beyond.[65] It was clearly a space where artefacts and food remains could be left scattered, but in this case, the remains were not those of everyday household activities, but the by-products of events conducted in, around, and in relation to the ceremonial house.

It is also important to note that the house presents a well-defined sequence of construction and use, with at least one major modification of the initial design as well as a change in the type of specific activities carried out within the interior. But the history of the house should also be seen to include, as a final but related stage, the moment when it was dismantled prior to the creation of the next structure. In this last moment, both the careful removal of the remaining posts and the placement of various artefacts in holes emptied of the main roof supports are evidence that the ending of the house was considered a significant event. Specifically, it can be suggested that the dismantling of the posts and the placing of the subsequent offerings were conceived of not only as a preliminary to the burial of the old house, but also as preparation for the creation of the new structure to come.

The Episode 3 platform, arising over the Episode 2 house site, was the foundation for a smaller wooden superstructure. There were a higher number of artefacts directly incorporated in the material of the platform than had been associated with the Episode 2 floor, and a wider range of artefacts was buried in holes cut into the platform. There do not, on the other hand, appear to have been any offerings made into any of the postholes, nor were there any human burials associated with this episode. However, without evidence to the contrary, it seems likely that the new house would have been used in a similar way to that of Episode 2, with a focus on fire-related ritual. Artefacts embedded in the new clay were mostly of types common in other depositions, such as shell and stone beads, and stone discs. However, there were two unique objects: the tree snail lime container modelled out of clay, and the stylized human figurine of volcanic tuff. And it is interesting that armadillo scutes, earlier associated with an Episode 2 ash scatter, should also be found in one of the Episode 3 offering pits located to the northwest of the central axis to the rear of the platform.

The first main difference was that the floor was not only distinguished by the material and chromatic difference of its substance, but now raised above the exterior ground level, particularly with respect to the ground outside the front. It is also notable that there may have been a small sort of proscenium at the top of the ramp and slightly to the fore of the main body of the platform. Furthermore, recovered posthole distribution indicates that any new superstructure, probably not as substantial as that of the

---

[65] It is notable that there was no obvious difference between the remains found inside and outside the fence set up to the northeast of the house.

Episode 1 house, was situated towards the rear half of the platform, with little evidence of posts being raised towards the front. Thus, the platform would have been divided into two main areas, one, open-spaced, towards the front, and the other, enclosed, to the rear. In this way the proscenium and forward open area would have been used as a point of vantage from which to address any gathering in front of the platform, and as a place in which protagonists and participants might be seen as they entered and exited the building, towards the rear, before and after the rituals conducted there.

In Episode 4, two new architectural components were added to the overall configuration of the ceremonial centre: a low clay retaining wall supporting a row of wooden posts, and a clay surface that was created as an extension of that wall. Although initially perhaps less than a meter wide, this surface grew later to at least 6 m wide along the front and extended the area of controlled ground into the previously undifferentiated peripheral space. The enclosure was now roughly square and measured almost 13 m in each direction. With the addition of the second layer of clay around the exterior, the platform and associated outer floor would have grown to cover an area 22 m square or more. But while the platform itself grew in extent, it did not grow any higher, and the earlier platform summit stood as a visible centre to the new configuration.

Access to the platform was once more via a ramp, built directly over that of the previous episode, and as before, there was probably a small flat area at the top of the ramp in front of the main body of the platform. But while it is possible that there was a single permanent house on top of the platform, it seems more likely that the various holes cut into its sloping sides represent smaller, ephemeral structures erected for specific ceremonies. More detailed study is required before this point can be clarified. However, previous fire-oriented practices continued over the centre of the platform. And once again, the area of the centre rear of the platform was the site for important offerings. This time, the dogs and curassows indicate a focus on non-human life forms.

Although there was significant underlying continuity of form, material, and use of the platform, there was clear evidence of change. The creation of the wall and of the outer floor, and the erection of a fence along the perimeter wall, were material alterations of importance to the physical structure of the site, affecting both its appearance and accessibility. The expansion of the complex is also noteworthy, as the total area under explicit control was now over four times that of the previous two episodes.

The limited data for Episode 5 offer yet another image of gradual evolution of the form of the platform. Continuity is indicated by the presence of a perimeter clay wall supporting posts, at least along the back edge. Once more, the platform was expanded, particularly along the front, so that it reached almost 14 m in length, but it was not

raised any higher. Open hearths and ash scatters were present, and the outer clay floor was extended. What sort of superstructure existed, if any, is unclear.

The front appears to have been altered. There was apparently no narrow ramp projecting forward from the platform proper. Rather, there was a single, continuous slope along the whole northeast side, with access up the centre section of the slope. However, the entrance route itself was now possibly defined on either side by low clay walling set into the platform slope.

Once again, there were offerings made to the rear of the platform, close to its central axis. The second of the two superimposed pits, cut into the inside edge of the wall, contained beads and a stone disc, artefacts such as were frequently included in earlier depositions. The first pit, however, with its anthropomorphic pendant, fossil wood, malachite bar and green stone beads, presented new objects, all organised with unprecedented elaboration in what was perhaps the most complexly articulated and symbolically charged of all artefact offerings in the sequence.

In Episode 6, the platform configuration altered once again. First, the platform summit was reduced to a 3 m square proscenium behind the top of the entrance, with the yellow clay sloping down to either side and behind. Overall length, at over 14 m, was slightly increased and its summit now stood over 70 cm higher than the ground outside its front edge to the northeast.

Other important changes concern the entranceway. For Episode 5, there was a hint of the use of clay walls to define the edges of the access route at the centre of the front slope. Now, after the extension of the platform, and in place of a ramp, a hard brown clay stairway was constructed, with an additional clay surround. As the bottom step they used the low clay wall that was built into most, but not all, of the base of the front edge of the platform. Importantly, the shell figurine pendant and green stone beads are the first example of dedicatory artefacts being placed in the entranceway itself.

To the back, there was possibly another low clay wall. Once more there were postholes cut into it, and it may be that there was a similar fence, along this rear section only, as stood around the Episode 4 platform. Also, there was another artefact deposition made just northwest from the centre line as it crossed the wall, this time including various worked stone tools.

On the top of the platform, there were several major changes. First, there was no sign of open hearths or ash scatter. Second, while there was no sign of any large superstructure, there was a small fence erected to mark off the rear section. That this curved row of posts or fence so closely matched a similar structure of the Episode 2 house interior seems unlikely to be coincidental. Third, it is at this stage that the rear of the platform likely began service as a site for human interment.

Episode 7 is notable not so much for any expansion of the platform itself, but for the massive wall built to contain it, for the increasing investment in the entranceway, and for the very thick floor built to the rear. The platform and its enclosing wall, at around 14 m square, were more or less of the same horizontal dimensions as those of the previous structure, and the front edge of the new wall lay along the line of the forward edge of the old platform. At the same time, the new entranceway was built over the old stairs. However, the entrance was no longer placed at the exact centre of the front, but slightly to the southeast. Overall, the structure was not quite symmetrical.

Along the front, the wall of hard brown clay was more deeply founded, taller, and broader than any previously built. A new aspect of the wall was its greater height along the front than along the sides and back, these being collectively about 30 cm lower. There must have been a step back down from the front corner to the northwest and southeast sides, and this, together with the greater dimensions of the front, demonstrate how much more importance was placed on the material and visual impact of the approach from the northeast than on the platform's aspect from the other directions. Indeed, while the front wall presents a marked physical barrier, forcing ingress via the constructed entranceway, the back wall was clearly a more symbolic frontier across which passage could be made unimpeded.

In previous episodes, exterior floors had been built directly out from the base of the perimeter walls, using the same clay as made up the body of the wall proper. Now, along the rear of the platform, this device was applied again, but this time with two differences. First, the exterior layer of clay was a direct extension of the sunken wall, being attached to the body of the latter by the very wide cut running away from the wall trench out to the southwest. Second, it was much thicker, with a maximum depth of about 20 cm at the point where it joined the wall. These factors, together with the difference in treatment between the front and rear of the platform, suggest that the rear exterior area was considered important in its own right and for reasons that were specific to it.

As with Episode 4, the clay perimeter wall was built first, and the yellow clay of the platform extension added second. On this occasion, however, the new yellow clay appears not to have been laid over the whole interior, but to have been limited to the front three quarters. As in Episode 6, there was a proscenium occupying the area immediately behind the entranceway, and though slightly larger, this high, flat area was still relatively small compared to the total area of platform.

The entrance to the platform during this episode had a markedly complicated history in which first the old stairway was combined with a new ramp, and subsequently the ramp was recombined with a new set of steps, such that the old approach was in neither moment destroyed but at least partially incorporated in the new configuration. Offerings

made included the usual shell and coloured stone beads, a stone disc, and part of an unusual tuff bead, all scattered over or amongst the layers of soil. The burial of shell and tuff figurines in the ramp continued the example of entranceway figurine deposition established in Episode 6.

The use of the platform is probably to be seen in terms of two main areas and two subsidiary areas.[66] First, there was the front, raised area between the top of the stairs and the centre of the platform. For the most part, this area was empty of features, the exceptions being two potentially later graves set just to the northwest of the centre line as defined by the entranceway, one of which was unique in its southwest-northeast orientation and in the absence of any skeleton, though typical goods were present. Second was the rear half of the platform, reaching over the perimeter wall to the floor outside, where the conventionally oriented human burials were generally situated, along with their respective fire pits and rubbish pits. The subsidiary areas were the two fringes of the platform either side of the main, raised space to the front. The southeast fringe was not recovered, but on the northwest side there were two, uniquely north northeast-south southwest aligned graves.

The platform interior, then, was perhaps primarily dedicated to funerary rites, though other events related to death may have been involved as well. And the data we have just reviewed could suggest that the rites involved a procession up the ramp and steps from the plaza that lay to the northeast, and that the procession halted a while on the raised area of the platform behind the entranceway. Here, participants or spectators gathered below may have been addressed, before moving to the rear, where, amidst feasting and the offering of fire, food, and broken pots, the body was finally laid in the ground.

Once again, there were features cut into the rear wall just northwest of the central axis, with a variety of new types of offering that included a malachite disc, many chert flakes with a modified conch, and a set of various stone tools, raw stone, and pot sherds. The dog burial just inside the wall and next to the main southwest-northeast axis, may have been associated with that axis, with the human dead, or with both.

Episode 8 saw the setting of another large wall immediately around that of the previous platform, so creating an even more massive 3 m thickness of hard brown clay along the front. As before, the front wall was higher than the sides and rear. But with the new platform now reaching just over 17 m in length, the structure by this stage was slightly longer from front to back than wide.

Whereas, however, the general form of the wall went unaltered, there was a significant addition to the space

---

[66] This time, there was not even a fence set on the platform summit, although there may have been small, secondary structures features along the area of the back wall. Sunken clay walling may have been used to differentiate internal space instead.

underlying it. The anthropomorphic stone figurines buried beneath the back wall represent the first material offerings directly incorporated in primary elements of any perimeter wall. We do not know whether the figurines encircled the entire building or were limited to the rear. However, we can suggest that they were a development out of the practice of figurine placement in entranceways, or out of the vision which led to the elaborate deposition of pendant figurine and fossil wood in a pit cut into an earlier wall, or both.

That no yellow clay was added to the interior is also to be noted, as this was the first time since the start of the sequence that the central space itself had been left unaltered. Nevertheless, the top of the platform remained 70 or 80 cm higher than the ground immediately outside the front. The overall platform profile would also have remained the same as in Episode 7, with a gradual rise from the rear to the centre, a raised space from centre to entranceway, and sloping fringes to either side of that.

After the wall, and the clay floor built out from its front, the main effort of construction went into the entrance. The earlier entranceway was left as before. However, the new entrance was not only wider than the old one, but also centred physically slightly to the southeast, and the arrangement of openings was not at all symmetrical. Furthermore, while the earlier opening in the wall widened towards the interior, the new wall had an opening that narrowed towards the interior.

Once again, access was via a combination of outer ramp and inner stairway, with a new ramp being built out from the old steps. The final configuration of the approach was probably slightly altered from before in that the ramp may have risen in two different stages, with a more gradual slope as far as the wall and a steeper gradient up to the two steps.

As before also, there were offerings made into the body of the ramp. Some were of types made previously, such as shell beads and shell rattles. But there were also broken fishhooks, scatterings of ash, fish bones, and bird bones. Unprecedented too was the burial of a bird in the upper ramp. And while there had been earlier burial of figurines in entranceways, we here find a new practice developed out of that, in which anthropomorphic figures were buried out beyond the walls, but underneath where the forward section of the new ramp was to be laid. These figures were notably different from those buried under the back wall, being of straight tusk form, rather that of the large flat-based type, and therefore are likely to represent a different principle.

It is with Episode 8 that there is the most impressive evidence since Episode 2 for the construction of a gateway at the entrance. This included a large central post set into the ramp in line with the outer edge of the new wall and roughly on the central axis of the old entrance, with sets of smaller posts to either side. These posts may have all been connected by horizontal beams across the ramp, or they may have been free-standing. Whatever, they asserted a division of the passage into two.

Along the back, there were no offerings made into pits cut into the wall. But the circular clay-lined pit, sited over the main northeast-southwest axis, and the burial of the conch, jar neck, and mother-o-pearl valves, are yet another addition to the wealth of material deliberately placed in this area of the structures.

The most important innovation of this episode was the practice of setting upright and visible stone figurines in holes cut into the floor that surrounded the platform. The fact that this type of deposition was limited to the exterior area is notable, suggesting a very strict understanding of the symbolic meaning of the boundary imposed by the clay wall and the figurines buried under it. The fact however that these depositions overlapped the field of human graves as they spilled over the rear side of the platform, suggests that they were conceptually linked with the human dead. Such a link is already indicated by the anthropomorphic nature of most of the figures, and by the presence of the two, but mutilated figures in one of the graves. The link is further strengthened by the fact that both figurines and humans are buried with greenstone.[67] We shall see later what the figurines may have meant, but meanwhile it is important to note this recognition, by those who used the site, of the variable force of the wall as a boundary marker.

In sum, by Episode 8 the original configuration and use of the site had undergone many significant changes. The idea of a roofed and walled ceremonial house, in which rites would be conducted out of the view of non-participants, had long been replaced by that of a raised platform from which a watching crowd could be addressed and included. A rectangular form with a northwest-southeast aligned long axis had been transformed into a similar form but with a northeast-southwest aligned long axis. An initial focus on fire-related rituals had been replaced by two linked sets of rituals involving burial of the human dead and the visible deposition of stone figurines.

The final platform now covered over 280 m², as compared with the 108 m² of the Episode 2 foundation layer. But considering the clay surface surrounding the platform and even with a minimum estimate of 5 m as the width of this floor, the area of constructed space would have by Episode 8 have grown to over 720 m². The overall extent of ceremonial activity, however, had increased a great deal more. Figurine depositions suggest that the range reached at least 80 m away to the southeast and 50 m to the northeast, while at least one other, secondary focus of ritual activity lay 20 m to the east.

5.2. Principles of Spatial Organization

Underlying the changes just outlined, there were several important principles of spatial organisation embodied directly in the structures themselves and suggested by the differential use of the structures and the areas around them.

---

[67] One set of figures from site 141A had necklaces of greenstone beads glued to them.

These principles relate to three interconnected concepts: the horizontal northeast-oriented central axis, the vertical axis, and concentric space radiating from a central point.

With Episode 1 there is no evidence of any linear axis, but if we argue that the hearth was located at the centre of the clay floor, this arrangement would have represented a central point surrounded in the horizontal dimension first by the clean yellow clay, and then by the ground that surrounded the floor. At the same time, the fire can be seen to have acted as a vertical axis, rising from the ground into the air, its smoke rising even higher towards the zenith. In this aspect also, the floor separated the ritual space from the ground beneath, such that the hearth lay at the centre point of a three-tiered open structure consisting of underworld, the earth (represented by the floor), and the heavens. Fire would have stood literally, and thus with symbolic intent, at the centre of things, within a protective zone that separated it both from the Outerworld and the Underworld even as it mediated between the lower levels and the sky.

Though the Episode 2 house presents a more complicated structuring, it is clearly an elaborate development out of the previous simple design. Here, fire lay at the centre of things, surrounded not only by the new yellow clay floor, but also by the posts and wall of the building. In fact, the building perimeter itself was clearly the first ring around the fire, perhaps with the clay floor skirt as a second, before reaching the unfloored ground beyond. Such an evaluation derives first from observation of the presence of the wall in the first stage of use of the building, separating activity inside from space outside. It is also suggested by use of the wall line and gully, after dismantling of the wall, as a site for offerings. A further concentric subdivision of surrounding space was represented by the outer fence, this time defining the ground beyond the floor into that which was immediately outside to that which was further outside.

The vertical dimensions and the vertical axis were represented in several ways also. First, the yellow clay floor reaffirmed the division established in Episode 1 between the upper and lower worlds of sky and underground. This layering was mediated now not only by the fire, but also by the posts that supported the roof. The potency of these posts, and of the underworld from which they emerge, was affirmed by the presence of the offerings placed in the packing around their bases.

Now, however, there was a new structural principle or device: the central axis. This axis can be seen as a linear extension of the centre, directed forwards first towards a specific point perhaps on the horizon, but also potentially reaching in the opposite direction. It is also a line which separates space into two halves, one on either side of the axis. In the case of Episode 2, we can see these aspects unfold as follows. The building was oriented towards the northeast, with its entrance at the centre of the northeast side. Within the building itself, the main hearth and ash pit were the centre. To the northeast of the hearth was one

main post, and to the southwest, two others. The central axis was further defined at ground level and above by the interior gully that ran from the hearth to the centre of the doorway, and by the row of three posts outside the doorway.

The buried offerings of the main postholes of the three centre files of the back two rows extended this line and its dividing principle to the underground. For, while the holes of the central file contained tuff discs and shells, those to either side contained shale discs and copper. This points first to the value of the central axis, second to the complementary but different value of the lateral files, and third to the value of the bilateral symmetry operating either side of the central axis. But that is not all. The shells in the central file were a *Spondylus princeps* and a *Vasum caestus*. Without entering here into discussion of the symbolism of the bivalve and the conch, this pair of offerings suggests that the axis was not simply an extension of the centre, but that different points along the line had different values. Such difference is most clearly expressed when we consider the house and the line in terms of front, with its opening to the northeast, and back, with the wall to the southwest.

The central rear portion of the house was explicitly defined not only by the central six posts of the rear two rows, but also by the internal partitions running up the two files either side of the centre and by the arc of four posts that crosscut the central axis to the rear of the central hearth. It was this area that was later selected for burial of the five dead interred beneath its floor. And it is no coincidence that in the case of the child buried on a northwest-southeast axis outside the original wall, while the body and feet lay to the northwest of the line, the head lay exactly on the central southwest-northeast axis of the house.

The central axis in the case of the house related to an ordered series of spaces established along it and to either side of it, and each of these spaces was associated with specific activities. Buried artefacts and the human dead lent further meaning and value to specific spaces and points. And the remaining episodes followed the basic pattern established with Episode 2, though with some divergences from the more precisely symmetrical patterns suggested for the first ceremonial house. All the following structures maintained a southwest-northeast axis with their entrances towards the northeast.[68] And posts set up in the

---

[68] The orientations for the main axes of the Late Formative structures at Salango were calculated at approximately 65°E (Episode 2), 60°E (Episode 3), 62°E (Episode 4), and 61° (Episodes 6, 7, and 8). It must be emphasized, however, that these are approximations, although the 5° range of variation is probably reasonably correct. In particular, the bearing for Episode 3 is uncertain. Since compass bearings for the structures were never specifically measured on site, estimation of the orientations was made as follows. In 1982, the outline of site OMJPLP–141B was included on a map of the general area of the factory yard within which it lay. The site is now underground, but the walls of the factory yard still stand. Unfortunately, no precise reference to North, Magnetic or Geographical, was ever included on the map. Compass readings, however, along the factory walls were taken on 10th October 2006, allowing a bearing with respect to Magnetic North for the site and

entranceways emphasized the importance of bipartition as a fundamental and defining concept in the creation of space. In the early stages, the centre of the platform was the focus of fire-related activities. In the later stages, the rear section of the platform was chosen for the burial of the main group of the human dead. And the central axis was throughout a focus for buried offerings.

While some offerings were made at a distance from the central axis and to either side, the great majority was clustered in one of two areas: the entrance way and the centre of the rear side of the structure. At the front entrance from Episode 6 onwards, figurines dominate the record, though there were also beads, discs, and birds; in Episode 7, a single figurine was set precisely on the central axis; and in Episode 8 each of a pair of figures was set either side of the axis. To the rear, in Episode 4 a dog buried on the precise centre of the perimeter wall appears to have embodied the vertical axis at that point also, while a curassow lay on the same central axis just outside the wall.[69] In Episode 7, a dog was buried over the central axis, but just inside the perimeter wall, and in Episode 8, the central axis just outside the wall was the site for an elaborate clay-lined circular pit.

However, it appears that next to the centre line itself, offerings along the rear side were also focused on the area immediately to the northwest. Thus in Episode 4, a second dog lay just to the northwest of that on the central axis, and a second curassow burial lay adjacent to the northwest side of the first; and in Episodes 5 to 8, a complex pendant figurine deposition, a set of stone artefacts, a set of chert flakes and conch, a malachite disc, and a set of shells and jar neck, all lay in pits just northwest of the central axis on, inside, or outside the rear wall.

It is also notable that in the last two episodes, the main axis was not actually along the geometrical centre line of the building itself, but along the centre line of the entrance.

Through the sequence, there was continual growth in the horizontal dimensions of all three of the main concentric spaces or elements that comprised the ceremonial precinct: the central structure itself, the perimeter wall, and the exterior clay floor. In addition to the offerings made at or near the centre line, there was also one moment, other than that of Episode 2, when artefacts were buried along the line of the perimeter wall. This was Episode 8, when the figurines were buried under the foundation trench of the perimeter clay wall before laying of the clay. Episode 8 also saw the dramatic use of the outer floor as a setting for the visible deposition of the many dozens of figurines subsequently brought to the site. This was the first and only time that differential artefact distribution of deliberately placed objects favoured the exterior space over that of the interior. In fact, the distribution pattern, with its exclusive focus on the exterior, is as powerful a statement of difference in spatial value as any of the elements of the buildings themselves.

However, we should remember that throughout the sequence, colour was an important factor in the differentiation of horizontal space (Lunniss 2001:105, 106). In particular, it was yellow clay that was selected for the central floor or platform, and different clay of contrasting colour, generally a dark reddish brown by the later episodes, that was favoured for the perimeter walls and exterior floors.[70]

We should also note the orientation of figurines and burials. The great majority of figurines from Episode 5 onwards faced northeast, while the next largest number faced southwest. And in all the dedicated depositions beneath and outside the Episode 8 wall, the figurines were upright, symbolizing the vertical axis. The graves, however, present a different pattern, and again we should remember that the bodies were laid horizontally. In Episode 2, four graves were aligned on a northwest-southeast axis, with the head to the southeast, while the fifth was on a south southwest-north northeast axis, the head to the north northeast. In Episodes 6 to 8, all the main group of burials to the rear of the platform, and the single burial on the central axis in the forward half of the platform, were aligned northwest-southeast, with a roughly equal number headed in either direction. In other words, although two graves in the northwest half were aligned north northwest-south southeast, and the empty grave was oriented southwest-northeast, almost all bodies were lain at right angles to the main axis of the structures.

Clearly there was a relation between the orientation of the buildings and those of the figurines and burials. The figurines tended not only to respect the axis of orientation of the structures, but in most cases to respect the specific orientation to the northeast. On the other hand, the burials all tended to crosscut that axis. But it is notable that at the same time, all bodies had their faces, if not looking upwards, turned to the northeast. The burials were perhaps not so much ignoring or defying the northeast orientation of the structures, as defining an alternative relationship with it.

Finally, there is probably great significance to be found in the fact that while the figurines of dedicated depositions were buried upright, the human dead were all buried horizontally. For if the figurines embody the vertical axis,

---

the site grid to be calculated. Adjusting for a Magnetic Declination of 4′ E, as computed by the program obtained from the National Geophysical Data Center (NGDC) website (http://www.ngdc.noaa.gov/seg/geomag/jsp/struts/calcDeclination), site OMJPLP–141B was found to be oriented towards 60°E of Geographical North. Individual structure orientations were then determined by measuring the difference of each with respect to the orientation of the site grid.

[69] While the field records indicate that the remains of the dog were buried in a vertical position, it is not clear which way up the remains were set.

[70] In this respect, the Munsell readings and their corresponding terms do not convey the reddish, even purple quality of the colouring of the later clay walls and floors when seen directly against the yellow of the clay used for the platforms.

the burials clearly do not, and it is in this aspect of their treatment that the two sets of features most clearly differ.

5.3. The Meaning of the Site

We have seen what the immediate purposes of the site may have been, and how, underlying its changing configuration and use, there were certain constant principles of spatial organisation. We can now use these different perspectives to attempt a reconstruction of the meaning the site may have had for those who constructed it.

Before Salango was ever occupied by human settlers, it existed as a place in the world with specific characteristics that would in many ways shape the way it was later to be used. Of most relevance is the presence of the island and the bay and its rich abundance of fish. The conjunction of these elements, with the shallow reefs between island and headland, the power of the winds as they blow the sea against the rocks, the frenzy of birds as they feed off the shoals of fish, the majesty of the whales that pass by the island, the schools of dolphin that once with seeming infinite numbers leapt and played their way in search of tuna, and the sea turtles emerging from the water to lay their eggs in the beach, all would have made the place seem something imbued with great power and spirit.[71] We should imagine that the first Valdivia settlers, when they made their offerings into the lagoon (Norton et al. 1983:42), would have had a strong awareness of their surroundings, and over the generations there would have developed a knowledge of the specific rhythms of the place, of what it had to give and when, and how those gifts of nature could be reciprocated.

By the time Middle Engoroy people felt the change in their world that prompted the creation of the first ceremonial floor, many generations had been born, lived, and died at Salango. So that to the knowledge of the nature of the place there would have been added the memory of human ancestors, whose bodies had one by one been entrusted to the earth and who had joined the community of spirits occupying the underworld. In Manteño times, the island was famous as the site of a healing deity (Sámano-Xerez 1937). And one might imagine that in Engoroy times also it was seen as a sacred place. We have only to look as far as La Plata Island to find another example of how a rock rising out of the ocean might be chosen for ritual and worship and dedicated to such practices (Damp and Norton 1987; Dorsey 1901; Marcos and Norton 1981, 1984). We cannot be sure what precise meanings Salango had for those who made the ceremonial centre on the mainland, but all these things must have contributed to their sense of it.

However, the laying of the first floor, and the burning of the first fire, would have incarnated a new vision and a new relation to the place. And the space at the base of the headland, close to the high-water line, was selected as the spot most fitting for the floor perhaps for those very reasons: it was the closest, reasonably flat space that could be found in relation to the waters of the straits and to the headland point and the island,

The ritual use of fire has been a theme little explored in the study of ceremonial practice on the Ecuadorian coast. A large, deep hearth found in the plaza south of the Fiesta House Mound at Real Alto has been interpreted as one of magico-religious function and, based on this hypothesis, it is further suggested that much of the ash around the settlement may also have been the product of ritual activities (Marcos 1988:34). The very rare cremation of the human dead in both pre-ceramic Las Vegas and Valdivia times (Marcos 1988:70; Stothert 1988:116, 139, 157) is a more direct indication of a relation between fire and the spirit world. Thus, we should not be entirely surprised that the evidence from Salango shows that hearths were not only central to ritual practice in Late Formative times, but primordial in the sequence of activities carried out in the newly created ceremonial space.

When we look to the Peruvian Andes, we find an entire religious tradition centred on sacred hearths, themselves set in specially constructed ritual chambers (Burger 1992:45–52; Burger and Salazaar-Burger 1980, 1985). Although these Kotosh Tradition structures were built a great distance away from and several centuries before the Middle Engoroy occupation of Salango, they provide an enlightening example of how important an element fire could be, and of how it might be used. Burger (1992:48) suggests that while fire was itself not worshipped, its importance lay in its function as a transformative agent, one that allowed mundane substances to be consumed by the spirits.

At Salango, in Episodes 1 to 5 fire was used to create ash that was in turn spread over the floor around the hearths, and events such as these were followed by the relaying of the floor over the affected areas, or even the creation of a new structure. Fire, then, appears to have been used at one and the same time both to mark an end or to destroy, and to make possible a new beginning. Combining this aspect with its other function of permitting mediation with the spirit world, fire would have been seen as a sacralising agent that converted mundane space into one fitting for communication with the spirits.[72]

The house raised in Episode 2 over the ashes of Episode 1 reflects the form of a domestic structure, in that it has walls, roof, floor, doorway, etc., and its size compares with that of, for example, the Valdivia III house as reported for

---

[71] Compare the Desana view (Reichel-Dolmatoff 1971:81–83) of the spiritual power of natural formations in the Vaupés region of Colombia. Of special relevance are the hills that stand out "like dark islands" amongst the rain forest, and the rapids of the rivers, for these are the houses of the Master of the Animals.

[72] In this respect, it is interesting to note that the Tsáchila of the Ecuadorian lowlands tell in their myths, of how a platform was built to support a temple, and the temple housed a ceremonial hearth (Lippi 2004:118). The modern day Tsáchila are a social formation far different from that of Middle Engoroy, but as least they are a group relatively closely situated to the site we are discussing.

Real Alto (Raymond 2003). Its organisation, however, and its incorporation of artefacts or substances of cosmic power in its foundations, present an elaborate design that went beyond the ambition of a normal habitation, and it can be seen as a development out of domestic architecture, but one adapted specifically for ceremonial purposes.

Perhaps the most important aspect of the organization of the house was its orientation to the northeast, an orientation maintained throughout not only the rest of the Middle and Late Engoroy episodes, but also during the Bahía II – Early Guangala and Middle Guangala phases. The significance of intercardinal axes for peoples of the Andean and tropical regions of South America is reported widely in the ethnographic literature, and it is noted that villages may be organized to embody such orientations (Zeidler 1998). These orientations derive from observation of the seasonal movements of celestial bodies and are designed to mark the concordance between mundane human society and the powers of the spirit world around it. Zeidler, in discussing the southwest-northeast axis of the ceremonial structure known as the Charnel House at Real Alto, suggests that the equatorial location of that site was a determinant factor in the intercardinal orientations both of the settlement as a whole and of the Charnel House itself. The persistent northeast orientation observed for the ceremonial spaces at Salango, even closer to the equator than Real Alto, may have reflected a similar concern, seeking to directly correlate the structure of the buildings with the structure of the heavens.

At the same time, it should not be forgotten that the orientation of the ceremonial space at Salango may also have been determined more simply by the terrain on which it was situated. For this area itself sloped down to the northeast, and the intention may have been to emphasize, through the central axis of the building and the approach up the slope to the entrance, the connection between the constructed spaces and natural form of the headland that lay behind. More data on the orientation of ceremonial buildings in the region will perhaps cast more light on this problem in the future.

The Episode 2 house, in summary, was the first in a series of elaborate and ever-changing structures, perhaps related to the annual movement of a specific astronomical body, that were dedicated to a variety of practices, with an ever-increasing focus on the burial of the human dead. While its own initial use continued and developed the fire-oriented rituals of Episode 1, it subsequently became the resting place for the five individuals who were buried under its floor. The group of one adult, one sub-adult and three infants is also interesting, in that it includes what is potentially a domestic or family unit. Whether these people were, in fact, directly related to each other cannot be said. However, their selection for and close grouping within the house argues for some degree of close identity amongst them. And, since the house was one dedicated to ritual, it is feasible that the dead were the resident religious leader and children of his family.

Whatever the case, the fact that they were buried in the house will have transformed the meaning of the place, establishing a direct link between it and a population of recently dead. It will have become, in other words, associated with a set of proximate ancestors. The physical transformation of the house, following the removal of the original wall and internal partitions, was accompanied by a spiritual transformation symbolized or expressed by the human graves and by using the old wall line as a place for offerings. The house moved one stage further away from the concept of space for mundane living and took one step more towards the concept of space reserved for the spiritual and ancestral. And in doing so, it also strengthened the divide between these two spheres.

During the following episodes the ceremonial spaces both grew and altered in design, and there was a gradual accumulation of spirit wealth as more and more objects of cosmic power were buried in association with the structures.[73] Major change in the use and likely meaning of the site came with Episode 6. At this point, the earlier fire-related rituals were abandoned, and from then on, through Episodes 7 and 8, the site was devoted increasingly to rituals directly concerning the ancestors. This focus followed two paths. First, there was veneration of the recent human dead, as evidenced by the burials placed in the body of the platform and to the south. Parallel with this, however, was increasing use of anthropomorphic stone and shells figurines that themselves represented original ancestors.

From Episode 5 through to the construction of the Episode 8 perimeter wall, all stone and shell figurine depositions involved the complete burial of the artefacts. Up to this moment, the figures remained in their subterranean world, protecting the ceremonial structures at the point of entry. Following the construction of that wall, however, the figurines later set around the Episode 8 platform, though placed in holes, were left unburied and with the tops of their heads protruding from the holes. Western Amazonian groups such as the Barasana trace their origins to the journey of ancestral anacondas up a mythical river. The anacondas stopped at a string of sites where they "emerged from the water, became groups of ancestral people, and danced. The sites represent serial stages of differentiation during the journey" (Hugh-Hones 1979:33, 34). Furthermore, "communities should be close to the emergence site" (Hugh-Hones 1979:43). I would suggest that the literal emergence of the figurines from the ground at Salango is a direct representation of a similar mythical emergence of the human ancestors of the Engoroy phase population after their underworld journey from their source. Furthermore, if the figurines in their vertical posture were ancestors emerging from the ground at the end of their journey, it could be suggested that the human dead, laid horizontally beneath the surface of the ground,

---

[73] See Helms 1998 (164–173) and 1993 for a general assessment of the significance of natural substances and crafted objects as symbols of cosmic power in pre-modern societies.

were perhaps being sent on the return journey to the source from which the ancestors originally came.

Stone figurines of the type documented at Salango have been found elsewhere in south Manabí, including the important ceremonial and funerary sites of Salaite and, perhaps, Joá. None of these other collections has any scientific documentation, as all the pieces were taken out of the ground by looters, so that we do not know their precise depositional context. However, it seems at least possible that all these different places were identified as emergence sites visited in turn at the time of the population of the earth, and that the figurines, and the ritual enactments that saw their deposition, were designed to strengthen notions of common ancestral origin. At the same time, the cult of the original ancestors at these sites was linked to the cult of the proximate ancestors represented by the recently buried dead.[74]

But there is a wider social context still to what was happening at Salango. From Episode 2 onwards, exotic artefacts and materials not available on the coast were incorporated in the body of the site (Lunniss 2001:319, 320). There was also an increasing quantity of imported ceramics and other artefacts suggesting social relations with coastal communities all the way from the Santa Elena Peninsula to Manta. Clearly, by then, Salango's ceremonial centre was no longer of merely local importance. Not only had the modest nature of the Episode 1 floor and the intimate setting of the Episode 2 house long given way to more publicly directed structures and rites, access to Salango's spiritual resources was by Episode 8 likely a matter of concern to groups spread over much of the central coast.[75]

In sum, the Middle and Late Engoroy ceremonial spaces at Salango present a remarkable sequence of development and enrichment which can be interpreted as follows. The site was initially identified as one of value for its access to the natural and spiritual power of the ocean waters and the island. It is likely that there was also already some sense of ancestral power associated with the setting, since Salango had been occupied since the latter half of the fourth millennium BC, and human burials of the Machalilla and Early Engoroy phases prove that it was indeed a long-established burial site. After the purification and renewal of the site in Episode 1, Episode 2 saw for the first time the construction of a building that sought to harness the forces of the skies (through its orientation and upright posts) with those of the earth (through its floor and location) and underworld (through the holes cut into the floor). This building was, in fact, both a model of the cosmos and, in the moments of ritual enactment, a place that could be identified as the cosmos itself. The design of later structures, with their use of different media for

the differentiation of space (elevated surfaces, clay walls, fences, coloured floors) made increasing emphasis of the demarcation of the sacred centre. Exotic artefacts and materials contributed extra cosmic power, always being carefully placed in precise locations related to the overall building design. With each episode, the new structure was validated by its incorporation of and foundation upon what had preceded it. And while the human dead endowed the site with proximate ancestral power, with the incorporation of the shell and stone figurines, original ancestral power was also added.

---

[74] See Helms (1998) for a full discussion of proximate (or emergent) and original (or *a priori*) ancestors.
[75] Helms (1998) also discusses the manipulation of ancestral identity in the search for spiritual power.

6

Conclusions

Abstract: Salango presents unprecedented examples of coastal Ecuadorian Late Formative ceremonial architecture as a well-preserved and tightly bound sequence of eight episodes of construction and use of spaces and structures dedicated to ritual performance. Through Salango, we can now see what varied forms the ceremonial structures took, how they developed through time, how precisely designed they were, how important were the underlying principles of organization for architectural planning and cosmic meaning, and how ritual enactment and the public expression of religious ideology were dynamic and constantly evolving phenomena. We can also see how the process of ideological change matched that of ceramic change, and that ceramics and ceramic change, far from being independent phenomena, were intimately bound to changes in ideology. Furthermore, Salango allows us to evaluate artifacts of ritual function recovered elsewhere and presents evidence of Late Engoroy stone figurine use that not only points to a south Manabí ancestor cult, but also the antecedent uses of figurines that led to this cult. We can also see how much more complex and varied were Late Formative ceremonial structures and settings than contemporary ceramic models would suggest and can appreciate the fundamental importance of buried offerings to those structures. And we can now begin to assess more specifically how coastal Ecuadorian Late Formative ritual architecture and practice compared with that of more distant regions. Moving forward to reconstruction of the Early Regional Development structures that followed, it will be necessary to consider the impact of the fall of volcanic ash that capped the final Late Engoroy platform and apparently marked the end of Late Formative Salango.

Resumen: Salango presenta ejemplos sin precedentes de la arquitectura ceremonial del Formativo Tardío costero ecuatoriano como una secuencia bien conservada y estrechamente unida de ocho episodios de construcción y uso de espacios y estructuras dedicados a la actuación ritual. A través de Salango, ahora podemos ver qué formas variadas tomaron las estructuras ceremoniales, cómo se desarrollaron a lo largo del tiempo, cuán detalladamente fueron diseñadas, cuán importantes fueron los principios subyacentes de organización tanto para la planificación arquitectónica como para el significado cósmico, y cómo la actuación ritual y la expresión pública de la ideología religiosa eran fenómenos dinámicos y en constante evolución. También podemos ver cómo el proceso de cambio ideológico coincidió con el de cambio cerámico, y que la cerámica y el cambio cerámico, lejos de ser fenómenos independientes, estaban íntimamente ligados a los cambios de ideología. Además, Salango nos permite evaluar artefactos de función ritual recuperados en otros lugares y presenta evidencia del uso de figurines de piedra Engoroy Tardío que no solo apunta a un culto ancestral del sur de Manabí, sino también a los usos anteriores de figurines que llevaron a este culto. También podemos ver cuánto más complejas y variadas eran las estructuras y escenarios ceremoniales del Formativo Tardío de lo que sugerirían los modelos cerámicos contemporáneos y podemos apreciar la importancia fundamental de las ofrendas enterradas para esas estructuras. Y ahora podemos comenzar a evaluar más específicamente cómo se comparan la arquitectura y las prácticas rituales Formativo Tardío de la costa ecuatoriana con las de regiones más distantes. Avanzando hacia la reconstrucción de las estructuras Desarrollo Regional Temprano que siguieron, será necesario evaluar el impacto de la caída de ceniza volcánica que cubrió la plataforma final de Engoroy Tardío y aparentemente marcó el final del Formativo Tardío en Salango.

Salango presents unprecedented examples of coastal Ecuadorian Late Formative ceremonial architecture as a well-preserved and tightly bound sequence of eight episodes of construction and use of spaces and structures dedicated to ritual performance. It thus permits discussion of ritual activity and artefacts for this period and region in terms both of architectural context and historical trajectory. Not all the details are clear, and indeed it is not in all cases certain what the overall form of the structures would have been. For that reason, it has been necessary occasionally to present alternative readings of the data. Indeed, a main purpose of this monograph is to make it possible for other investigators to understand both the original data set and the process of selection made in arriving at the final interpretation. Nevertheless, the excavation record has permitted reconstruction of the likely design of most of the structures and, no less importantly, identification of the fact that the locations of the varied artefact offerings and human burials associated with them were significant precisely because of their relation to the overall design and order of those structures.

We are, then, now able to see not only what varied forms the ceremonial structures took and how they developed through time, but also how remarkably elaborate and precisely designed such spaces were, and how important were the principles of organization that underlay them, in terms both of architectural planning and, more importantly, of the cosmic meaning that these principles brought to the buildings. We can also see that even while there was constant regard to those underlying principles, ritual enactment and the public expression of religious ideology were dynamic and constantly evolving phenomena; and from this, we can infer that ideology itself was subject to continual change.

Through the site, we can also see how the process of ideological change matched that of ceramic change. In particular, the increased focus on proximate ancestors from Episode 6 onwards, the desire to impress, so evident in the more imposing structures of Episodes 7 and 8, and the sudden elevated importance of original ancestors, embodied most especially in the massive deployment of stone figurines of Episode 8, all coincide with the end of Middle Engoroy ceramics and the introduction of the greatly increased range of designs in iridescent paint, of zoomorphic bottles, and of other symbolically charged elements of the Late Engoroy repertoire. In other words, we can see that ceramics and ceramic change, far from being independent phenomena, were intimately bound to changes in ideology.

It is furthermore important that the Salango site allows us to evaluate artifacts of ritual function recovered, with or, more commonly, without proper record, from other sites. Reference has been made especially here to the stone figurines found not only at Salango but elsewhere, and the evidence they offer suggests that the south of Manabí, by Late Engoroy, was the background to a local ancestor cult based on those figures. But there also is a diachronic perspective now available that shows in detail how this cult itself developed out of earlier use of stone and shell figurines and how these figurines were deployed in association with a range of other ritually charged artefacts and substances. For example, one marble pendant figurine was buried with a pottery lime container and a stone disc, and through this single context alone we are invited to contemplate a set of associations linking three types of artefacts that would likely otherwise not have been considered to be related save in the most general of terms as different examples of ritual paraphernalia. And from this and so many other instances we can now see directly how much richer the interpretation of artefacts is when made in the light of the full context of their deposition. This should not be a surprise. But for a long time now most Late Formative ceremonial or ritual artefacts have

only been approached and approachable as looted and thus isolated objects affording little or no clue as to their specific meaning and function, far less the narrative of their historical antecedents and origins.

Through the analysis of Salango's record, we now have the basis for predicting at least the general nature of the other ceremonial sites in the region. This is important both theoretically and methodologically. The significance for theory we have already touched on in terms of our ability, now, to consider more precisely the local, architectural, and historical context of ritual enactments and the ritual use of artefacts. We no longer need limit ourselves to reference to ambiguous looted Chorrera ceramic models to imagine how contemporary ritual precincts may have appeared. Indeed, we can see that while the models likely point to the design of ritual architecture elsewhere, they give no clue as to the complex symbolic structure of the first ceremonial house at Salango with all its underground offerings, and even less to the idea of ritual space as presented by subsequent episodes. We are also now in a position to compare an example of coastal Ecuadorian Late Formative ritual architecture with formal ceremonial contexts documented elsewhere in the north Andean region and beyond, and to consider the degree to which ideology and ideological practice on the Ecuadorian coast reflected trends on a much broader scale.

The methodological implications are various too. Salango asserts forcefully the need for absolute precision in the register of ceremonial sites and contexts if we are not to lose valuable details of symbolic structure. It also shows the need for as total an excavation as possible of such sites in order to achieve real command of overall design both of the architecture and of the features associated with it. The data from T3 are not invalidated by those from T4, but the combination of the two sets has provided a vastly more rich and significant set of images than either one alone could produce.

The next stage in the analysis of Salango's register will be reconstruction of the ceremonial precinct of the Early and Middle Regional Development periods. T3 has already provided a partial view of this latter half of the architectural sequence, but again, the data from T4 will provide invaluable and no doubt surprising complementary evidence of the front halves and entrances to the structures. In this, it will be necessary to consider the social and other impacts and consequences of the volcanic ash fall that separates the Late Formative structures from those of the Early Regional Development. Meanwhile, it is to be hoped that the reconstruction presented here will stimulate a fresh and more structured appraisal not only of the ideology of the Ecuadorian coast during the Late Formative period, but also of its social and political context.

References

Allan, R. 1988. Site OMJPLP–140: A Specialist Shell Workshop. Unpublished manuscript. Museo Salango, Salango, Ecuador.

Allan, P., & Allan, R. 1989. Prehistoric Settlement Distribution in the Río Salango Valley. Unpublished manuscript. Museo Salango, Salango, Ecuador.

Beckwith, L. 1996. Late Formative Period Ceramics from Southwestern Ecuador. Ph.D. dissertation, Department of Archaeology, University of Calgary, Alberta.

Bischof, H. 1982. La Fase Engoroy - períodos, cronología y relaciones. In J. Marcos & P. Norton (eds.), *Primer Simposio de Correlaciones Antropológicas Andino-Mesoamericano, Salinas, Ecuador, 25-31 Julio 1971,* 135–176. Escuela Superior Politécnica del Litoral, Guayaquil.

Burger, R. 1992. *Chavin and the Origins of Andean Civilization*. Thames and Hudson, London.

Burger, R. 2003. Conclusions: Cultures of the Ecuadorian Formative in the Andean Context. In S. Raymond & R. Burger (eds.), *Archaeology of Formative Ecuador*, pp. 465–486. Dumbarton Oaks Research Library and Collection, Washington, D.C.

Burger, R., & Salazaar Burger, L. 1980. Ritual and Religion at Huaricoto. *Archaeology* 33.

Burger, R., & Salazaar Burger, L. 1985. The Early Ceremonial Center of Huaricoto. In C. Donnan (ed.), *Early Ceremonial Architecture in the Andes*, pp. 111–138. Dumbarton Oaks Research Library and Collection, Washington, D.C.

Bushnell, G. 1951. *The Archaeology of the Santa Elena Peninsula in Southwest Ecuador*. Cambridge University Press, Cambridge.

Carluci, M. 1966. Recientes investigaciones arqueológicas en la Isla de La Plata (Ecuador). *Humanitas* 6(1):33–65. Quito.

Cummins, T. 1992. Tradition in Ecuadorian Pre-Hispanic Art: The Ceramics of Chorrera and Jama-Coaque. In F. Valdez & D. Veintimilla (eds.), *Amerindian Signs: 5000 Years of Precolumbian Art in Ecuador*, pp. 63–91. Dinediciones, Quito.

Cummins, T. 2003. Nature as Culture's Representation: A Change of Focus in Late Formative Iconography. In S. Raymond & R. Burger (eds.), *Archaeology of Formative Ecuador*, pp. 423–464. Dumbarton Oaks Research Library and Collection, Washington, D.C.

Currie, E. 1995. Archaeology, Ethnohistory and Exchange along the Coast of Ecuador. *Antiquity* 69:511–526.

Damp, J., & Norton, P. 1987. Pretexto, contexto y falacias en la Isla de la Plata. *Miscelánea Antropológica Ecuatoriana* 7:109–121. Museos del Banco Central del Ecuador, Guayaquil.

Decsola, P. 1996. *In the Society of Nature*. Cambridge University Press, Cambridge.

Dorsey, G. 1901. *Archaeological Investigations on the Island of La Plata*. Field Museum of Natural History, Chicago.

Estrada, E. 1957. *Prehistoria de Manabí*. Museo Víctor Emilio Estrada, Guayaquil.

Estrada, E. 1962. *Arqueología de Manabí Central*. Museo Víctor Emilio Estrada, Guayaquil.

Evans, C., & Meggers, B. 1954. Informe preliminar sobre las investigaciones arqueológicas realizadas en la Cuenca del Guayas, Ecuador. *Cuadernos de Historia y Arqueología* 4(12):307–336.

Evans, C., & Meggers, B. 1957. Formative Period Cultures in the Guayas Basin, Coastal Ecuador. *American Antiquity* 22(3):235–247.

Graber, Y. 2004. Proyecto Río Chico: Temporada 2003. In Informe de Investigaciones: Sitio Arqueológico Río Chico, Provincia de Manabí. Temporada de Campo 2003, pp. 112–216. Unpublished manuscript, Museo Salango, Salango.

Harris, E. 1979. *Principles of Archaeological Stratigraphy*. Academic Press, London.

Helms, M. 1993. *Craft and the Kingly Ideal: Art, Trade and Power*. University of Texas Press, Austin.

Helms, M. 1998. *Access to Origins: Affines, Ancestors and Aristocrats*. University of Texas Press, Austin.

Holm, O. 1969. Cortadura a piola (una técnica prehistórica). *Joá* 1. Casa de la Cultura Ecuatoriana, Núcleo del Guayas, Guayaquil.

Holm, O. 1985. *Arquitectura Precolombina en el Litoral*. Museo Antropológico y Pinacoteca del Banco Central del Ecuador, Guayaquil.

Huerta, F. 1940. Una civilización precolombina en Bahía de Caráquez. *Revista* 51. Colegio Nacional Vicente Rocafuerte, Guayaquil.

Hugh-Jones, C. 1979. *From the Milk River: Spatial and Temporal Processes in Northwest Amazonia*. Cambridge University Press, Cambridge.

Kurc, A. 1984. Informe acerca de las excavaciones en el Sitio OMJPLP–141C. Unpublished manuscript. Museo Salango, Salango, Ecuador.

Lathrap, D., Collier, D., & Chandra, H. 1975. *Ancient Ecuador: Culture, Clay and Creativity, 3000-300 BC.* Field Museum of Natural History, Chicago.

Lippi, R. 2004. Las tolas (montículos artificiales) ecuatorianas como íconos sagrados: una perspectiva panamericana. In M. Guinea (ed.), *Simbolismo y Ritual en los Andes Septentrionales*, pp. 111–125. Abya-Yala, Quito.

Lunniss, R. 2001. *Archaeology at Salango, Ecuador: An Engoroy Ceremonial Site on the South Coast of Manabí.* PhD. Dissertation, University of London. University Microfilms International, Ann Arbor, Michigan.

Lunniss, R. 2008. Where the Land and the Ocean Meet: The Engoroy Phase Ceremonial Site at Salango, Ecuador, 600-100B.C. In J. Staller (ed.), *Pre-Columbian Landscapes of Creation and Origin,* pp. 203–248. Springer, New York.

Lunniss, R. 2022. *Cultural Identity, Transition, and Interaction at Salango, Coastal Ecuador: A Study of Pottery from the Early Regional Development Funerary Precinct.* BAR International Series 3019. BAR Publishing, Oxford.

Lunniss, R., & Mudd, A. 1987. Analysis of Part of Structure 1, OMJPLP-141B-T3, a Late Formative Ceremonial Structure Excavated at Salango, Manabí, Ecuador. Unpublished manuscript. Museo Salango, Salango, Ecuador.

Marcos, J. 1988. *Real Alto: La Historia de un Centro Ceremonial Valdivia. Primera Parte.* Biblioteca Ecuatoriana de Arqueología 4. Escuela Superior Politécnica del Litoral, Guayaquil, y Corporación Editora Nacional, Quito.

Marcos, J. 2003. A Reassessment of the Ecuadorian Formative. In S. Raymond & R. Burger (eds.), *Archaeology of Formative Ecuador*, pp. 7–32. Dumbarton Oaks Research Library and Collection, Washington, D.C.

Marcos, J., & Norton, P. 1981. Interpretación sobre la arqueología de la Isla de la Plata. *Miscelánea Antropológica Ecuatoriana* 1:136–154. Museos del Banco Central del Ecuador, Guayaquil.

Marcos, J., & Norton, P. 1984. From the Yungas of Chinchay Suyu to Cuzco: The Role of La Plata Island in Spondylus Trade. In D. Browman, R. Burger, & M. Rivera (eds.), *Proceedings of the 44th International Congress of Americanists, Manchester 1982: Social and Economic Organization in the Prehispanic Andes,* pp. 7–20. *British Archaeological Reports International Series* 194. BAR Publishing, Oxford.

Masucci, M. 1992. *Ceramic Change in the Guangala Phase.* Ph.D. dissertation, Southern Methodist University, Illinois. University Microfilms International, Ann Arbor, Michigan.

Meggers, B. 1966. *Ecuador.* Thames and Hudson, London.

Norton, P., Lunniss, R., & Nayling, N. 1983. Excavaciones en Salango, Provincia de Manabí. *Miscelánea Antropológica Ecuatoriana* 3:9–72. Museos del Banco Central del Ecuador, Guayaquil.

Parducci, R., & Parducci, I. 1970. Un sitio arqueológico al norte de la ciudad: Fase Guayaquil. *Cuadernos de Historia y Arqueología* 37:57–115. Casa de la Cultura Ecuatoriana, Núcleo del Guayas, Guayaquil.

Parducci, R., & Parducci, I. 1972. Artefactos de piedra, concha y hueso: Fase Guayaquil. *Cuadernos de Historia y Arqueología* 39:97–158. Casa de la Cultura Ecuatoriana, Núcleo del Guayas, Guayaquil.

Parducci, R., & Parducci, I. 1975. Vasijas y elementos diagnósticos: Fase Guayaquil. *Cuadernos de Historia y Arqueología* 42:155–284. Casa de la Cultura Ecuatoriana, Núcleo del Guayas, Guayaquil.

Pauslen, A. 1970. *A Chronology of Guangala and La Libertad Ceramics of the Santa Elena Peninsula in South Coastal Ecuador.* Ph.D. dissertation, Columbia University, New York.

Paulsen, A. 1982. La secuencia de la cerámica de Guangala de la Península de Santa Elena y sus implicaciones para un contacto prehistórico entre el Ecuador y América Central. In J. Marcos & P. Norton (eds.), *Primer Simposio de Correlaciones Antropológicas Andino-Mesoamericano, Salinas, Ecuador, 25-31 Julio 1971,* pp. 203–210. Escuela Superior Politécnica del Litoral, Guayaquil.

Paulsen, A., & McDougle, E. 1974. The Machalilla and Engoroy Occupations of the Santa Elena Peninsula in South Coastal Ecuador. Paper presented at the 39th Annual Conference of the Society for American Archaeology, Washington, D.C.

Paulsen, A., & McDougle, E. 1981. A Chronology of Machalilla and Engoroy Ceramics of the South Coast of Ecuador. Paper presented at the 9th Annual Midwest Conference on Andean and Amazonian Archaeology and Ethnohistory, Colombia, Missouri.

Raymond, S. 2003. Social Formations in the Western Lowlands of Ecuador during the Early Formative. In S. Raymond & R. Burger (eds.), *Archaeology of Formative Ecuador*, pp. 33–67. Dumbarton Oaks Research Library and Collection, Washington, D.C.

Reichel-Dolmatoff, G. 1971. *Amazonian Cosmos: The Sexual and Religious Symbolism of the Tukano Indians.* University of Chicago Press, Chicago and London.

Sámano-Xerez. 1937. Relación. In R. Porrás (ed.), *Las Relaciones Primitivas de la Conquista del Perú.* Les Presses Modernes, Paris.

Simmons, M. 1970. *The Ceramic Sequence from La Carolina, Santa Elena Peninsula, Ecuador.* Ph.D. dissertation, University of Arizona. University Microfilms International, Ann Arbor, Michigan.

Stothert, K. (ed.). 1988. *La prehistoria temprana de la Península de Santa Elena, Ecuador: Cultura Las Vegas.* Serie Monográfica 10. Museos del Banco Central del Ecuador, Guayaquil.

Stothert, K. 1993. *Un sitio Guangala Temprano en el suroeste del Ecuador.* National Museum of Natural History, Smithsonian Institution, Washington, D.C., and Museo Antropológico del Banco Central, Guayaquil.

Stothert, K. 1995. Las albarradas tradicionales y el manejo de aguas en la Península de Santa Elena. *Miscelánea Antropológica Ecuatoriana* 8:131–160. Museos del Banco Central del Ecuador, Guayaquil.

Stothert, K. 2003a. Expression of Ideology in the Formative Period of Ecuador. In S. Raymond & R. Burger (eds.), *Archaeology of Formative Ecuador*, pp. 337–421. Dumbarton Oaks Research Library and Collection, Washington, D.C.

Stothert, K. 2003b. Los primeros pueblos. In K. Stothert, F. Compte, Á. Hidalgo, W. Paredes, & C. Tutivén, *Guayaquil al Vaivén de la Ría*, pp. 17–83. Ediciones Libri Mundi Enrique Grosse-Luemern, Quito.

Ubelaker, D. 1988. Human Remains from OGSE-46, La Libertad, Guayas Province, Ecuador. *Journal of the Washington Academy of Sciences* 78(1):3–16.

Weinstein, E. 1999. *The Serpent's Children: The Iconography of the Late Formative Ceramics of Coastal Ecuador.* PhD dissertation, University of Toronto. Y Microfilm International, Ann Arbor, Michigan.

Zeidler, J. 1983. La etnoarqueología de una vivienda Achuar y sus implicaciones arqueológicas. *Miscelánea Antropológica Ecuatoriana* 3:155–193. Museos del Banco Central del Ecuador, Guayaquil.

Zeidler, J. 1994. Archaeological Testing in the Middle Jama Valley. In J. Zeidler & D. Pearsall (eds.), *Regional Archaeology in Northern Manabí, Ecuador, Vol.1*, pp. 71–98. University of Pittsburgh, Pittsburgh and Ediciones Libri Mundi Enrique Grosse-Luemern, Quito.

Zeidler, J. 1998. Cosmology and Community Plan in Early Formative Ecuador: Some Lessons from Tropical Ethnoastronomy. *Journal of the Steward Anthropological Society* 26(1,2):37–68.

Zeidler, J. 2003. Appendix A: Formative Period Chronology for the Coast and Western Lowlands of Ecuador. In S. Raymond & R. Burger (eds.), *Archaeology of Formative Ecuador*, pp. 487–527. Dumbarton Oaks Research Library and Collection, Washington, D.C.

Zeidler, J., & Isaacson, J. 2003. Settlement Process and Historical Contingency. In S. Raymond & R. Burger (eds.), *Archaeology of Formative Ecuador*, pp. 69–123. Dumbarton Oaks Research Library and Collection, Washington, D.C.

Zeidler, J., & Pearsall D. (eds.). 1994. *Regional Archaeology in Northern Manabí, Ecuador, Vol.1.* University of Pittsburgh, Pittsburgh, and Ediciones Libri Mundi Enrique Grosse-Luemern, Quito.

Zeidler, J., & Sutliff, M. J. 1994. Definition of Ceramic Complexes and Cultural Occupation. In J. Zeidler & D. Pearsall (eds.), *Regional Archaeology in Northern Manabí, Ecuador, Vol.1*, pp. 111–130. University of Pittsburgh, Pittsburgh, and Ediciones Libri Mundi Enrique Grosse-Luemern, Quito.

Zeller, R., & Bischof, H. 1960. Excavaciones arqueológicas en Palmar. Unpublished report, Museo Salango, Salango, Ecuador.

Zevallos, C. 1965/66. Nota preliminar sobre el cementerio Chorrera, Bahía de Santa Elena, Ecuador. *Revista del Museo Nacional* 34:20–27. Lima.

Zevallos, C. 1995. *Nuestras Raices Guancavilcas.* Casa de la Cultura Ecuatoriana, Guayaquil.

www.ingramcontent.com/pod-product-compliance
Lightning Source LLC
Chambersburg PA
CBHW061009030426
42334CB00033B/3420